B 2

finance

D0820846

ORACLE E-BUSINESS SUITE 11*i*®

ORACLE E-BUSINESS SUITE 11*i*®

IMPLEMENTING CORE FINANCIAL APPLICATIONS

SUSAN FOSTER

John Wiley & Sons, Inc.

New York • Chichester • Weinheim • Brisbane • Singapore • Toronto

Library of Congress Cataloging-in-Publication Data:

Foster, Susan, 1955–
    Oracle E-business suite 11i : implementing core financial applications / Susan Foster.
      p. cm.
    Includes index.
    ISBN 0-471-41205-8 (cloth : alk. paper)
    1. Electronic commerce—Computer programs.   2. Oracle E-business suite   I. Title.
  HF5548.32 .F67   2001
  658.1'0285'57585—dc21   2001026856

For Lanie

About the Author

Susan Foster was one of Oracle Corporation's first financial system consultants starting in 1989. In 1990, she became an independent Oracle Applications consultant, starting her own consulting firm in 1994. Her Oracle applications project experience includes being the project leader for 20-plus implementations, one accounting flexfield structure change, and one calendar change (neither through a reimplementation). She has presented papers at nine national and regional Oracle Application User Group Conferences. To contact her, e-mail suefoster@aol.com.

Acknowledgments

I would like to thank Alex Cudzewciz for starting my Oracle Applications career. In addition, I would like to thank my old business associates Pam Kotapski, Kevin Gillins, Bob Ledwith, and Ralph Calabrese for their support. I also thank Mary O'Brien.

Specific to the book project, I would like to acknowledge Chayim Herzig-Marx and Bev Johnson for providing access to Oracle E-Business Suite 11*i*. Also, thanks to Beckie McKie for her assistance with the new Oracle Receivables functionality, and Bonnie Egan for great input.

Preface

The book is designed to provide the user with a basic understanding of Oracle's E-Business Suite 11*i*, formerly known as Oracle Applications. Both new and old users will benefit from the easy-to-follow screen shots, simple business process examples, and the integrated setup steps between the Oracle General Ledger, Oracle Payables, and Oracle Receivables applications, the core financial applications.

If you are an accountant, manager, Information Technology person, or consultant, the book serves as a tutorial or template to start the organization's implementation or upgrade of Oracle's E-Business Suite.

WHAT'S COVERED

The book starts as a new instance of Oracle E-Business Suite 11*i* financial applications. The book follows a simple organization, its implementation decisions, and typical business processes. Oracle application setup decisions and functionality are covered for the Oracle System Administrator, Oracle General Ledger, Oracle Payables, and Oracle Receivables modules. In addition, all application setup steps and Oracle's Multi-Org functionality are also covered.

The book was written during various 11*i* releases (11.5.1 and 11.5.2). Each version has been slightly different. The screen shots displayed were current as of February 2001. Later releases may be slightly different. The setup steps may also vary due to an organization's specific requirements. Use the book as a starter set, but remember to use common sense as the applications may have changed.

WHAT'S NOT COVERED

The author presumes the user knows the basic Personal Computer (PC) hardware functions such as starting the PC, using the mouse functions including cut, copy, and paste, and knowing the difference between a single click and a double click. The user should also know the basic PC software functions and icons. Familiarity with menus, scrollbars, toolbars, and closing windows is also important. In addition, the user should know how to use the organization's web browser.

The book is as simplistic as possible for a sample U.S. organization. Therefore, the book does not cover the use of security, foreign currency, encumbrance accounting, or integration with modules other than those covered. In addition, the setup of Oracle General Ledger recurring journal formulas, allocation formulas, consolidation, and Financial Statement Generator definition steps as well as the Oracle Human Resources key flexfield definition processes are beyond the scope of this book. Use the Oracle application-specific user guides for more information.

BOOK CONVENTIONS

A field in **Bold** indicates required data entry in the window. The user must save and close the window during the data entry process. The save and close window commands are presumed and are not specifically noted. Again, use common sense. In addition, the keyword "Enter" means key the data in the windows. The keyword "Select" means the field is selected from a pre-defined list.

    The information bullet indicates an important note.

Contents

Introduction   **1**

    Oracle Application Methodology   1

    Hardware   2

    Software   4

    Data   9

    People   11

    Procedures   13

    Project Methodology   14

Chapter 1 **Concepts**   **17**

    Overview   17

    Oracle E-Business Suite 11*i* Integration   17

    Oracle Glossary   18

Chapter 2 **Oracle Applications Navigation**   **29**

    Overview   29

    Accessing Oracle Applications   29

    Select Responsibility   31

    Navigate   32

    Data Entry Mode   48

    Query Mode   48

Chapter 3 **Setting Up Oracle Applications**   **51**

    Overview   51

    System Administrator Step 1.1: Responsibility   53

System Administrator Step 1.2: User 55
System Administrator Step 1.3: Printer 56
System Administrator Step 1.4: Profile Values 57
System Administrator Step 1.5: Concurrent Processes 59

Chapter 4   Flexfields **67**
Overview 67
Accounting Flexfield 68
Descriptive Flexfields 75
Accounting Flexfields Step 2.1: Setup 77
Accounting Flexfields Step 2.2: Values 85
Accounting Flexfields Step 2.3: Cross-Validation Rules 88

Chapter 5   General Ledger **91**
Overview 91
Using General Ledger 93
Setup 94
General Ledger Step 3.1: Calendar 94
General Ledger Step 3.2: Set of Books 96
General Ledger Step 3.3: Profile Values 98
General Ledger Step 3.4: Intercompany Account 101
General Ledger Step 3.5: Open Period 102
Journals 104
Budgets 116
Inquiry and Reporting 126
Period-End Process 139

Chapter 6   Multi–Org **141**
Overview 141
Setup 141
Multi-Org Step 4.1: Human Resources User Profile 142
Multi Org Step 4.2: Locations 144
Multi Org Step 4.3: Organizations 145
Multi Org Step 4.4: Responsibilities 151
Multi Org Step 4.5: Profile Values 152
Multi Org Step 4.6: Adamin 153
Multi Org Step 4.7: Other Profile Values 154

Chapter 7	**Payables**	**157**
	Overview	157
	Setup	158
	Payables Step 5.1: Lookup Codes	162
	Payables Step 5.2: Select Set of Books	163
	Payables Step 5.3: Profile Values	164
	Payables Step 5.4: Payment Terms	165
	Payables Step 5.5: Financial Options	166
	Payables Step 5.6: Expense Report Template	172
	Payables Step 5.7: Bank Accounts	173
	Payables Step 5.8: Payables Options	176
	Payables Step 5.9: Reporting Entities	181
	Payables Step 5.10: Open Period	182
	Suppliers	183
	Invoices	190
	Credit Memos	202
	Matching to Purchasing	206
	Prepayments	208
	Employee Expense Report	210
	Recurring Invoice	216
	Payments	216
	Inquiry and Reporting	233
	Period Process	240
	Open/Close Period	243
Chapter 8	**Receivables**	**249**
	Overview	249
	Setup	251
	Receivables Step 6.1: Flexfields	251
	Receivables Step 6.2: System Options	257
	Receivables Step 6.3: Payment Terms	261
	Receivables Step 6.4: Open Period	262
	Receivables Step 6.5: AutoAccounting	263
	Receivables Step 6.6: Transaction Types: Credit Memos	265
	Receivables Step 6.7: Transaction Source	269
	Receivables Step 6.8: Collectors	270
	Receivables Step 6.9: Approval Limits	270
	Receivables Step 6.10: Receivable Activities	271

Receivables Step 6.11: Bank Accounts   274
Receivables Step 6.12: Receipt Classes and Payment Methods   277
Receivables Step 6.13: Receipt Sources   278
Receivables Step 6.14: Statement Cycles   280
Receivables Step 6.15: Profile Values   281
Receivables Step 6.16: Customer Profile Class   282
Receivables Step 6.17: Customers   284
Receivables Step 6.18: Remit-to Addresses   284
Receivables Step 6.19: (Standard) Memo Lines   285
Receivables Step 6.20: Tax Codes   287
Customers   287
Invoices   296
Credit Memos   304
Printing   311
Receipts   313
Inquiry and Reporting   322
Period Process   327

Index   **335**

ORACLE E-BUSINESS SUITE 11*i*®

Introduction

To implement Oracle E-Business Suite 11*i* as efficiently and effectively as possible, each and every Oracle project team member needs to understand the concepts of a successful business system and a software project. The concepts hold true for any software project regardless of whether the organization is implementing or upgrading Oracle E-Business Suite 11*i*.

ORACLE APPLICATION METHODOLOGY

Foster's Oracle Application Methodology (OAM) provides the guidelines for a successful Oracle applications business system software project. OAM involves understanding the components of a business system and how to incorporate the project methodology into the business system (see Exhibit I.1). The business system components include: hardware, software, data, people, and procedures. These five components working in harmony with a proven project methodology will produce a state-of-the-art business system and will guarantee a successful Oracle E-Business Suite 11*i* implementation project.

Each business system component is critical to the success of the system. Clearly, hardware, software, and data are required, but people and procedures are also an integral part of any system. In addition, each system component can't stand individually and one can't replace the other. There is a balance between the components. For example, many organizations try to build software to perform user procedures. Each component, including the project methodology, is described in detail.

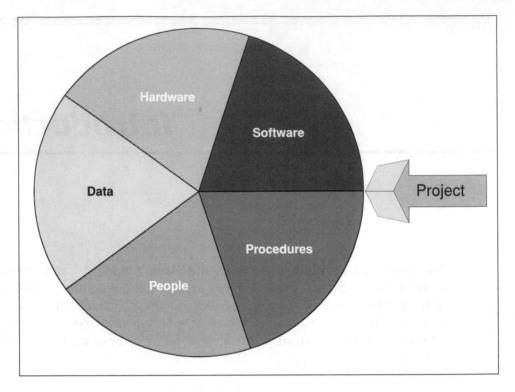

Exhibit I.1   Oracle Applications Methodology

HARDWARE

Oracle E-Business Suite uses a three-tier hardware architecture. The three tiers represent the database tier, the application tier, and the PC tier.

Platform

The first decision is the hardware platform. Oracle E-Business Suite supports a number of hardware platforms. The Information Technology personnel should review Oracle's Internet Computing Architecture (ICA) and determine the organization's optimal hardware configuration.

The project team must determine the number of Oracle applications instances or occurrences required when sizing the platforms. Typically, different organizations have different configurations of instances. Oracle applications instance examples include:

- Patch instance—patches are applied and tested
- Development instance—programmers develop custom software prior to user testing

- Test instance—users test the custom software prior to production
- Training instance—people are trained
- Production instance—live data

Also keep in mind the organization's budget cycle. Additional instances may require additional hardware platforms that may impact the capital budget. If upgrading, understand the ICA architecture and how the distribution of platform tiers may increase an organization's hardware requirements.

Sizing

Prior to purchasing hardware, the organization should perform sizing calculations for Oracle E-Business Suite. The previous Oracle application installation manual provided a sizing spreadsheet. Therefore, use the release 10 sizing spreadsheet as a template. If nothing else, have the Database Administrator (DBA) calculate sizing estimates based on the larger volume tables. Use common sense when reviewing or creating the sizing formulas.

Keyboard Mapping

Oracle E-Business Suite 11*i* provides default keyboard mapping. The keyboard mapping may not reflect the organization's standard keyboard mapping. Have the Information Technology personnel change the keyboard defaults to comply with in-house standards. For example, set F7 to Enter Query, F8 to Execute Query, F9 to retrieve a List of Values, F10 to Save, and so forth. If no keyboard standards exist, create them. Create a keyboard template for users to position above the function keys.

Printers

Oracle E-Business Suite 11*i* seeds printer definitions. Many common printer styles are predefined. The Information Technology personnel must review the seeded printer definitions and link them to the appropriate in-house printers. They must also ensure the printers are working properly. They should test all output types used including portrait, landscape, and landwide print formats. Any specific custom print styles such as checks, invoices, statements, dunning letters, and so forth should be tested as well.

SOFTWARE

Oracle E-Business Suite software comprises Enterprise Resource Planning applications, including General Ledger, Payables, and Receivables.

Software Customization Rule

The standard software customization rule of thumb states that 80 percent of the software application package should fit the organization as is, and only 20 percent of the software application should be customized. The rule holds true for Oracle E-Business Suite as well. If over 20 percent of the software must be developed in-house due to the unique business requirements, a harder look at the business processes should occur.

Most customers start with a "No Customization" philosophy. While this holds true in theory, every organization has some customization. The trick is to avoid customization wherever possible. The one-time cost and ongoing costs of customization can easily get prohibitive. The more customization, the more overhead and testing that must occur with every patch and upgrade. Try to use functional solutions rather than technical solutions. Reengineer the business process if possible, and perform cost-benefit analysis projections. In other words, cost-justify the solutions. Once personnel management see the true cost, they may be less eager to customize.

All customization should utilize Oracle E-Business Suite's Standard Report Submission (SRS) capabilities. SRS gives each application the same look and feel for running batch or concurrent processes. Information Technology personnel are responsible for adding new batch processes including custom reports and programs. Using SRS allows the custom software to have the same look and feel as the other Oracle concurrent processes. Running the custom software should be transparent to the user.

Oracle Software Support

The first level of support for Oracle E-Business Suite is the Oracle applications documentation. The installation CDs contain a documentation CD. The documentation file formats include HTML and PDF. (HTML is the language the web browser understands and PDF is the Adobe Acrobat file format.) The Information Technology personnel should install the documentation and provide the organization with full Oracle applications documentation. Exhibit I.2. displays the Oracle Applications Documentation Library.

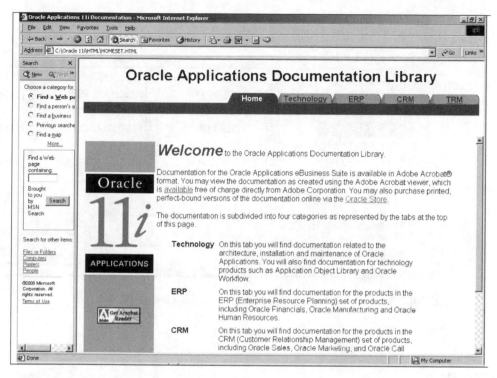

Exhibit I.2   Oracle Applications Documentation Library: HTML

Navigate through the Oracle applications HTML documentation as with any other internet-compliant application. Start with the appropriate tab and drill-down to the specific documentation. For example, press the ERP (Enterprise Resource Planning) tab to review the documentation for Oracle General Ledger, Oracle Payables, and Oracle Receivables.

Exhibit I.3 displays the Oracle Applications Adobe Acrobat documentation file directory. The PDF user guide naming standards include the release number, the application short code, and the type of manual. The release number is 115 (release 11.5), the application short codes are AP, AR, and GL, and the manual type is UG for user guide manual. For example, the Oracle Payables user guide is 115APUG.PDF.

The Oracle Applications PDF technical reference manual naming standards include the application short code and the type of manual of TRM. For example, the Oracle Payables technical reference manual is APTRM.PDF.

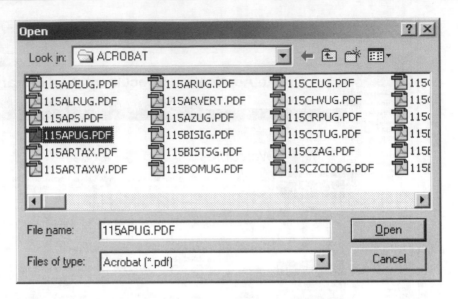

Exhibit I.3   Oracle Applications Documentation Library: PDF

MetaLink

Use Oracle's MetaLink website (www.metalink.oracle.com) to check for application issues and patches. (See Exhibit I.4). MetaLink provides a forum for all users to share and trade information. The organization's support number, for example, the Customer Support Identifier (CSI) number, is required to sign in.

Oracle supports only certified software versions for the specific hardware platform. For example, Oracle E-Business Suite 11*i* with Oracle database version 7.4 is not supported. Check MetaLink for the certified software versions and make sure the organization is compliant.

Oracle Apps World and Oracle Applications User Group

Oracle Apps World (sponsored by Oracle Corporation) and the Oracle Applications Users Group (OAUG) meet periodically. Both conferences provide functional and technical papers presented by Oracle, the user community, and various consulting firms. Both conferences are an excellent resource for improving an organization's understanding of Oracle applications and functionality. In addition, new releases are demonstrated and new features discussed.

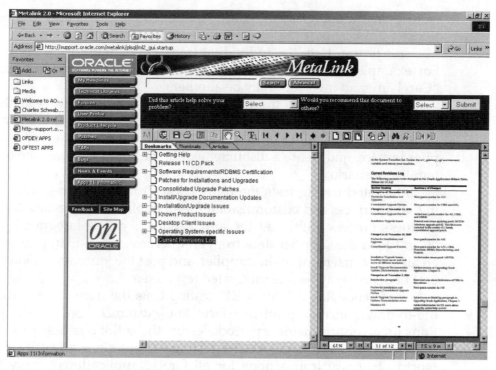

Exhibit I.4 Oracle MetaLink

Oracle Applications and Personal Computers

Each user's personal computer must be configured with software to run Oracle E-Business Suite 11*i*. A web browser, such as Netscape Navigator or Microsoft Internet Explorer, is required to log onto the organization's Oracle applications internet address. In addition, Jinitiator software from Oracle must be loaded on the PC to connect with Oracle applications. Typically, the Information Technology group is responsible for configuring the PCs. Develop and follow in-house procedures for installing software on the user's PC.

Testing

Testing Oracle applications needs to be intensive. After the business requirements have been defined, the test scenarios and test plans may be developed for the four testing methodologies. The testing methods should be used in sequential order and should be utilized initially during implementation and later during patch or upgrade testing. The four testing methodologies are: unit, system, integrated, and Conference Room Pilot.

Unit testing tests the individual transactions within the application. For example, " Can I enter a supplier?" may be one unit test scenario. "Can I enter an invoice?" may be another.

System testing tests the transactions from cradle-to-grave within the application. System testing involves testing the entire business process within the application. For example, "Can I enter a supplier, enter a supplier invoice, and create a disbursement to the supplier?" may be one system test scenario.

Integrated testing tests the transactions from cradle-to-grave, including all interfaces and customization for all applications. Testing the entire business process within all the applications is called integrated testing. "Can I load the supplier data from an interface, enter a supplier invoice, create a disbursement to the supplier, and post the journals in Oracle General Ledger?" may be one integrated test scenario.

Conference Room Pilot (CRP) testing tests the transactions from cradle-to-grave, including all interfaces and customization for all applications for an entire business period. Testing the entire business process as a monthly cycle is considered CRP testing. "Can I enter an entire month's worth of typical transactions for all Oracle applications?" may be the high-level CRP test scenario. The CRP testing should be signed off by the users and the steering committee.

The CRP test plans should be saved for patch and upgrade testing. In addition, the test plans may also serve as the foundation for user training materials and user procedure documentation. As the use of Oracle applications change during the lifetime of the software, remember to incorporate the new features into the test plans.

Housekeeping

Oracle Applications require the Information Technology personnel and users to perform housekeeping tasks. The Information Technology personnel are responsible for installing Oracle E-Business Suite 11*i* and configuring and tuning the system. In addition, the Information Technology personnel are responsible for monitoring the batch processes, including purging old batch requests that include the report and log files. Typically, a "number of days old" is selected for purging. For example, all batch requests over five days old are purged. Users should be aware of the days-old purge criteria and produce reports accordingly.

The users are responsible for purging the application data periodically. At year-end, the purge of old data should occur. Journals, balances, and other transaction tables, such as invoice and payment tables, should be purged. Determine the reporting requirements and remove the unnecessary data, especially before an upgrade! Review each application for the purge capabilities. Remember to back up and test purge before attempting to purge production data.

Patches and Upgrades

Patches are enhancements to Oracle Applications. Typically, patches are downloaded from Oracle's MetaLink site. All patches should be tested thoroughly before installing into production, no matter how insignificant the patch may seem. Do not install patches and test them in the production environment!

Upgrading Oracle applications is not for the faint of heart. The upgrade process is a project. All custom software must be reviewed and determined if the customizations remain necessary. Users must thoroughly test the upgraded software as if going into production.

DATA

Oracle E-Business Suite Data is stored in Oracle's database. As with any system, the quality of the data is critical—garbage in, garbage out.

Relational Architecture

All team members must have a high-level understanding of relational architecture before utilizing Oracle applications. The table concept of rows and columns is similar to the spreadsheet architecture, and the organization should be educated as such. A user must understand the architecture before properly navigating the windows and entering data.

Data Flows

The current business processes should be diagrammed. The cradle-to-grave business processes should document the steps and the data flows. After the processes are documented, review the steps and data flows to note unnecessary or duplicate steps. Determine how Oracle applications will perform the business processes. Note the gaps between the software application and the business process. Develop solutions. Ask "Why?"

Reengineer the business process, think of workarounds, or at worst, design a custom software solution.

In addition, the future business processes should be diagrammed. A flowcharting package should be used to document the envisioned cradle-to-grave business processes. This data flow diagram should also be used as a prototype for the training plans, the test plans, and the user procedures documentation.

Conversion

To convert or not to convert, that is the question. Converting legacy data can be time-consuming, expensive, and complex. Determine the historic reporting requirements and perform a cost-benefit analysis. And remember, like-to-have reporting requirements are different than have-to-have reporting requirements. For example, the financial reporting requirements of prior year actuals to current year actuals is most likely have-to-have reporting. Supplier payment history for the past year is an example of like-to-have reporting.

The project team must determine the conversion requirements, then provide the conversion plan. First, consider converting manually. If the volume is too large, convert the legacy data via a custom software conversion program. The process can be complex and time-consuming. The legacy data must be downloaded, cleansed, and run through the conversion program into Oracle applications. Typically, the data is not in a relational database format. The Information Technology group must provide a vehicle for the users to view and cleanse the data. Duplicates must be noted and merged. This process can be very time-consuming as the conversion data files can be large. Automated approaches to noting possible duplicates and data cleansing are available, but user involvement is still critical.

Also, timing issues with conversion extracts must be understood and planned for. Given the time it takes to cleanse the data, the team must determine how the new records and changes are to be identified and added to the previously extracted conversion data so the entire file is converted prior to production.

Interfaces

Oracle Applications provide the table layouts for converting or interfacing legacy systems. These open interfaces are now documented in the user manuals rather than the technical manuals. The project team must determine what data, if any, must interface. All interfaces into and out of the current legacy systems should be documented. All future in-coming and out-going interfaces to Oracle applications should be documented also. The interface flow documents will confirm that all interfaces are included in the project plan and project testing scenarios.

PEOPLE

People represent the organization's personnel. Both functional and technical personnel must be included.

Team Personnel

The project team members should include: the steering committee, management, functional users, Information Technology personnel, including programmer/analysts, Database Administrators, and System Administrators. Typically, consultants, contractors, upper management, and Internal Audit complete the project team.

The steering committee and management determine the high-level project scope and expected project dates. The functional users determine how the organization will utilize the Oracle applications functionality. As part of the Information Technology personnel, programmer/analysts design and develop the custom software, including conversion programs and custom reports. The Database Administrator is responsible for installing and maintaining the Oracle databases. The System Administrator is responsible for setting up the application infrastructure including users, menus, printers, and system profile values.

Although the implementation of Oracle E-Business Suite 11i does not require the use of consultants or contractors, they can make the project more effective and efficient. Consultants provide application knowledge, project guidance, and leadership. For example, a consultant can provide the project plan. Contractors perform the work the organization specifies. For example, a contractor builds the customer conversion program. Although each type of outside resource is needed, understand the use of each and why they are not interchangeable. Interview and check references for the specific consultant or contractor, just as you would for an employee.

Team Attributes

Functional and technical personnel must compose the team. And they must be dedicated to the project. If personnel are not dedicated to the project, the probability of success diminishes significantly. In addition, if only technical personnel comprise the team, the probability of user acceptance is significantly lessened. All project team members must be able to communicate, think, and be team players. Each must be willing to make decisions, trade information, and share the project responsibilities. These attributes do not necessarily reflect the strongest or more experienced personnel in the respective area.

Most crucial is a *proven* Oracle applications leader who can ensure the project stays focused, keeps its scope, and remains on track. In addition, the project leader must control the schedule, and make adjustments as changes occur and issues arise. The ability to identify, prioritize, and resolve project issues in a timely manner is critical. In addition, the project leader must be able to convey confidence, even in dire times.

Train the Trainers

Use an experienced Oracle applications instructor. Afterwards, have the best users train the remaining users. Do not use an in-house training department to teach Oracle applications. Other organizations have tried and, at best, it works poorly. This is not a spreadsheet package. It is a flexible but complicated software package. A quality Oracle applications instructor understands the organization's business processes and how they are accomplished with the Oracle software and in-house custom software and procedures.

In addition, the training should be specific to the organization. The training materials should be developed from the testing materials and should be used as a starter set for the user procedure manuals.

Ensure the users have had adequate PC training. They should be able to sign-on, use the mouse, and navigate the system prior to learning how to use Oracle applications.

In addition, make the training time as productive as possible. Get a training room with one PC per two users. Users learn by doing, not by hearing; it is like driving a car. Get them behind the wheel! In addition, the training room gets the users out of their offices where too many distractions can occur.

Train When Appropriate

Training users more than one month before they actually sign-on and use the system is fruitless. They will forget everything they learned and have to be retrained. In addition, train new users or new employees to the organization. Do not consider training to be a one-time occurrence.

Application and Query Training

Training should include functional and technical training. Many users, while not needing to know the Oracle applications technical details, can benefit from a technical overview. Many functional users are able to use query tools against the data tables to create their own custom reports.

PROCEDURES

Procedures document the organization's business and system processes. Procedures should be easy to follow and include complete documentation.

In-house Procedures

In-house user procedures must be developed. Although Oracle E-Business Suite release 11*i* is the internet version, it is not necessarily intuitive. New users must be trained and procedures must be documented to ensure the organization's business processes are working properly.

Project team members should have documentation standards. A project setup book should be created with all setup screen shots, reports, and test scenarios. Key setup decisions, such as the accounting flexfield, may have "white papers" detailing the analysis, design results, and recommendations, and should be included.

Data Naming

Create in-house naming standards and follow them. Develop naming standards from Oracle's standards or create new ones. Naming standards apply to functional and technical team members.

The functional team should develop the internal Oracle Applications naming standards. For example, the functional team should develop supplier and customer naming standards. Remember relational database models stress the use of English. In other words, use code names which have meaning on their own. For example, use Yes and No, not codes such as 0 or 1 to reflect Yes and No. As another example, user-names should be real user-name identifiers such as SFOSTER, not the old legacy sign-in code of F42628.

The technical team members should follow Oracle's file and directory naming standards for consistency. All customization should reside in a unique directory. Do not place customizations under Oracle applications directories or they risk being overwritten during the upgrade process.

Examples of naming standards should be developed for:

- Key flexfields, including the value set name, segment name, and segment structure name
- Descriptive flexfields
- Oracle General Ledger Financial Statement Generator report components and report names
- Responsibilities, menus, users, printers, SRS concurrent processes
- Segment values, List of Values, Quick Codes
- Supplier and Customer names and address data
- Batch names as in journals, invoices, receipts, and disbursements

PROJECT METHODOLOGY

Each organization needs to have a project methodology. How is the organization going to document the project? Typically, different consulting organizations provide their own project methodology. How does the methodology document the business process flows? The gap analysis? The custom software required? Does the methodology provide real value or only promote additional consulting hours? The key is to balance the cost of the methodology with the benefit to be derived.

Project Scope

Have management clearly define the project scope at the beginning of the project. Have the project team clearly understand and stick to the project scope. Don't deviate from the scope without management approval.

Many projects have scope creep, which precludes the organization from implementing on-time or meeting the true project objectives.

Project Plan

The project should have a project plan. The project scope and project lifecycle must be incorporated into the project plan. Realistic milestones should be incorporated from the project scope document. Typically, all major milestones and tasks should be detailed. Use a project software package that details the tasks, the resources, and the task dependencies. Once the project plan is created, use the plan to monitor performance. Actual to baseline comparisons may be performed to indicate lagging project tasks.

Project Communication

The project team members must communicate on a regular basis. Weekly status meetings and weekly status reports from each team member are a must. As the production date nears, the project team may have daily meetings. Project team communication is critical to monitoring and managing the project plan.

In addition, all project documentation should be available to all project team members. Use shared public folders on a network directory with files detailing:

- Project Scope
- Project Plan
- Current and Future Business Process Flows
- Status Meetings
- Issues: Open and Closed with the resolutions
- Conversions/ Interfaces/Customizations
- Naming Standards
- Test Plans
- Setup Documentation
- User Procedures
- Training Materials
- Technical Assistance Requests (TARs) logged to Oracle Support
- Any other information all team members should share

Project Lifecycle

All project team members must understand the project lifecycle. The project lifecycle is: Analysis → Design → Development → Testing → Implementation → Production. The steps are sequential. Typically, problems occur if one phase is rushed. Just because the CFO said the organization is going live January 1, doesn't mean it is a good idea. Nine women can't have a baby in one month no matter how much the CFO or CIO wants it and is willing to throw money at it.

During the analysis phase of the project, the project team should conduct interviews with upper management to determine the organization's critical success factors. What does the organization consider the top priorities to be? Verify that the critical success factors are within the project scope, if applicable. The project must ensure that the organization's critical success factors are met. Look at the organization hierarchy document; make sure all levels of the organization have been interviewed and the relevant critical success factors have been included in the project scope.

The ability to think differently and adapt to change is hard. Many organizations implement exactly what they have in their legacy systems. They make Oracle applications a mirror image of the current system. Users are accustomed to the current process. Identifying business process improvements and convincing users and management to change can be challenging at best.

When reviewing the cradle-to-grave business processes, ask if each step in the process is adding value? Is the human touching the paper (or transaction) adding value to the process, or is that person simply following the business process designed long before? If the process is not adding value, ask why is it occurring? In order to maximize the organization's return on investment, don't recreate what is there today. Think differently.

CHAPTER 1

Concepts

OVERVIEW

Oracle's E-Business Suite 11*i* is the first true integrated set of business applications in a database environment available in an internet format. Using Oracle's database technology and combining Oracle's superior integrated applications provides a state-of-the art business system with extreme flexibility. Each organization has the ability to implement these applications according to its specific processing environment.

While there are a multitude of Oracle applications within the E-Business Suite 11*i* software package, this book focuses on core financials Oracle General Ledger, Oracle Payables, and Oracle Receivables. Once the learning curve of these applications is under way, the learning curve of the other applications should be significantly reduced.

Prior to navigation through the system, a number of Oracle concepts, including the integration between the applications, should be understood. These concepts are documented in this chapter or are included in the respective application chapter.

ORACLE E-BUSINESS SUITE 11*i* Integration

Oracle General Ledger is fully integrated with Oracle applications, including Oracle Payables and Oracle Receivables (see Exhibit 1.1).

Oracle General Ledger defines the processing environment used by Oracle Payables and Oracle Receivables. The environment defines the

17

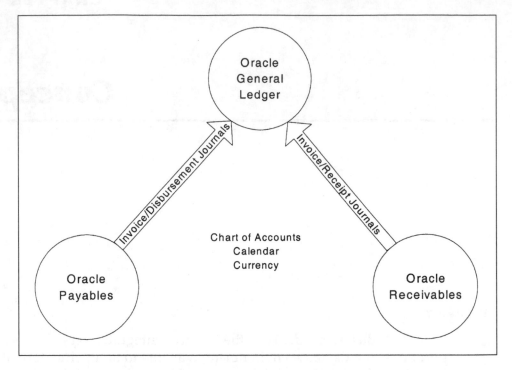

Exhibit 1.1   Oracle E-Business Suite General Ledger Integration

specific organization's chart of accounts, calendar, and currency. Oracle Payables journal entries to Oracle General Ledger include Invoices and Disbursements. Oracle Receivables journals entries to Oracle General Ledger include Invoices and Receipts.

All accounting transactions flow to the Oracle General Ledger with full audit trail capabilities, even if the Oracle Payables or Oracle Receivables subsystem journals are summarized. Drill-down capabilities from the Oracle General Ledger journal entry to the Oracle Payables and Oracle Receivables subledgers are available. In addition, release 11*i* allows the ability to view the actual T-accounts and journal entry transactions.

ORACLE GLOSSARY

Oracle applications have specific terminology. A sample of terms a user must comprehend before navigating or setting up Oracle E-Business Suite 11*i* will be discussed.

Responsibility

A responsibility determines which Oracle applications a user may access. In addition, a responsibility determines what transactions a user may perform and optionally, what data the user may perform the transaction on. For example, the accounting manager may have full access to Oracle General Ledger, while the accounting clerk may only have access to the Oracle General Ledger journal entry transactions.

Concurrent Processing

Oracle applications use concurrent processes to perform batch processing or background processing. Batch processes include creating reports, running custom software, or posting journals. Oracle's concurrent manager processes these batch requests. The concurrent request starts with a status of Pending. Once the concurrent manager begins processing the request, the status will change to Running. After the concurrent process is done, the status will change to Completed.

Concurrent requests may be run as an individual request or as a request set composed of a parent request, which spawns many child requests. For example, a GL month-end report set may have the Trial Balance report and General Ledger report produced. Each request will have a unique concurrent request number.

System Administrator

The System Administrator is responsible for setting up the applications foundation and monitoring the applications. The System Administrator defines the users, menus, user responsibilities, printers, and appropriate profile values. In addition, the System Administrator is responsible for defining and controlling concurrent processing. Most organizations have the System Administrator as the Oracle Applications Help Desk. In other words, when a user encounters a question or issue, the first person asked for help is the System Administrator. In addition, the System Administrator contacts Oracle for support assistance.

Database Administrator

The Database Administrator is responsible for installing and configuring the Oracle database and applications. In addition, the DBA is responsible for the daily monitoring of the database and users, for managing security privileges, and for performing database sizing and tuning.

Flexfields

Oracle applications provide flexfields to allow each organization the ability to define its own reporting structures. Two kinds of flexfields are provided: key flexfields and descriptive flexfields. Key flexfields are required within Oracle applications to record key data elements. Descriptive flexfields are user-defined and record required data elements not provided by standard Oracle applications functionality.

The key flexfield types are predefined. Each key flexfield type is owned by a specific Oracle application, but is shared across all the applications. For example, the accounting flexfield represents the chart of accounts and is owned by Oracle General Ledger, but is shared with all Oracle applications that create financial transactions. The key flexfield definition process and setup steps are described in detail in Chapter 4.

Account Generator

Some Oracle applications utilize the Account Generator. The Account Generator replaces FlexBuilder as the tool to automatically create accounting flexfield combinations. The Account Generator process utilizes Oracle's workflow capabilities. The Account Generator is not required for the core financials unless utilizing the gain/loss or finance charges functionality of Oracle Receivables.

Set of Books Architecture

The Oracle General Ledger (GL) Set of Books concept must be understood. An Oracle GL Set of Books contains the same three Cs: the same chart of accounts, the same calendar, and the same currency (see Exhibit 1.2).

All three are unique within a GL Set of Books. The chart of accounts determines the accounting flexfield structure and segment values. The calendar defines the transaction and reporting periods, such as months or periods. The currency defines the functional currency for the organization.

If one of the three Cs for the GL Set of Books is different, such as a different chart of account structure, another GL Set of Books must be created.

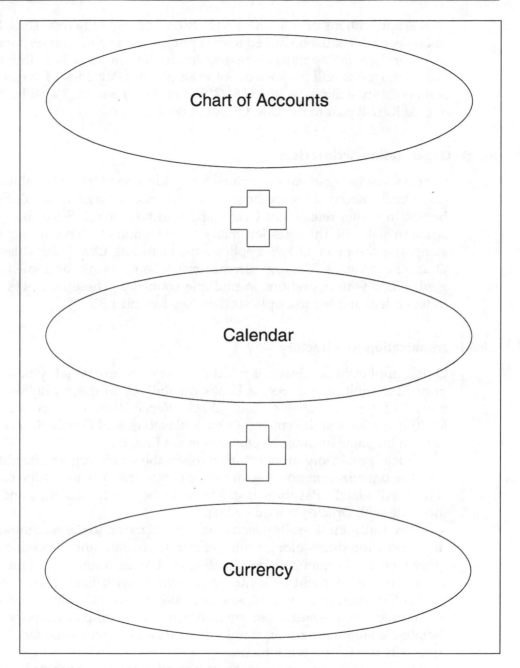

Exhibit 1.2   Oracle General Ledger Set of Books

Oracle applications post to one, and only one, GL Set of Books. The GL:Set of Books profile must be linked to the appropriate application responsibility. Therefore, the application responsibility determines where the financial transactions will be posted. For example, the Payables Manager U.S. responsibility will post to the U.S. GL Set of Books and the Payables Manager U.K. will post to the U.K. GL Set of Books.

Single Organization Architecture

Oracle's single organization architecture allows one Oracle Payables and one Oracle Receivables instance or occurrence to post to a GL Set of Books. In earlier releases of Oracle applications, the GL Set of Books restriction with the three Cs led many organizations to have multiple instances of the other Oracle applications, including Oracle Payables and Oracle Receivables. The one currency restriction was cumbersome for organizations with operations in multiple countries. These instances were independent and led to duplicate data (see Exhibit 1.3).

Multi-Organization Architecture

Oracle applications release of multi-organization functionality now integrates the multiple GL Set of Books capabilities to the multiple occurrences of Oracle Payables and Oracle Receivables (see Exhibit 1.4). Multi-org allows all instances of Oracle Payables and Oracle Receivables to be in the same instance as Oracle General Ledger.

Oracle's multi-org architecture resolves the single org architecture issue. The organization now decides which organizations are within one instance. All Oracle Payables instances may be in one instance and still integrate with Oracle General Ledger.

This multi-org flexibility leads each organization to define centralized data and procedures along with decentralized data and procedures. In other words, an organization can define the organization-wide Oracle applications environment or centralized environment. Each logical group within the multi-org environment can have its own Oracle applications environment or decentralized environment. For example, Corporate can dictate the supplier naming standards while each operational facility can dictate its payables environment.

Oracle's multi-org concepts must be understood prior to defining the multi-org environment. Understanding the multi-org levels is critical for the multi-org environment to work properly. The multi-org concepts are displayed in Exhibit 1.5.

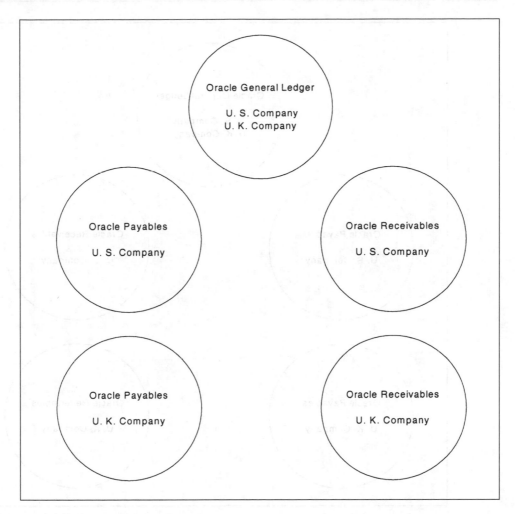

Exhibit 1.3 Single Org Architecture

Prior to defining the multi-org structure, develop the multi-org design on paper first. Use Exhibit 1.6 as a simple template to design and document the various organization levels and values. See Chapter 6 for the required setup steps and more information.

Relational Architecture

Oracle applications' underlying architecture is Oracle's relational database version 8*i*. A relational database is composed of tables. A table is

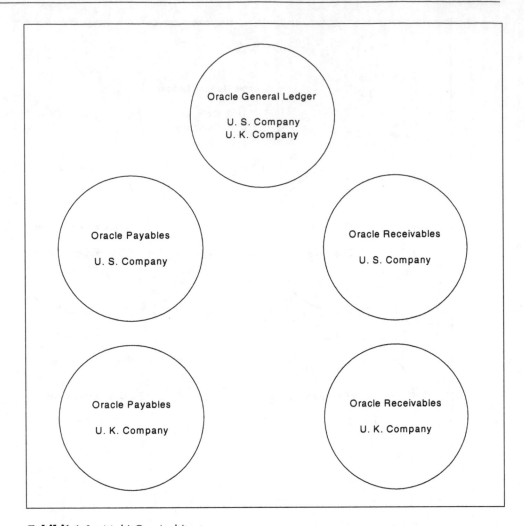

Exhibit 1.4   Multi-Org Architecture

very similar to a spreadsheet with rows representing data records and columns representing the data element types. The supplier table consists of supplier number, supplier name, supplier type, and so forth (see Exhibit 1.8).

A relational database table is a collection of data records (see Exhibit 1.7). For example, a supplier table is a collection of supplier records or rows. A row is a unique record. The rows make up the data records. Ex-

Level	Description
Business Group	The top level of the multi-org environment. Employees are assigned to a business group, which segregates the Oracle Human Resources data.
GRE/Legal Entity	A legal entity is the organization level at which financial and tax reporting occurs. A legal entity links to a GL Set of Books.
Operating Unit	An operating unit is the subdivision of an organization within a GL Set of Books. Oracle Applications subsystems such as Oracle Payables or Oracle Receivables are defined at the operating unit level. In addition, security may be defined at the operating unit level to disallow one operating unit from entering or viewing data from another operating unit.
Inventory Organization	Inventory organizations are required by Oracle Applications which utilize inventory functionality. The inventory organization typically represents the different inventory locations, such as the organization's various warehouses.

Exhibit 1.5 Multi-Org Concepts

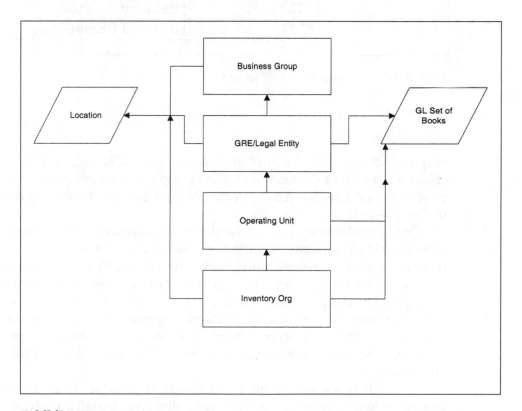

Exhibit 1.6 Organization Design

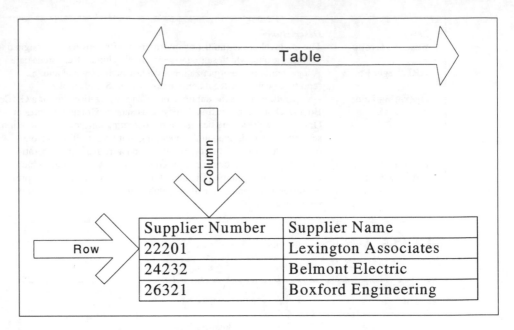

Exhibit 1.7   Relational Table Architecture

amples include: 22201 Lexington Associates or 24232 Belmont Electric. A column is a field or data element. For example, a supplier number or supplier name field represents a column. A combination of columns or fields makes a record.

Oracle's relational database architecture supports one-to-many data relationships (see Exhibit 1.8). Each table may have a one-to-many relationship with another table. Tables are related by a key column and are indicated to the user through different screens or windows. For example, one supplier may have more than one supplier site or location. The one supplier record, Boxford Engineering, has three supplier site records. Project team members must understand this concept prior to designing and developing conversion programs for suppliers or customers.

In addition, the one-to-many relational database architecture will be evident when navigating through the windows. Usually, each window represents a table. For example, there is one window for supplier and another window for supplier sites. If the two tables are displayed in one

Supplier Table

Supplier Number	Supplier Name
22201	Lexington Associates
24232	Belmont Electric
26321	Boxford Engineering

Supplier Site Table

Supplier Number	Supplier Site
26321	Boston
26321	Orlando
26321	Los Angeles

Exhibit 1.8   Oracle Table Relationships

window, usually they are segregated into blocks or logical divisions of the window.

Windows also may call views or subsets of the table. Oracle application windows in a multi-org environment call a view of the related table. For example, the data displayed in the Payable Options window is a view of the related table for the specific organization. The table contains all the data and the view provides the organization-specific subset of the table.

CHAPTER 2

Oracle Applications Navigation

Learning to navigate Oracle's E-Business Suite successfully is important for all team members. Once the navigation concepts are understood, the user should be able to navigate any Oracle application.

OVERVIEW

Learning how to navigate through Oracle applications is critical. While the navigation process is similar to navigating through a PC application, the navigation is not identical. Users must be able to navigate through the application, and be comfortable with the data entry and query capabilities. The typical sign-on process is displayed in Exhibit 2.1.

ACCESSING ORACLE APPLICATIONS

Each organization should have in-house documentation for starting the PC and the Oracle applications sign-on process. The six steps are:

1. Start the Personal Computer.
2. Start the Web Browser.
3. Start Oracle Applications.
4. Sign-on to Oracle Applications.
5. Select a Responsibility.

29

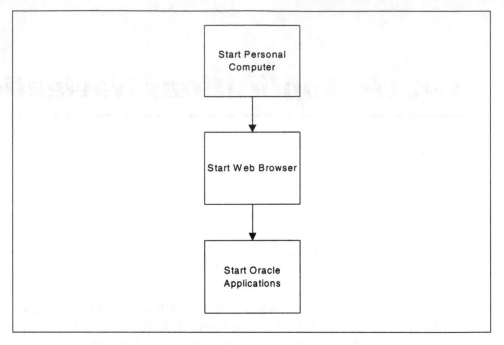

Exhibit 2.1   Start Up Process

6. Navigate through the menus to select a transaction or inquiry window.

Once you have started your computer:

1. Enter the **Internet** address supplied by the System Administrator in the Address field and press **Go.**
2. Save the address as a Favorite for ease-of-access in the future. Enter a descriptive, yet short name, such as OFDEV or OFPROD to indicate the Oracle instance, such as development or production.

The Oracle sign-on window is displayed in Exhibit 2.2. Follow the appropriate sign-on directions.

The sign-on procedure requires two steps:

1. Enter the User Name and Password that are supplied by the System Administrator. Enter **sysadmin/sysadmin**.
2. Press **Connect**.

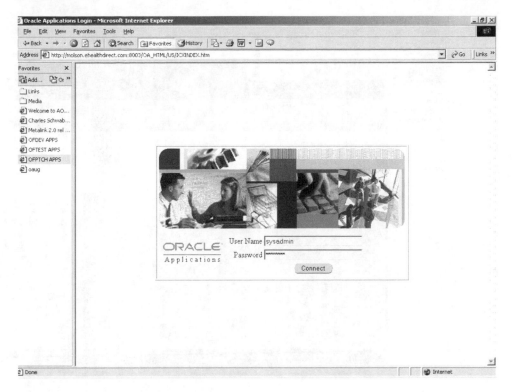

Exhibit 2.2   Oracle Applications Sign-On

Oracle will prompt to change the password with the initial sign-on. Oracle applications will open the password change window. Enter the old password. Enter the new password and re-enter the new password again for verification purposes.

SELECT RESPONSIBILITY

The user's homepage displays with the list of valid responsibilities (see Exhibit 2.3). More responsibilities may exist than may be displayed on one window. Use the down arrow to review all the responsibilities.

System Administrator Responsibility

From the **Responsibility** list, select the **System Administrator** responsibility and proceed with the System Administrator setup tasks. The default System Administrator sign-on will not display the responsibility list, if

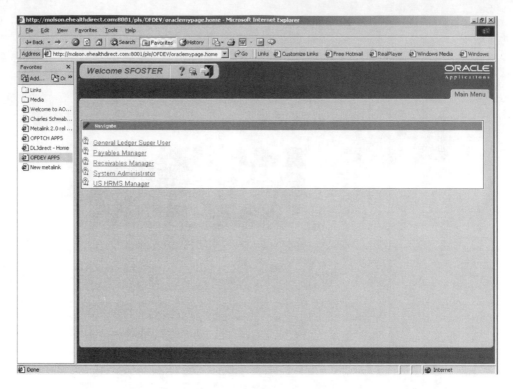

Exhibit 2.3   Home Page List of Responsibilities

only one responsibility exists. The System Administrator main menu will display instead.

User Responsibility

From the **Responsibility** list, select the Oracle application responsibility that you wish to access. If only one responsibility exists for the User Name, the responsibility list will not display; only the menu will display.

The Java applet window will appear after selecting a responsibility. The Java applet is a small program or script that initiates the Oracle application menus and windows from the web browser.

NAVIGATE

Once the Java applet is loaded, the Navigator window appears displaying the menu structure defined for the responsibility (see Exhibit 2.4).

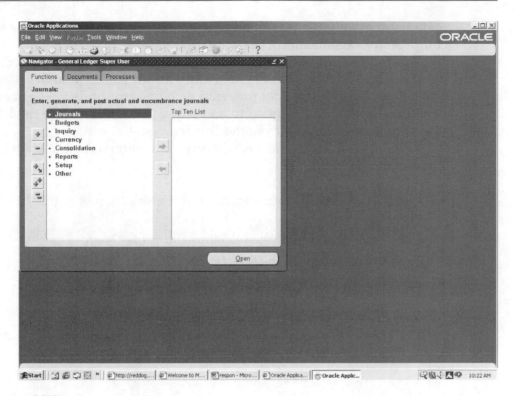

Exhibit 2.4 Menu Architecture

In this case, the General Ledger Super User menu structure is displayed. (A Super User responsibility has all the application capabilities except purge.) Typically, a user navigates through the menus to the applicable window.

The menu window displays, from the top down, the Oracle applications menu commands, the Oracle applications toolbar, and the Oracle applications Navigator. The Navigator displays three tabs. Each tab represents different functionality.

The Functions tab navigates the user through the application via menus and allows data entry in the application windows. The Documents tabs allow the user to place frequently referenced windows in the document tab. Whenever the Place on Navigator command is displayed from the File menu, the document may be saved for future reference. The Processes tab displays the workflow defined for the application. For example, the journal entry process may be defined as a workflow. Oracle's workflow technology allows the flow of business processes to be automated and graphically represented. Users may follow the workflow to accomplish the organization's business process flow.

The Top Ten List allows users to save the ten most commonly accessed windows and navigate directly to them without going through the menu navigation. Simply highlight the window name and press the right arrow key in the middle of the menu to add to the Top Ten List. Use the left arrow to remove a window from the Top Ten List.

To navigate through the menu, many navigation options are available. Choose among:

- Use the ↓ ↑ arrows to navigate until the selection is highlighted and press **Open**.
- Click once to highlight the selection and press **Open**.
- Type the first letter of the selection and press **Open**.
- Double click on the selection.

The different menu icons are described in Exhibit 2.5.
The Oracle Menu is displayed as the first line on the menu or window.

Icon	Meaning	Description
✛	Expand	Expands to display all menu selections for the selected menu level.
▬	Collapse	Minimizes the menu display for the selected menu level.
✛↘	Expand Branch	Displays all menu selections for the selected level.
✛	Expand All	Expands to display all menu selections.
▬	Collapse All	Minimizes the display of all menu selections.
→	Add to List	Add to the Top Ten List.
←	Remove from List	Remove from the Top Ten List.

Exhibit 2.5   Oracle Menu Icons

The Oracle applications menu is displayed in Exhibit 2.6. The individual menu commands are described in Exhibit 2.7.

Just as with other PC software applications, Oracle applications use the Alt + another key functionality. The Alt plus the underlined menu command will perform the same function as if the user selected the command by using the mouse.

The Oracle Applications File Menu is displayed in Exhibit 2.8. The commonly used commands are displayed in Exhibit 2.9.

The Oracle Applications Edit Menu is displayed in Exhibit 2.10.

The Edit menu allows you to change the data records standard with any PC application using the **Cut, Copy,** and **Paste** commands.

Clear Record and **Delete** are very similar with a key difference. The **Clear Record** command removes the record from the window display. If the record has not been saved to the database, as in an data entry error, the record is gone. If the record has been saved to the database, the record is gone from the window but still in the database with the Clear Record command. Use the **Delete** command to delete the record from the window and the database.

Use the **Edit Field** to view the entire data value. The window may not

File Edit View Folder Tools Window Help

Exhibit 2.6   Oracle Menu

Command	Description
File	Executes navigation, save, print, switch responsibility, close form, and exit commands.
Edit	Executes clear and delete commands. In addition, executes standard PC cut, copy, and paste commands.
View	Executes queries to retrieve data.
Folder	Allows the user to customize window displays and saves predefined queries.
Tools	Executes commands specific to the application. Also executes the Reprint command.
Window	Shows current windows open.
Help	Executes user help and technical diagnostic information.

Exhibit 2.7   Oracle Menu Commands

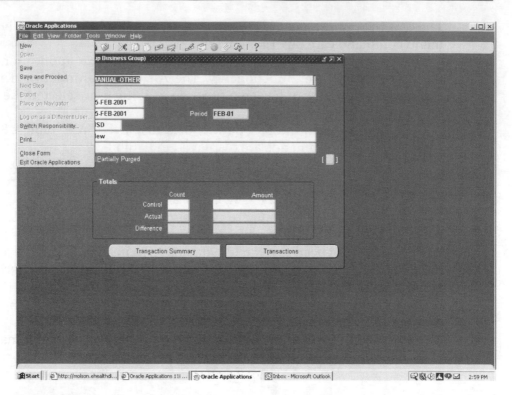

Exhibit 2.8   Oracle Applications File Menu

Command	Description
Command	*Description*
New	Use the New command to insert a new data record.
Open	Use the Open command to review data records previously entered.
Save	Use the Save command to save the data entry to the database.
Switch Responsibility	Use the Switch Responsibility command to change responsibilities.
Print	Use the Print command to print the window.
Close Form	Use the Close Form to close the window. Alternatively, check the X in the top, right-hand corner of the window as with any PC application.
Exit Oracle Applications	Use Exit Oracle Applications to exit Oracle Applications. The system will prompt with a message to confirm the exit.

Exhibit 2.9   Commonly Used File Commands

 When exiting Oracle applications, make sure to close the Java applet window and the homepage responsibility window.

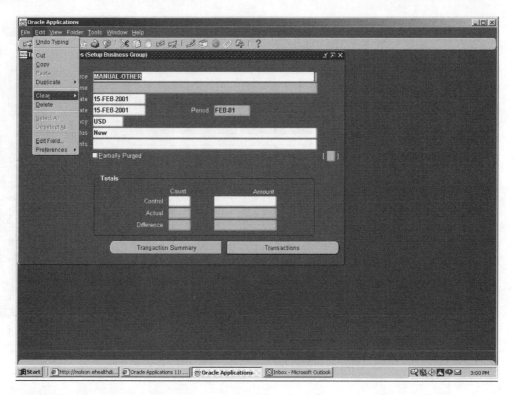

Exhibit 2.10   Oracle Applications Edit Menu

display all the characters of the data element due to the display length of the field.

The **Select** capabilities allow you to select one or more records at one time. To select multiple records hold the Ctrl key plus the record. To select a range of records click on the first record plus shift plus click on the last record. To deselect a single record, press the Ctrl key plus click on the record to deselect. Selected records are colored in blue.

The **Preferences** commands allow the user to view profile values or change the Oracle applications password.

The Oracle Applications View Menu is displayed in Exhibit 2.11. The View Menu allows the user to find data saved in the database. The commonly used commands are displayed in Exhibit 2.12.

The Oracle Applications Folder Menu is displayed in Exhibit 2.13. The Folder command allows the user to modify the window formats. For example, the user may wish to hide fields, enlarge fields, and so on. The

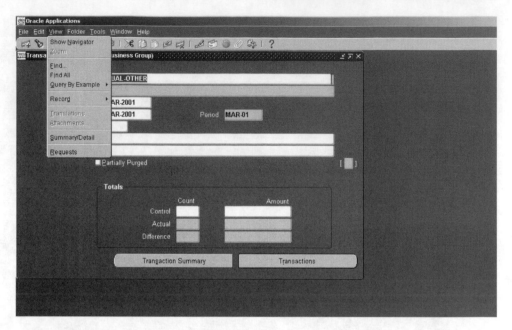

Exhibit 2.11   Oracle Applications View Menu

Command	Description
Find	Use Find command to open the Find window and enter the search criteria to retrieve data.
Query by Example Enter	Use the Query by Example Enter command to enter query mode within the window. Enter the search criteria.
Query by Example Run	Use the Query by Example Run command to execute the query after entering the search criteria. All matching records will be displayed. If no records match the search criteria, the system will display No Records Found message.
Requests	Use the Requests command to view concurrent requests.

Exhibit 2.12   Commonly Used View Commands

modified window version is saved in the folder and accessed rather than the original window. In addition, Folders can save predefined queries. Folder commands are optional.

The Oracle Applications Tool Menu is displayed in Exhibit 2.14. The Tool Menu is specific by application. For example, Oracle Inventory uses the Tools menu to start the Calendar Build program. The most commonly

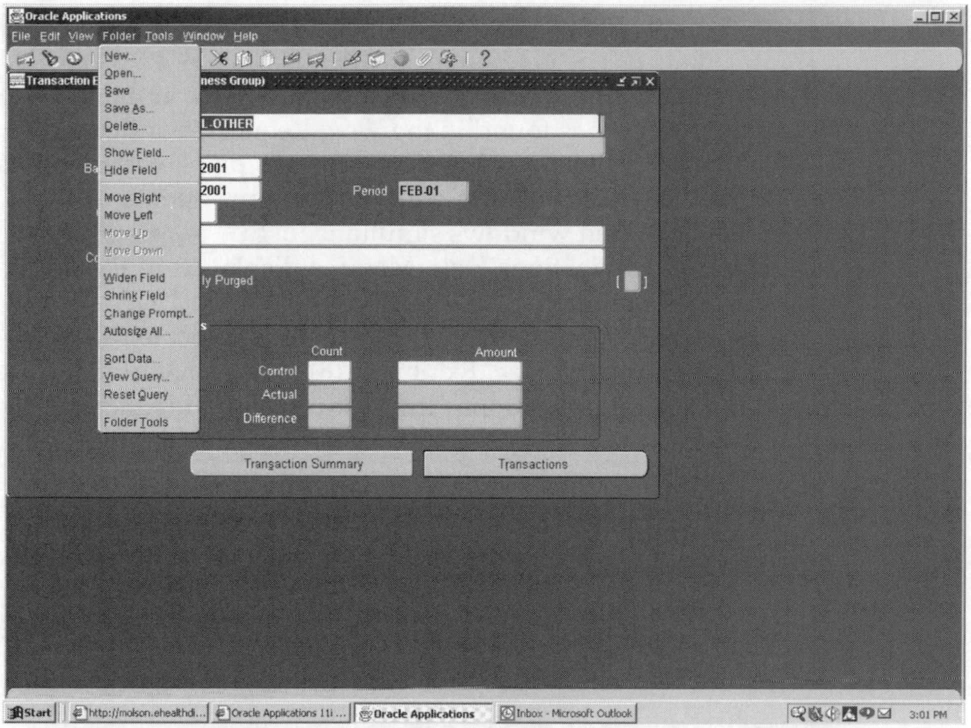

Exhibit 2.13 Oracle Applications Folder Menu

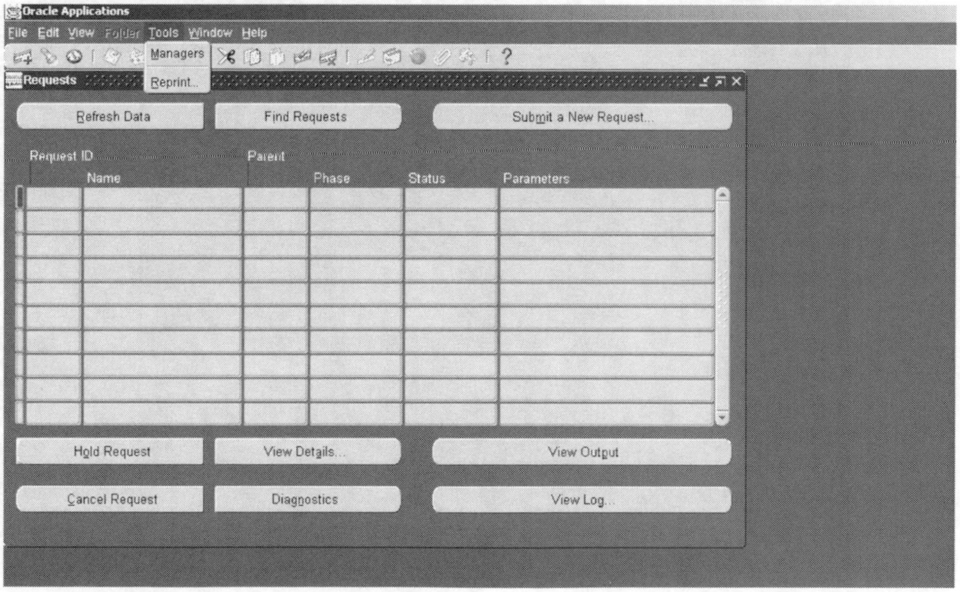

Exhibit 2.14 Oracle Applications Tools Menu

39

used command is the Reprint command. Use this command to reprint a concurrent request. It is found in the View Requests window.

The Oracle Applications Window Menu is displayed in Exhibit 2.15. The Window Menu shows the current windows open and the different ways of viewing open windows simultaneously.

The Oracle Applications Help Menu is displayed in Exhibit 2.16. The commonly used commands are displayed in Exhibit 2.17.

To display the default keyboard commands, execute the Help → Keyboard Help command (see Exhibit 2.18). Note the function keys are mapped in Oracle Applications. The user may use the function keys to ex-

 To navigate through fields, use the <Tab> key. The <Enter> key executes the default command.

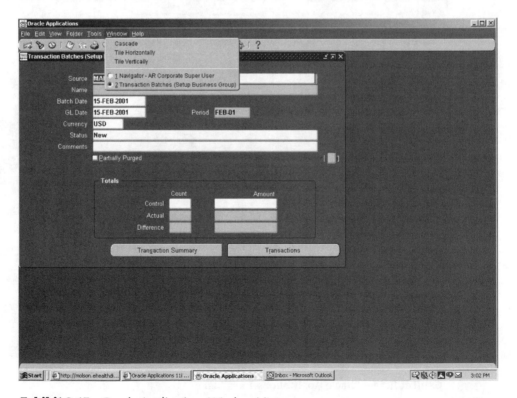

Exhibit 2.15   Oracle Applications Window Menu

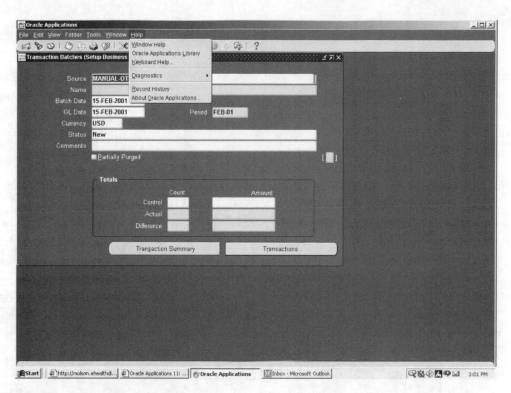

Exhibit 2.16   Oracle Applications Help Menu

Command	Description
Command	*Description*
Window Help	
Oracle Applications Library	Select the Oracle Applications Library and a help window will open; you may drill-down to the appropriate level of documentation.
Keyboard Help	Use to view the keyboard mapping.
Diagnostics	Use the Diagnostics commands to view error messages. The Diagnostics → Display Database Error will display database error messages.
Record History	Select Record History to view the table or view name, and who created and last updated the record. The command only works with records saved to the database.

Exhibit 2.17   Commonly Used Help Menu Commands

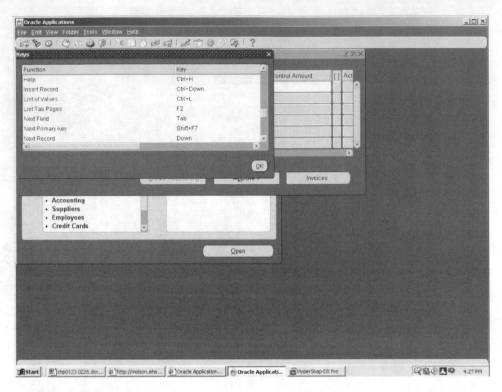

Exhibit 2.18   Oracle Keyboard

ecute certain commands rather than use the mouse to display the command (see Exhibit 2.19).

Toolbar

The Oracle toolbar is displayed as the second line on the menu or window (see Exhibit 2.20). The Oracle applications menu is displayed in Exhibit 2.20. The individual toolbar icons are described in Exhibit 2.21.

 The toolbar name will appear when the cursor is dragged over the toolbar icon.

Windows

Oracle application screens are called windows (see Exhibit 2.22). A window displays the data via the rows and columns of the applicable table.

Key	Description
↓	Use the ↓ key to go to the next row. Typically, the ↓ key is used to navigate to a new row for data entry.
↑	Use the ↑ key to go to the previous row.
Tab	Use the Tab key instead to move from field to field.
Enter	The Enter key should not be pressed after each field as it accepts the default button. The default is indicated by the dashed lines around the command.
Alt + Tab	Use Alt + Tab to move back from the current field to the prior field.
Shift Pg Dn	Use Shift Page Down to go to the next block in the window.
Shift Pg Up	Use Shift Page Up to go to the previous block in the window.
F6	Use F6 to clear the records from display. It is the same as the Edit ➡ Clear Record command.
F11	Use F11 to enter the query search criteria. It is the same as the View ➡ Query by Example Enter command.
Ctrl + F11	Use Ctrl + F11 to execute the query. This is the same as the View ➡ Query by Example Run command.
Ctrl + L	Use Ctrl + L to view the List of Values.

Exhibit 2.19   Commonly Used Keyboard Commands

Exhibit 2.20   Oracle Applications Toolbar

Notice how the supplier data is located in one window and the supplier site data is located in another window. In this example, the Lexington Associates supplier record is displayed. To view the next record (or row of data), simply press the down arrow key in the window just as in spreadsheet. To view the previous record, simply press the up arrow key. The window components are displayed in Exhibit 2.23.

Icon	Meaning	Description
	New	Opens a new record for data entry
	Find	Opens the Find window
	Show Navigator	Opens the Navigator window
	Save	Commits the record to the database
	Next Step	Opens the next step defined in the Process workflow
	Print	Prints the current window
	Close Form	Closes the window. (Windows were called forms in older releases.)
	Cut	Cuts the selected object
	Copy	Copies the selected object
	Paste	Pastes the copy of the selected object
	Clear Record	Erases the record from the window. Doesn't delete the data from the database, only the window
	Delete	Deletes the record. Oracle will not allow deletion of records which may compromise the database. For example, deleting a posted journal would corrupt the audit trail to the GL balances
	Edit	Opens the Editor window or full field display
	Zoom	Custom drill-down capabilities
	Translations	Opens the Translations window
	Attachments	Opens the Attachments window. A paper clip will appear indicating an existing attachment
	Folder Tools	Opens the Folders windows
	Window Help	Opens online Help documentation

Exhibit 2.21 Toolbar Icons

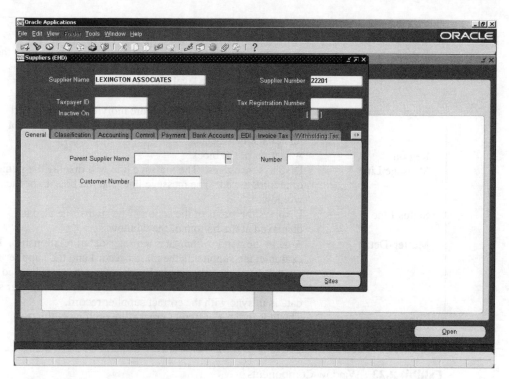

Exhibit 2.22   Supplier Window

Data Fields

The data fields on the window are displayed in colors. See Exhibit 2.24 for sample data field colors.

Other Icons

Oracle application windows utilize buttons, check boxes, option groups, and other icons. See Exhibit 2.25 for a list of other Oracle application icons and their respective meanings.

 The applications utilize dates to enable or disable a system capability. Oracle will label these as Effective Dates, Inactive On, Start, and End Dates, or From and To dates. Entering the end date disables the record or capability. Deleting the end date field will cause the record or capability to be enabled again.

Window Title	A short descriptive name for the window.
Window	A window may display one or more windows and allows the user to perform data entry, inquiry, and reporting business processes. Window-level security is standard throughout Oracle applications.
Block	A window is made of one or more individual areas called blocks. A block usually represents a table or collection of related data elements.
Region	A section of the block
Message Line	Displays messages. The message line will display the number of records saved. The message line is at the bottom of the window.
Status Line	Displays the status of the action. The status line also is displayed at the bottom of the window.
Master-Detail	A ☑ in the window indicates a master-detail relationship. For example, the supplier is the master record and the supplier sites are the detail records. Typically, the ☑ indicator is located in the top-right corner of the window to indicate the supplier site data is in sync with the correct supplier record.
Tab	The tabs indicate different processing options within the window.

Exhibit 2.23 Window Components

Color	*Use*
White	Data entry
Ivory	Required data entry field
Gray with black text	Display-only data fields
Gray with gray text	Disabled data entry fields
Blue	Queriable fields *or* selected records

Exhibit 2.24 Data Field Colors

The supplier site data is entered in another block of the supplier entry window (see Exhibit 2.26). To go back to the supplier block, execute the Close Form command.

 The Close Form command must be used to close each window after the data is saved and to navigate back to the previous window or menu.

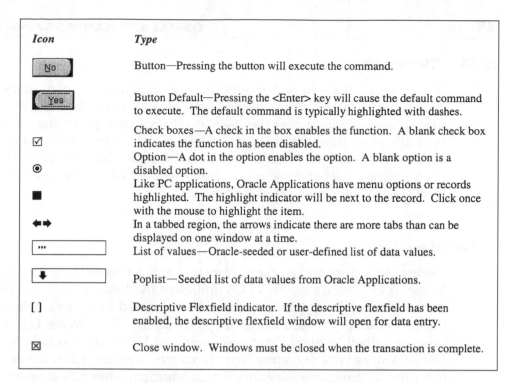

Icon	Type
No button	Button—Pressing the button will execute the command.
Yes button	Button Default—Pressing the <Enter> key will cause the default command to execute. The default command is typically highlighted with dashes.
☑	Check boxes—A check in the box enables the function. A blank check box indicates the function has been disabled.
◉	Option—A dot in the option enables the option. A blank option is a disabled option.
■	Like PC applications, Oracle Applications have menu options or records highlighted. The highlight indicator will be next to the record. Click once with the mouse to highlight the item.
◆➡	In a tabbed region, the arrows indicate there are more tabs than can be displayed on one window at a time.
...	List of values—Oracle-seeded or user-defined list of data values.
⬇	Poplist—Seeded list of data values from Oracle Applications.
[ ]	Descriptive Flexfield indicator. If the descriptive flexfield has been enabled, the descriptive flexfield window will open for data entry.
⊠	Close window. Windows must be closed when the transaction is complete.

Exhibit 2.25   Other Icons

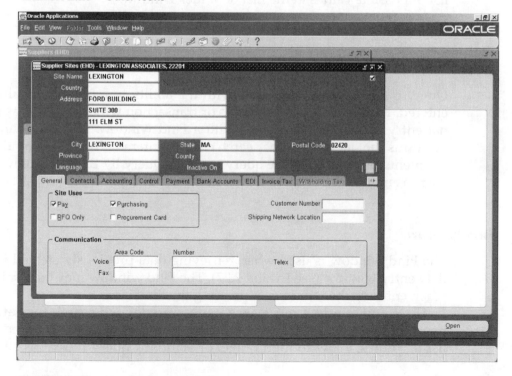

Exhibit 2.26   Supplier Site Window

47

DATA ENTRY MODE

Oracle applications have two modes of operation: data entry mode and query mode. Data entry mode allows the users to enter data into the database. Query mode allows the user to retrieve data previously entered. Typically, most transaction windows start in data entry mode and inquiry windows start in query mode. In data entry mode, the data should be entered in a new row in the window. Down arrow to a new row or press the New icon to enter a new row of data.

List of Values

During data entry mode, the user may come across fields with a List of Values (LOV) indicator. This LOV indicates the field is validated from a List of Values. The valid values have been defined in a previous window during setup. Only valid values may be selected. To open the List of Values, the default keyboard mapping in release 11*i* is Ctrl plus L. When in a List of Values window, enter first characters to shorten list. In addition, enter the % to retrieve the entire list. In addition, enter a % to shorten the list of possible values in the List of Values window.

QUERY MODE

Query mode provides the users with the ability to retrieve data already entered. Many data entry windows or transaction windows, such as journal entry or invoice entry, start with a Find window. The Find window performs the query with the search criteria entered. The Query by Example menu also performs the query process. Query by Example allows the user to enter search criteria, then execute the query.

Find Window

The Find window is used when retrieving data previously created in the data entry window (see Exhibit 2.27). The Find window may be displayed when entering the window, or pressing the Find icon.

The Find window retrieves data in a predefined search format. Depending on the field, the Find window allows data to be retrieved by a list of values, a low to high range, or standard query functions such as

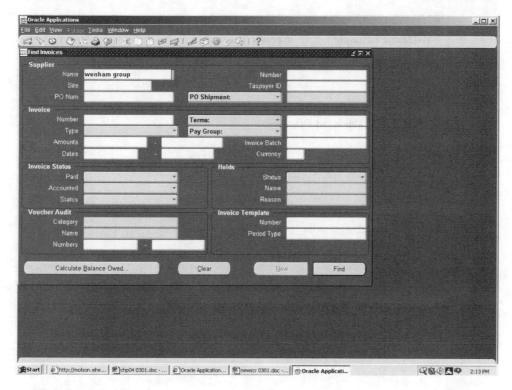

Exhibit 2.27 Find Window

◆ and %. The greater than (>) and less than (<) operators allow a range of values to be retrieved, such as company greater than 01 and less than 10, for example.

Wildcard Search

The % is a wildcard operator. When a % is used in a query, all data matching the character string will be retrieved. If the data records are US INDUSTRIES, MOUSE INDUSTRIES, and AMBULUS, the wildcard search will select different records depending on the location of the % character. For example, to retrieve all suppliers with the name starting with US, in query mode, enter US%. To retrieve all suppliers with the name ending with US, enter %US. To retrieve all suppliers with US anywhere in the supplier name, enter %US % (see Exhibit 2.28).

Wildcard Example	*Record Selected*
US%	US INDUSTRIES
%US	AMBULUS
%US%	All records would be selected.

Exhibit 2.28   Wildcard Examples

CHAPTER 3

Setting Up Oracle Applications

OVERVIEW

The Oracle applications foundation must be defined prior to setting up the Oracle applications (see Exhibit 3.1). The analysis process for the setup decisions can be time-consuming. However, the actual setup process is usually not time-consuming. Remember to take screen shots of all setup steps and document them appropriately.

The setup steps include defining the Oracle applications system environment, the General Ledger environment, the multi-org environment, and the respective applications.

The first step is defining the application foundation, which includes setting up the users and responsibilities. The next step is to define the accounting flexfield structure and values. Once the accounting flexfield has been defined, Oracle General Ledger is set up to define the GL Set of Books environment. Multi-org setup is not required but is recommended. Once multi-org has been enabled, Oracle Payables and Oracle Receivables may be defined.

The System Administrator is responsible for setting up the application foundation and monitoring Oracle applications. The System Administrator defines the users, menus, user responsibilities, printers, and appropriate profile values (see Exhibit 3.2). In addition, the System Administrator is responsible for defining and controlling concurrent processing.

Responsibilities must be defined for the specific Oracle application before being linked to a user. The responsibility defines the application

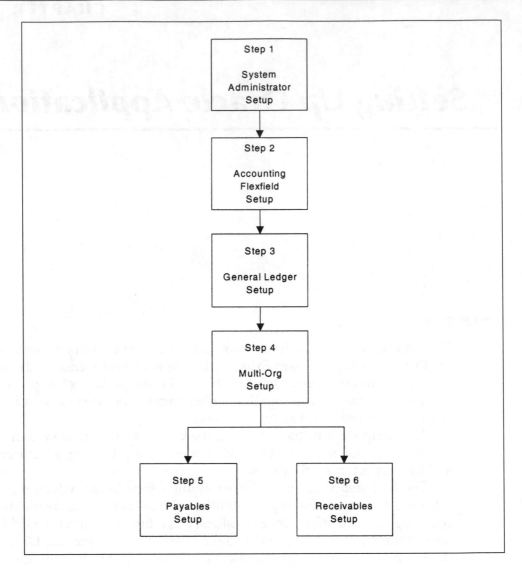

Exhibit 3.1   Oracle Applications Setup Steps

menus and windows the user may access. The responsibility is then
linked to the user. Note, one responsibility may be shared by many
users. The printers are used to print concurrent requests. Once the
printers are defined, they should be linked to the profile level. In addition, the concurrent processing setup step tests the concurrent processing capabilities.

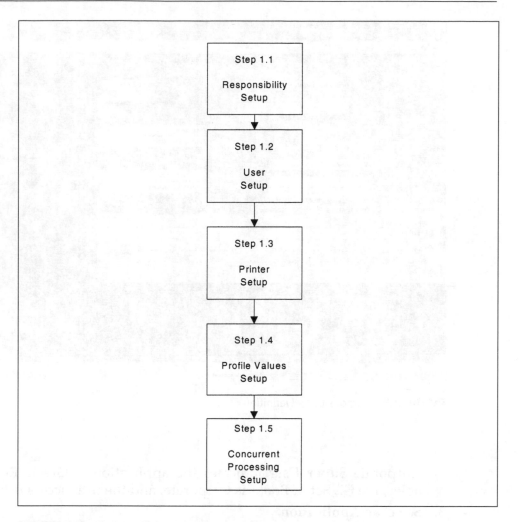

Exhibit 3.2   System Administrator Start Up Process

SYSTEM ADMINISTRATOR STEP 1.1: RESPONSIBILITY

Enter a new responsibility (see Exhibit 3.3). This step is optional, but is typical for a multi-org implementation.

1. From the System Administrator menu → **Security** → **Responsibility** → **Define**

2. Enter a **Responsibility Name.** The name should reflect the application, the user access, and the GL Set of Books. For example, AR

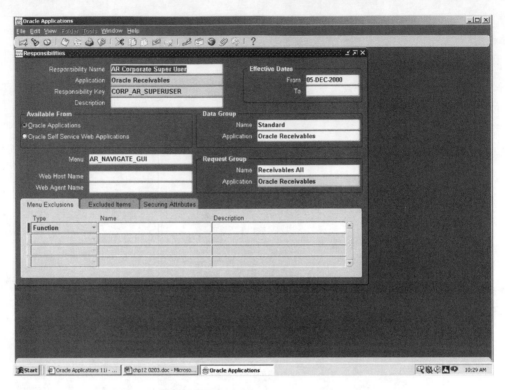

Exhibit 3.3 Responsibility Definition

Corporate Super User indicates the application is Oracle Receivables, the GL Set of Books is Corporate, and the user access is full.

3. Select an **Application.**

4. Enter a unique **Responsibility Key.**

5. Select a **Data Group Name.** Typically, the Data Group Name is Standard.

6. Select the **Data Group Application** for the Data Group. Typically, the application is the same as above.

7. Select the application **Menu** to display when the user signs on.

8. Select the **Request Group Name** to determine the available reports and concurrent processes. The Request Group Application will display.

Repeat for all responsibilities to be defined in the multi-org environment.

The books uses three new responsibilities: GL Corporate Super User, AP Corporate Super User, and AR Corporate Super User.

SYSTEM ADMINISTRATOR STEP 1.2: USER

Once the responsibilities have been defined, they may be linked to the applicable user (see Exhibit 3.4). The six steps involved are:

1. From the System Administrator menu → **Security** → **User** → **Define.**
2. Enter the **User Name.** Follow in-house naming standards, such as first initial and last name. The User Name will appear on all concurrent processes and audit trail data. The User Name should immediately identify the specific user. Avoid old legacy codes such as U4000 which do not readily identify the user.
3. Enter a **Description** of the user.
4. Enter the **Password.** The password will not display. Press the tab key and re-enter the password for verification purposes.

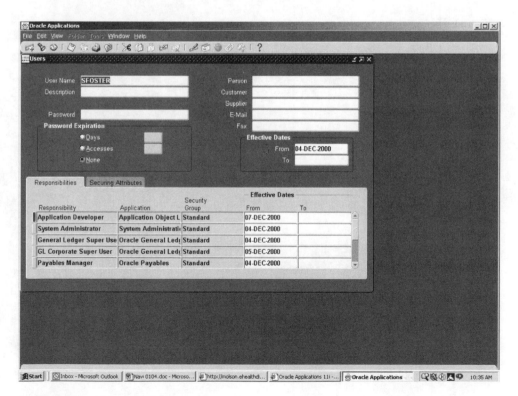

Exhibit 3.4 User Definition

5. Optionally, select the Person after Employees have been defined.

6. In the Responsibilities tab, select the **Responsibility.** Select all responsibilities to be utilized in the multi-org environment.

SYSTEM ADMINISTRATOR STEP 1.3: PRINTER

The organization's printers must be defined in Oracle applications (see Exhibit 3.5). Review the seeded printer types, and define the new printer styles and drivers as necessary. Test all printer types and printer styles such as portrait, landscape, and landwide to ensure the print properties are working properly.

1. From the System Administrator menu → **Install** → **Printer** → **Register**

2. Enter the operating system **Printer** name.

3. Select the printer **Type.**

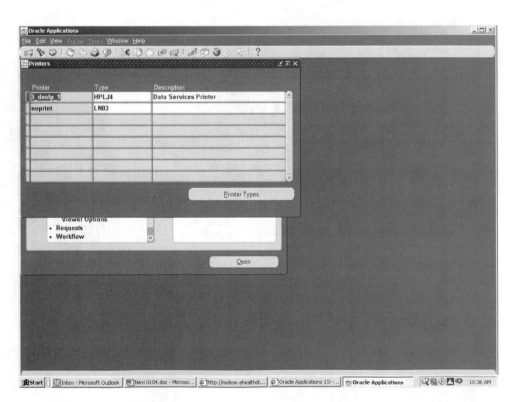

Exhibit 3.5   Printer Definition

If the printer type is not seeded, refer to the *Oracle Applications System Administrator's Guide* for the printer definition process.

SYSTEM ADMINISTRATOR STEP 1.4: PROFILE VALUES

Profile values set at the Site level cascade to the Application level that cascade to the Responsibility level that cascade to the User level (see Exhibit 3.6). Each level has different profile options, which may be set at the specific level.

Typically, the System Administrator sets the initial profile value settings. The users may change the individual settings as they see fit. However, many profile options can only be set by the System Administrator. The message " (Profile) Item is protected against update" indicates the profile value may not be changed by the user.

Common profile values are displayed in Exhibit 3.7.

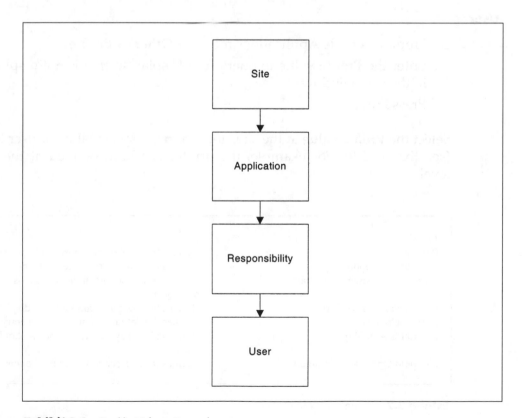

Exhibit 3.6   Profile Values Cascade

Refer to the *Oracle Applications System Administrator's Guide* for a complete definition of the common profile options. The documentation will define profile option levels as well.

The profile values must be set at the appropriate levels (see Exhibit 3.8).

System Administrator

1. From the System Administrator menu → **Profile** → **System.**
2. Check the appropriate **Display** profile level box.
3. Enter the **Profile** value to query.
4. Press **Find.**

User

1. From the Oracle Applications menu → **Other** → **Profile.**
2. Enter the **Profile** value to query. The Display section is not displayed in the user window.
3. Press **Find.**

Select the **Profile** value at the site, application, responsibility, or user level (see Exhibit 3.9). For example, the printer has been defined at the Site level.

Profile	*Use*
Printer	Defines the printer for report printing
Concurrent: Report Copies	Defines the number of copies to be printed
Currency: Thousands Separator	Defines how amounts in the thousands are displayed
Currency: Negative Format	Defines how negative amounts are displayed
Default Country	Defines the default country for data entry
Flexfields AutoSkip	Defines if the key flexfield window should open
Flexfield Open Descr Window	Defines if the descriptive flexfield opens

Exhibit 3.7   Common Profile Values

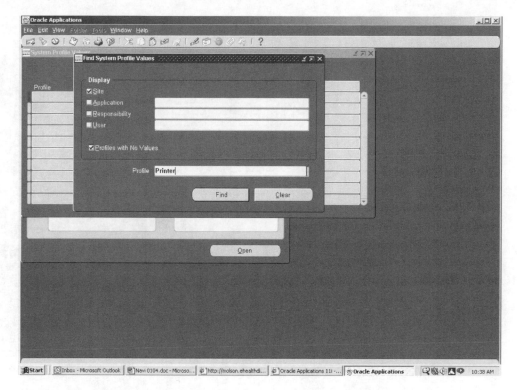

Exhibit 3.8 Profile Definition: Find

SYSTEM ADMINISTRATOR STEP 1.5: CONCURRENT PROCESSES

The System Administrator is responsible for managing the concurrent processing. As part of the setup process, the System Administrator should initiate a concurrent request to verify that the concurrent manager is working properly. In addition, the System Administrator should view the report output and log files, and test all print styles utilized within Oracle applications.

Submitting a Concurrent Process

To run a concurrent process, most Oracle Application responsibilities navigate to the Other Run Request menu option (see Exhibit 3.10).

1. From Oracle Applications → **Other** → **Requests** → **Run.**
2. The default is to run a **Single Request.** Press **OK.**

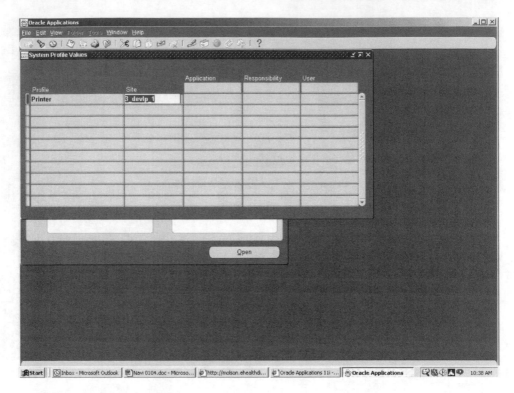

Exhibit 3.9   Profile Definition: Profile Values

3. Select the Concurrent Process **Name.** Concurrent processes include reports and batch programs. A complete list is found in the respective Oracle Applications User Guides.

4. Press **OK.**

5. The **Parameters** window will open if run-time parameters are available. Run-time parameters allow the report to be produced from a variety of reporting perspectives such as accounting flexfield ranges or date ranges.

6. Press **OK.**

7. The completed concurrent request with parameters will be displayed.

8. Press **Submit.**

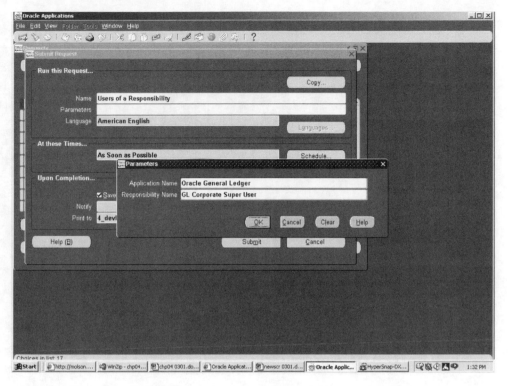

Exhibit 3.10 Concurrent Request Submission

Viewing Concurrent Requests

Some concurrent requests zoom directly to the View Requests window. If the View Requests window doesn't display, use the View Requests command (see Exhibit 3.11).

1. From the **View** menu → **Requests View.**
2. Enter the Concurrent Request search criteria.
3. Press **F̲ind** to execute the query.
4. The status of all concurrent requests for the user are displayed. If a concurrent request is Pending, press **R̲efresh Data** to requery the concurrent process phase. The new phase will not display until the request is requeried.

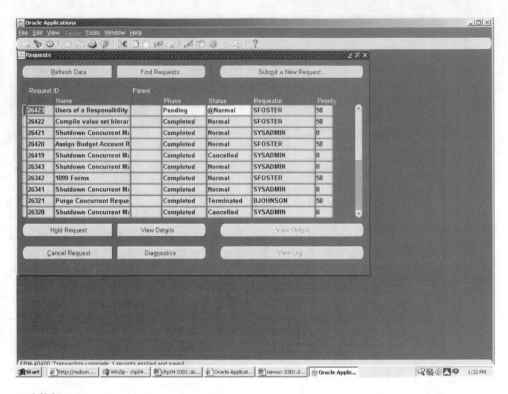

Exhibit 3.11   Viewing Concurrent Requests

5. When the concurrent process is complete, press **View Output** to view the concurrent process output (see Exhibit 3.12). Press **View Log** to view the concurrent process log. If the concurrent process ends in Error, review the log (see Exhibit 3.13).

Review the report file online (see Exhibit 3.12). Change the Font Size to view the entire report. Use these five buttons to navigate through the report:

1. **Go To**—go to page number *n*.
2. **First**—go to the first page.
3. **Previous**—go to the previous page.
4. **Next**—go to the next page.
5. **Last**—go to the last page.

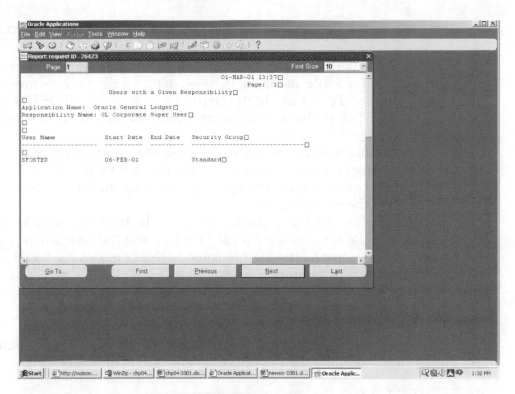

Exhibit 3.12   Reviewing Concurrent Requests Output

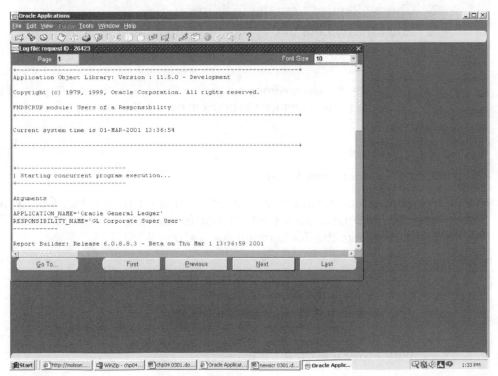

Exhibit 3.13   Reviewing Concurrent Requests Log File

Typically the output file is stored in the Oracle Applications OUT directory, with a file name of the user name and the concurrent request number. For example, the output file name is SFOSTER.26423 where SFOSTER is the user name and 26423 is the concurrent request number.

The log file displays the concurrent request program name, the start time, and program parameters or arguments (see Exhibit 3.13). When a concurrent request ends in error status, reviewing the log file may reveal the cause of the error condition.

Typically the log file is stored in the Oracle Applications LOG directory, with a file name of the l (little l for log) and the concurrent request number. For example, the log file name is l26423.req where 26423 is the concurrent request number.

Reprinting a Concurrent Request

All concurrent requests may be reprinted by querying the concurrent requests and executing the Reprint command (see Exhibit 3.14).

1. Highlight the appropriate concurrent request record.
2. Choose **Reprint** from the Tools menu.
3. Enter the number of **Copies**, the **Printer**, and the **Style**.
4. Press **OK.**

 Typically, the test environment has the Concurrent: Report Copies set to 0. Use the reprint command to print the report after review.

Downloading a Concurrent Request

All concurrent requests may be downloaded to the PC. Oracle reports may be downloaded for additional formatting or calculations. Choose **Copy File** from the Tools menu (see Exhibit 3.15).

1. Navigate to the appropriate concurrent request record.
2. Press **View Output.**
3. Choose **Copy File** from the Tools menu.
4. Press **File → Save As →** and enter the directory and file name just as with any other PC document.

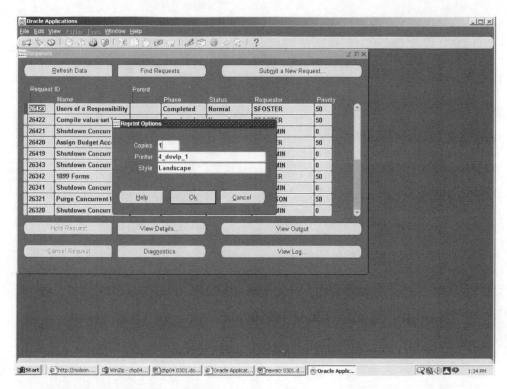

Exhibit 3.14 Reprinting

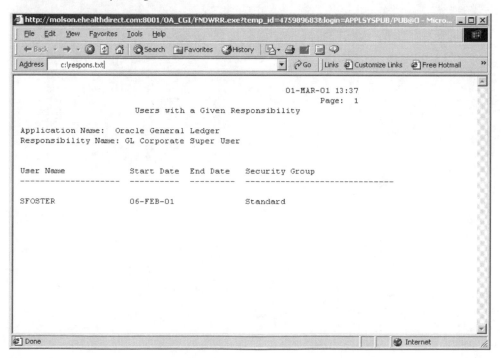

Exhibit 3.15 Downloading a File

CHAPTER 4

Flexfields

OVERVIEW

Oracle applications provide flexfields to allow each organization the ability to define its own reporting structures. Two kinds of flexfields are provided: key flexfields and descriptive flexfields. Key flexfields are required within Oracle applications to record key data elements. Descriptive flexfields are user-defined and record required data elements not provided by the standard application functionality.

Oracle application key flexfields are predefined. Each key flexfield is owned by a specific Oracle application, but is shared across all the applications. Sample key flexfields include the accounting flexfield, the inventory system items flexfield, the sales tax location flexfield, and the customer territory flexfield (see Exhibit 4.1). Each organization defines its specific key flexfield structures and data values. For example, one organi-

Flexfield	*Structure*	*Samples*
Accounting	Company - Account - Cost Center	01-1101-100
System Item	Inventory Part Number	728429
Customer Territory	Customer Location	North America
Sales Tax Location	State – County – City	MA-ESSEX-BOXFORD

Exhibit 4.1 Sample Key Flexfields

zation may have one accounting flexfield structure while another organization may have a different one.

 Refer to *Oracle Applications Flexfields Guide* for a list of all Oracle applications key flexfield structures.

The accounting flexfield utilized throughout the book is displayed in Exhibit 4.2 and consists of company, account, cost center, and product line.

The accounting flexfield represents the chart of accounts for recording financial transactions. Each organization defines its specific accounting flexfield, as the application software does not determine the structure.

ACCOUNTING FLEXFIELD

The accounting flexfield is probably the most complex key flexfield to analyze, design, and define. As such, the accounting flexfield will be used as

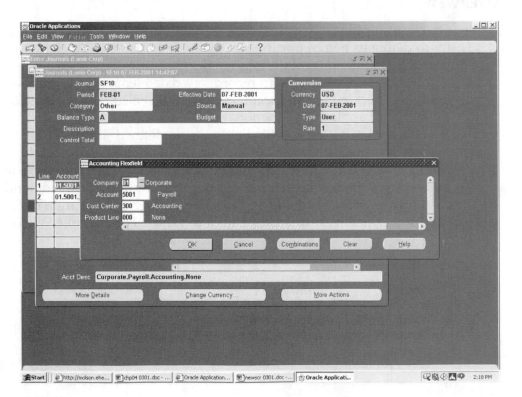

Exhibit 4.2   Sample Accounting Flexfield

the key flexfield example throughout the book. All key flexfields will have a similar, though usually less complex, definition process.

Typically, the accounting flexfield definition process includes:

- Analysis of the current and future reporting requirements
- Design of the accounting flexfield structure
- Define the accounting flexfield structure
- Definition of the valid accounting flexfield segment values including parent values
- Definition of the accounting flexfield cross-validation rules
- Test of the accounting flexfield throughout all Oracle applications

The process should be thorough. Key flexfield structures are hard to change after the definition process is complete.

Accounting Flexfield Analysis

Careful consideration should be placed when designing a new accounting flexfield, as it is critical to the success of the Oracle Applications implementation project. Oracle applications, which record financial transactions, ultimately create journal entry transactions to the posting level accounting flexfield. Oracle's General Ledger Financial Statement Generator (FSG), journal posting, budgeting, and allocations utilize the accounting flexfield structure. FSG is a financial statement generator (report writer) which reports posted General Ledger balances.

All current financial statements, which utilize accounting flexfield financial data, should be collected and reviewed. In addition, any ad-hoc financial reports should be collected. The reports should be analyzed and the reporting points documented. The reporting points represent the different dimensions of the report. Each reporting point should be considered as a potential segment in the proposed accounting flexfield. Examples of common reporting points include: company, account, cost center, department, division, and product line. Include all reporting points for financial reporting.

An accounting flexfield matrix with reports down the page and segments across the page assists in determining the proposed accounting flexfield (see Exhibit 4.3).

Report	Company	Account	Cost Center	Product Line
Balance Sheet	X	X		
Income Stmt	X	X		
Group Expense Summary	X	X	X	
Product Line Revenue	X	X		X

Exhibit 4.3   Report Matrix

Accounting Flexfield Design

Design the accounting flexfield for all Oracle applications. The project team must understand how the accounting flexfield is used throughout all the applications. Test the proposed accounting flexfield and verify that all users are satisfied with the accounting flexfield reporting capabilities. Have the appropriate personnel sign off to accept the proposed accounting flexfield.

For each key flexfield, Oracle provides 30 segments with up to 25 characters per segment. Typically, an accounting flexfield is composed of four to seven segments with three to six characters per segment. In addition, try to avoid having a lengthy number of characters in the accounting flexfield. Only the first 28 characters or so (depending on the number of segments and segment separators) appear on the standard Oracle General Ledger reports. If the accounting flexfield is longer, custom reports may have to be developed. In addition, if the accounting flexfield is lengthy, is it truly being used for financial reporting or is the accounting flexfield being used for organizational detail reporting?

Use parent and summary accounts as necessary. Parent segment values are the rollup of child segment values and are calculated during the concurrent process. Summary accounts also report the rollup of child segment values, but are actual accounting flexfield combinations. As such, summary accounts provide online inquiry capabilities, which parent values do not. However, summary accounts may impact performance if the number of summary accounts grows too large.

Accounting Flexfield Structure

The accounting flexfield segment structure defines the display order of the segments. In addition, the segment defaults, the segment sizes, and the segment validation types are defined in the key flexfield structure definition process. Segment validation types include: Independent, Dependent, Table, and None.

Typically, accounting flexfields have a validation type of Independent and only Independent. A validation type of Independent indicates the segment values must be validated from a user-defined list. For example, the only company values are 01-Corporate and 02-Subsidiary.

Try to avoid segments with a Dependent validation type. A validation type of Dependent indicates the segment value is based on another segment value (see Exhibit 4.4). The sub-account segment value is dependent on the account segment value.

The subaccount segment value 01 or 02 has no meaning without the context of the account segment value 140 or 150. Beware of dependent segments, as parent segment values can't be created for dependent segments. Therefore, any Oracle General Ledger parent functionality will not work for the dependent segment. This includes allocations and potentially FSG reporting parent capabilities. Rather than define a dependent segment, consider concatenating the two segments together. For example, concatenate the account segment value 140 and subaccount segment value 01 to create account 14001 with a segment description of Accounts Receivable—Trade.

The validation type of Table indicates another Oracle table will provide the list of valid values. The validation type of None indicates no validation will occur. Any data within the segment size will be allowed. Segments with this validation type allow any data value.

Flexfield Qualifiers

Oracle applications require flexfield qualifiers for some of the key flexfield structures. Flexfield qualifiers are required for certain key flexfield segments. For example, each accounting flexfield structure requires two

Account Segment Description	Subaccount Segment Description	Account Segment	Subaccount Segment
Accounts Receivable	Trade	140	01
Accounts Receivable	Employee	140	02
Furniture and Fixtures	Computer	150	01
Furniture and Fixtures	Leasehold Improvements	150	02

Exhibit 4.4 Accounting Flexfield Dependent Segment

flexfield segment qualifiers: a balancing segment and a natural account segment. The balancing segment determines the segment level at which a balanced financial transaction occurs. Total debits must equal total credits at the unique balancing segment value or the posting program will create the intercompany journal lines to make the journal balance. Typically, company or fund represents the balancing segment.

The natural account segment determines the account type. The account type choices are Assets, Liabilities, Owners' Equity, Revenue, and Expense. During year-end processing, the account type will determine if the accounts are closed to Owner's Equity or roll forward. The balance sheet account types roll forward and the income statement account types close to the retained earnings account. When creating statistical accounts, the account type is still a critical decision. Should the statistical account roll forward at year-end or start with zero balance?

Accounting Flexfield Segment Values

Each segment should have one meaning and only one meaning. In addition, keep the segment values in a range to facilitate FSG report definition. FSG works left to right when sorting segment values. It is difficult to derive reporting data if the significant data is embedded in the middle of the segment. The wildcard search character of % doesn't work in FSG. Each potential combination has to be individually called into the row set accounting flexfield range. FSG report definition and maintenance can become cumbersome and time-consuming.

Keep the ranges large enough to accommodate future growth. The FSG report ranges should easily accept the new segment value directly into the range. The range should follow the financial statements (see Exhibit 4.5). Exhibit 4.6 details a high-level account range mirroring the primary financial reports.

Keep the accounting flexfield segment values numeric for ease of data entry. While using alpha characters to represent the segment value of an English-like form is promising, entering segment values on the numeric keypad is faster than alpha characters. Many clients have numeric segment values for the child/posting segment values and alphabetic segment values for the parent values. For example, child cost centers 501 to 599 roll up to the G+A parent segment value. Other clients keep the child values strictly within the range. For example, cost center 500 is the parent value and cost centers 501 to 599 roll up to 500 (see Exhibit 4.7). Use parent segment values to accommodate hierarchical reporting. Do not try to build the segment value rollup structure horizontally.

Assets	**Liabilities**
Current Assets:	Current Liabilities:
Cash	Payables
Accounts Receivable	Total Liabilities
Prepaids	
Total Current Assets	Owner's Equity
Long Term Assets:	Retained Earnings
Land	Total Equity
Furniture and Fixtures	
Total Long Term Assets	
Total Assets	Total Liabilities and Equity

Exhibit 4.5 Financial Report

1000-1999	Assets
1100-1199	Cash
1200-1299	Accounts Receivable
1300-1399	Prepaids
2000-2999	Liabilities
3000-3999	Equity
4000-4999	Revenue
5000-5999	Direct Expenses
6000-7999	Indirect Expenses
8000-8999	Allocations
9000-9999	Statistical

Exhibit 4.6 Accounting Flexfield Segment Value Ranges

Dynamic Insertion and Cross-Validation Rules

Dynamic insertion allows each segment value to mix-and-match with any other segment value. Many accounting flexfield combinations could be created which may not be valid. Cross-Validation Rules (CVR) allow the organization to define validation rules to allow or disallow accounting flexfield combinations. For example, without cross-validation rules, the Information Technology cost center could have a Cash account defined.

When a new combination of segments is entered, Oracle Applications will process the new accounting flexfield segment values through the cross-validation rules. If the accounting flexfield segment combination passes, a new code combination will be created. If the combination

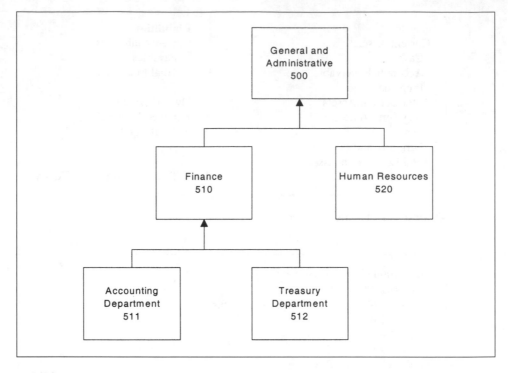

Exhibit 4.7   Accounting Flexfield Hierarchy

doesn't pass, the user must enter a valid combination or exit the data entry process.

Use cross-validation rules sparingly. If the accounting flexfield is range-driven, this should not be an issue. If the accounting flexfield is not range-driven, many cross-validation rules may occur, making maintenance ongoing and time-consuming.

During the chart of accounts and legacy General Ledger conversion, organizations may find they have historical data in what would now be an illegal combination. Typically, cross-validation rules are disabled during conversion to maintain a clean audit trail. After the data is converted, the cross-validation rules may be enabled and the now-illegal accounting flexfield combination should be disabled.

Accounting Flexfield Sizing

Sizing the accounting flexfield is critical for successful performance. The number of segments and the number of segment values determines the possible accounting flexfield combinations. Each organization should produce a spreadsheet calculating each segment and the number of segment values to determine the number of possible accounting flexfield combinations. While there is no maximum number of accounting flexfield combinations, an unusually high number of combinations warrants a review of the proposed accounting flexfield structure.

After calculating the number of combinations, multiply by the number of periods to calculate the size of the GL_BALANCES table. Again, an unusually large GL_BALANCES table warrants a review of the proposed accounting flexfield structure.

Accounting Flexfield Security

The accounting flexfield structure may have security enabled at the accounting flexfield segment level. Typically, data entry users are limited to data entry within their own organization. For example, users in organization 01, Corporate may only enter journals for organization 01 and not organization 02, Subsidiary. In addition, reports may be secured by segment security. Flexfield security is tied to user responsibility and is defined by the users and the System Administrator.

DESCRIPTIVE FLEXFIELDS

Descriptive flexfields allow an organization to record and report its unique data elements. During the analysis phase when the business processing gaps and data are identified, the missing, yet required, data elements must be identified and a home found. Typically, this home is an Oracle applications descriptive flexfield. Most Oracle application windows have descriptive flexfield capabilities at the block or table level. The descriptive flexfield is displayed in the window as [ ]. Sample descriptive flexfields are displayed in Exhibit 4.8.

A sample of an enabled descriptive flexfield in a window is displayed in Exhibit 4.9.

Oracle provides a number of descriptive flexfield segments in each block or section of a window. From a technical perspective, the block usually corresponds to a unique table. The descriptive flexfield data elements are stored in the attribute fields. For example, descriptive flexfield data in the vendors table will reside in the PO_VENDORS table in

Window	Use
Customer	Customer Service Rep Name and Number
Expense Report Entry	Airline Ticket Number
Invoice Distribution Line	Lease Number

Exhibit 4.8   Descriptive Flexfield Samples

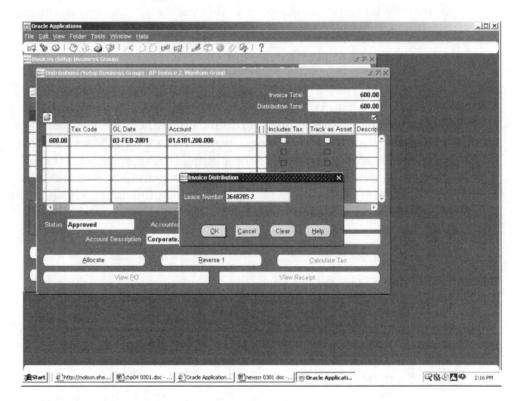

Exhibit 4.9   Descriptive Flexfield Sample

the attribute *n* column. Typically, 15 descriptive flexfield attribute fields (attribute1–attribute15) of 150 characters are available to record each unique descriptive flexfield data element.

 All reporting is custom as the descriptive flexfield data is unique to Oracle applications.

The descriptive flexfield definition process is similar to the key flexfield definition process. Typically, the descriptive flexfield definition process includes:

- Analyze the current inquiry and reporting requirements
- Design the descriptive flexfield structure
- Enable the descriptive flexfield structure and define the segments
- Define descriptive flexfield valid segment values, if applicable

Descriptive flexfields may also be global or context-sensitive. The global option opens the descriptive flexfield data entry window every time. The context-sensitive option only opens the descriptive flexfield when a certain segment value is entered. For example, if the "Airline" expense report line item is entered, the descriptive flexfield opens for the user to enter the airline ticket number.

Journals Captured Information Descriptive Flexfield

Oracle Applications provide an Account segment context-sensitive descriptive flexfield. The descriptive flexfield works in the journal entry window. If a specific account number is entered, the journal captured information descriptive flexfield opens. For example, if a capital asset account is entered in a journal, the user must enter the Capital Appropriation Request number.

ACCOUNTING FLEXFIELDS STEP 2.1: SETUP

The accounting flexfield setup process includes defining the accounting flexfield structure, defining the segment values, and creating cross-validation rules if dynamic insertion has been enabled (see Exhibit 4.10).

The process for setting up the other key flexfields is very similar. The key flexfields used in Oracle Receivables will be defined in Chapter 8.

Accounting Flexfields

Prior to entering the accounting flexfield structure and values, perform the analysis and design phases of the accounting flexfield definition process:

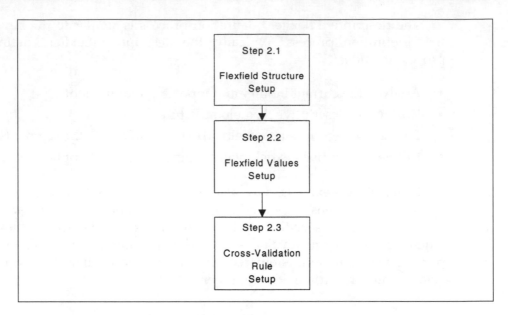

Exhibit 4.10   Accounting Flexfield Setup Process

1. From the **File** menu → **Switch Responsibility** → **GL Corporate Super User** responsibility.
2. From the General Ledger menu → **Setup** → **Financials** → **Flexfields** → **Key** → **Segments.**
3. Press the **Find** icon (see Exhibit 4.11).
4. Select the **Oracle General Ledger** application and the **Accounting Flexfield.**
5. Press **OK.**

 The *Oracle Applications Flexfields Guide* provides worksheets for the flexfield definition process.

1. All the accounting flexfield structures are displayed. Oracle applications seed an undefined structure titled "Accounting Flexfield". Typically, this is the first accounting flexfield structure used (see Exhibit 4.12).
2. Enter a new **Title** or leave the default accounting flexfield title.
3. Enter the accounting flexfield structure **Description.**
4. Press **Segments** to enter the segments.

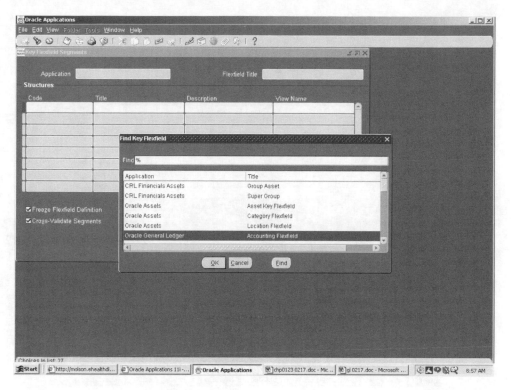

Exhibit 4.11   Key Flexfields Structure Find Window

The accounting flexfield structure segments are entered in the order they are to be displayed.

1. Enter the segment **Number** (see Exhibits 4.12 and 4.13). Segments within the flexfield structure are displayed in sequential order.

2. Enter the segment **Name.**

3. The **Window Prompt** defaults from the segment Name. The Window Prompt is what you see during data entry. Leave the default value.

4. Select the **Column** field. The field determines where the segment data is stored. For users, this information is usually irrelevant. However, developers will need this segment number for custom reports or processes. In this example, the company segment values will be stored in the SEGMENT1 field in the GL_CODE_COMBINATIONS table for this chart of accounts structure.

5. The **Displayed** check box should be checked.

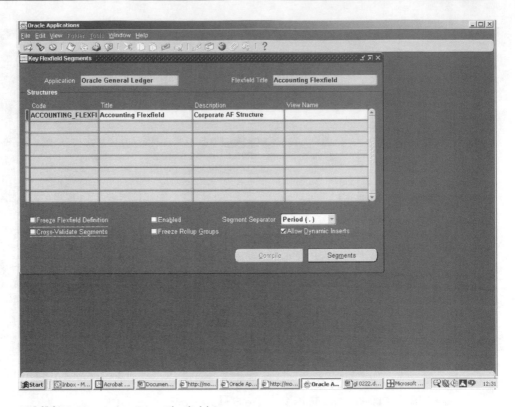

Exhibit 4.12   Accounting Flexfield Structure

6. The **Enabled** check box should be checked.

7. Enter the **Value Set** name.

8. Press **Value Set** to enter the segments structure parameters.

The accounting flexfield segments utilize value sets that determine the format type and segment size.

1. Enter the **Value Set Name** (see Exhibit 4.14). Typically, the organization's naming standard prefix is included to speed the List of Values search. For example, all the value sets will list together with the same prefix of XXX.

2. Enter the **Description.**

3. Change the **Format Type** if applicable.

4. Enter the **Maximum Size** for the segment.

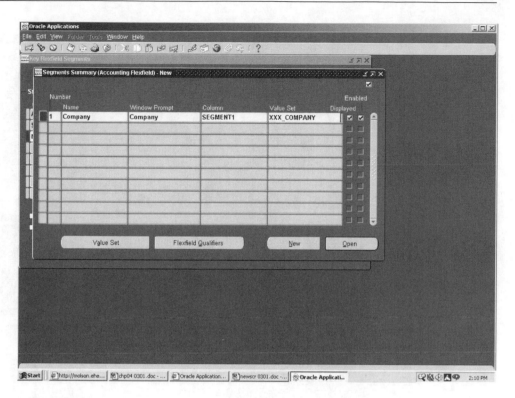

Exhibit 4.13 Accounting Flexfield Structure Segments Summary

5. Check the appropriate boxes in the **Format Validation** region. Check the **Numbers Only** for example to indicate the segment values must be numeric. If alphabetic characters are allowed, check the **Uppercase** box to allow only uppercase alphabetic characters.

6. Select the **Validation Type.** The default Independent is displayed.

7. Press **Flexfield Qualifiers.**

Minimally, each accounting flexfield structure must have a balancing segment and an account segment. For the appropriate segments, the accounting flexfield qualifiers must be set (see Exhibit 4.15).

The Natural Account Segment qualifier denotes this segment as the segment used for year-end closing. All segment values will have an additional data entry field indicating the account type: Assets, Liabilities, Owner's Equity, Revenue, or Expense.

The Balancing segment qualifier denotes this segment as the segment

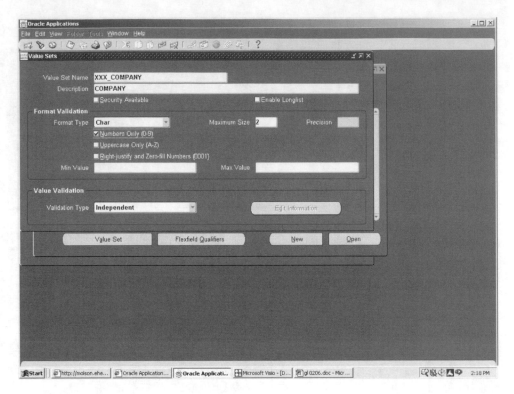

Exhibit 4.14   Accounting Flexfield Structure Value Sets

used for balancing unbalanced journals. Typically, the company or fund represents the balancing segment. Thereby, the sum of debits for company 01 must equal the sum of credits for company 01.

Check the **Enabled** box to identify the appropriate segment qualifier.

Repeat the steps for the required segment qualifiers in the accounting flexfield.

When done defining all the accounting flexfield segments, close the window to go back to the Key Flexfield Segment window (See Exhibit 4.16).

The accounting flexfield structure used in the book is displayed in Exhibit 4.17. Segment1 represents the Company segment and will be the balancing segment. Segment2 is the Account segment and will be the natural account segment denoting the account type. The Cost Center is Segment3 and Product Line is Segment4.

After entering the flexfield segment structure, the flexfield must be

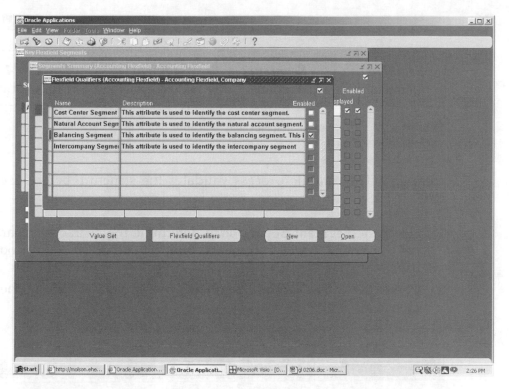

Exhibit 4.15 Accounting Flexfield Segment Qualifiers

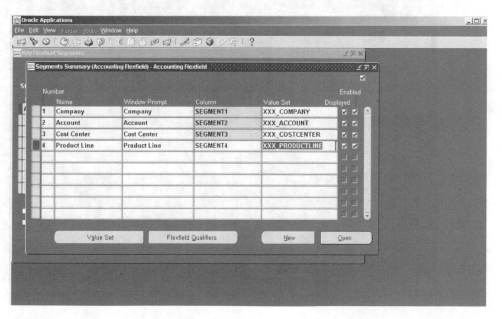

Exhibit 4.16 Accounting Flexfield All Segments

Segment1	**Segment2**	**Segment3**	**Segment4**
Company	Account	Cost Center	Product Line

Exhibit 4.17   Book Accounting Flexfield Structure

compiled. The compile process validates the structure before use (see Exhibit 4.18).

1. Select the **Segment Separator** to determine the character separating the accounting flexfield segments. Typically, a dash (-) or a period (.) is used.
2. Check the **Cross-Validate Segments** box to validate across the segments.

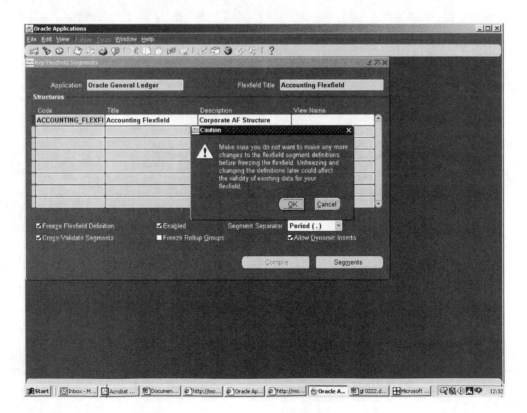

Exhibit 4.18   Accounting Flexfield Structure Compilation

3. Check the **Allow Dynamic Insertion** box to allow dynamic insertion of accounting flexfield segment values.

4. Check the **Freeze Flexfield** box ONLY after checking the other boxes and when complete with the key flexfield structure input process.

5. Press **OK** to the Caution window.

6. Press the **Compile** button to compile the flexfield.

7. Press **OK** to close the Compile Note window.

8. The system will display a message indicating the flexfield was compiled successfully. Press **OK** to acknowledge the message. In addition, the compile command spawns a concurrent process to create the views used by Oracle Applications. Review the concurrent request to verify the concurrent process completed successfully.

ACCOUNTING FLEXFIELDS STEP 2.2: VALUES

Prior to defining the accounting flexfield segment values, document the child segment values and how they roll up to the parent segment values. Use the document to input the segment values (see Exhibit 4.19).

1. From the General Ledger menu → **Setup** → **Financials** → **Flexfields** → **Key** → **Values**

2. Select the **Oracle General Ledger Application.**

3. Select the **Accounting Flexfield Title.**

4. Select the appropriate **Accounting Flexfield Structure.**

5. Select the appropriate **Accounting Flexfield Segment** as defined in the structure.

6. Press **Find.**

Enter the segment **Value** and **Description** (see Exhibit 4.20). Follow in-house naming standards. The segment value and description are displayed in the data entry windows. In addition, Oracle General Ledger's FSG uses the segment value and segment description as a reporting option in the report definition process.

For all segment values, use the **Qualifiers** column to define the segment as Postable and Budgetable. In addition, if the segment is the Natural Account segment, the **Qualifiers** column will require an account type. Valid account types include: Assets, Liabilities, Owners' Equity, Revenue, or Expense. Tab through the fields, even if using the default Ex-

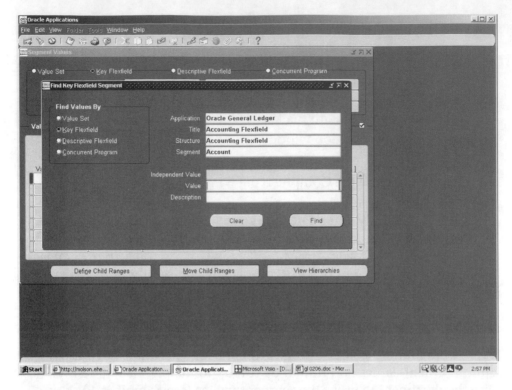

Exhibit 4.19 Flexfields Segment Value Definition

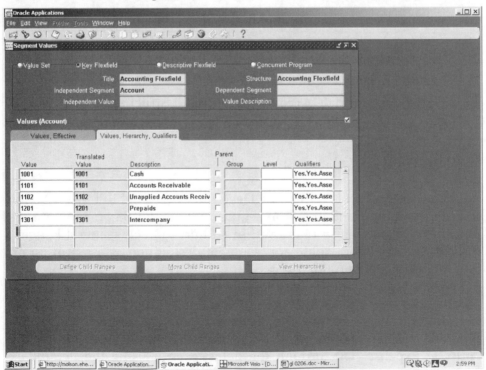

Exhibit 4.20 Flexfields Segment Value and Description

pense account type. Make sure to enter the appropriate account type as they may not be changed after setup.

Repeat the segment value definition process for all segments.

Parent Segment Values

1. If the segment value is a parent, check the **Parent** box (see Exhibit 4.21).

2. Press **Define Child Ranges** to define the children which rollup to the parent value. In this example, the segment value 1000 reflects all asset accounts and will have a child range of values from 1001 to 1999.

1. Enter the parent segment value **From** and **To** child segment values (see Exhibit 4.22).

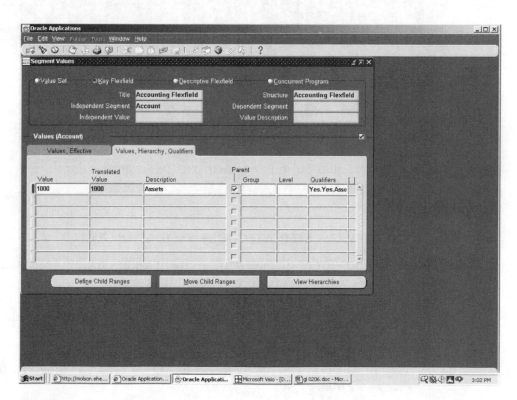

Exhibit 4.21 Flexfields Parent Segment Value Definition

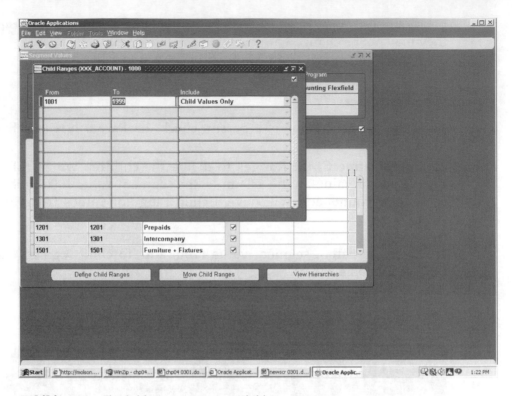

Exhibit 4.22   Flexfields Parent Segment Child Ranges

2. The system will submit a concurrent process to compile the parent segment value hierarchy. Press **OK**.

ACCOUNTING FLEXFIELDS STEP 2.3: CROSS-VALIDATION RULES

Cross-Validation Rules dictate what segment values are allowed with the other segment values to create valid account combinations. For example, the balance sheet accounts may only use the balance sheet cost center (000). All other cost centers, for example the departments, are not allowed to post to balance sheet accounts.

1. From the General Ledger menu → **Setup** → **Financials** → **Flexfields** → **Key** → **Rules**
2. Press the **Find** icon.

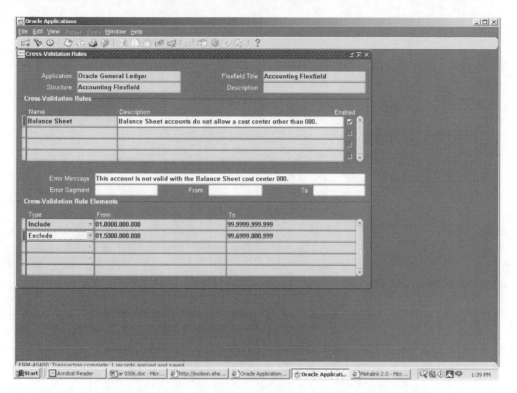

Exhibit 4.23   Cross-Validation Rules

3. Select the **Oracle General Ledger Application** and the **Accounting Flexfield Title** and the appropriate **Accounting Flexfield Structure.**

4. Enter the **Cross-Validation Rule Name.** The rule name should be short but descriptive.

5. Enter the **Error Message** to be displayed to the user when violating the CVR.

6. Enter the Cross-Validation Rule Elements. The first row should be the **Include** type, with a range of **all accounting flexfields.** The second row should be the **Exclude** type, with a range of the disallowed accounting flexfield range. For example, the 000 cost center is not allowed to post revenue or expense accounts.

 Run Oracle General Ledger Optimizer concurrent program to create or update indexes on the accounting flexfield segments. Periodic running of the Optimizer program should improve system performance.

CHAPTER 5

General Ledger

OVERVIEW

This chapter describes using Oracle General Ledger to enter and post journal transactions, generate recurring journals and allocations, enter budgets, and produce financial statements and standard General Ledger reports. Oracle General Ledger is the system of record for all Oracle applications that produces financial transactions including Oracle Payables and Oracle Receivables.

To fully comprehend Oracle General Ledger capabilities, the fundamental concepts of accounting must be understood. These concepts include the accounting equation and the transaction principle.

The first concept is the accounting equation. The accounting equation states that total assets must equal total liabilities plus owner's equity. An increase in assets must reflect a corresponding increase in liabilities or owner's equity. In other words, the balance sheet accounts must balance. An increase in expenses may also reflect a corresponding increase in liabilities. At year-end, the income and expense accounts are closed to the retained earnings account in the owner's equity section of the balance sheet. In other words, at year-end, the balance sheet still balances.

The second concept is the transaction principle. The transaction principle states that all financial transactions must be recorded and balance. In other words, total debits for the financial transaction must equal total credits for the financial transaction. Therefore, all financial journals in Oracle General Ledger must balance. If not, either the difference will be posted to the suspense account or the journal must be corrected.

Both these accounting concepts apply in Oracle General Ledger and all Oracle application subsystems, which create the financial transactions that ultimately create journal entries. A full audit trail from Oracle General Ledger is available.

Oracle General Ledger provides a variety of journal entry capabilities to record financial transactions. Journal entry balance types include actual journals and budget journals. Actual journals post to either a financial currency or a statistical currency. Journal sources define the subsystem and journal categories define the module within the subsystem. For example, the journal source is Payables and the journal category is Payments. In addition, a journal approval process may be defined and journals may automatically post. A periodic concurrent request may be run to select and post certain journal sources and categories.

Oracle General Ledger journal capabilities also include recurring journals and allocation journals. Recurring journals speed data entry by automatically creating the journal. Allocations allow cost pools to be distributed across the organization. Allocations may be run in parallel mode, which means all are run at once, or in step-down mode, which means the allocations are run in a cascading fashion. In other words, the first level allocation journal is generated before the next level allocation journal.

Oracle General Ledger budget capabilities include online budget entry, a number of mathematical formulas, and the ability to load budgets from any other system. In addition, Mass Budgeting allows the organization to create budgets or forecasts based on actual data. For example, the preliminary next year budget forecast may be this year's actuals increased by 10 percent.

Oracle General Ledger provides unsurpassed online inquiry and reporting capabilities. The drill-down from account inquiry to the Oracle application subsystem to the T-accounts and journal entry transactions is phenomenal. This drill-down functionality is available for Oracle application subsystems including Payables, Receivables, Assets, Projects, Inventory, and Work In Process (WIP).

Oracle General Ledger provides standard General Ledger reports as with any other Oracle application. In addition, Oracle General Ledger provides a user report writing tool called the Financial Statement Generator (FSG). FSG allows the user to develop custom financial reports from the posted account balances.

USING GENERAL LEDGER

The typical Oracle General Ledger business process flow is setup, journal entry, budget entry, inquiry and reporting, and period end processing (see Exhibit 5.1). Journals include manually entered journals as well as those imported from Oracle applications or legacy systems. These amounts are considered actual balance types.

Likewise, budget capabilities include manual budget entry as well as those budgets imported from a budget legacy system. These budget amounts are considered budget balance types. Both balance types must update the GL Balance records before inquiry and reporting will display the proper amounts.

Inquiry and reporting are extremely robust in Oracle General Ledger. The account inquiry window drill-down capabilities are world-class. The Oracle General Ledger account inquiry window drill-downs from GL balances to the journals which created the balance to the Oracle applications

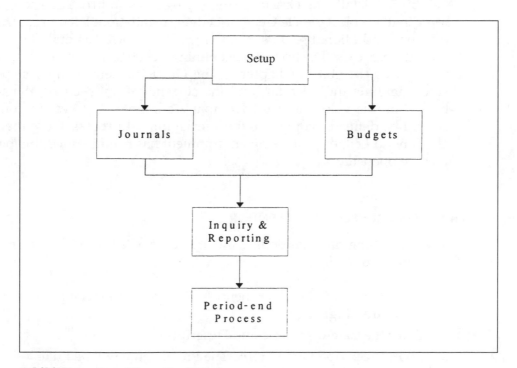

Exhibit 5.1 Open/Close: First Period

that created the journal entry. In addition, the journal T-accounts are graphically represented.

Oracle General Ledger's Financial Statement Generator (FSG) allows the user to define the organization's financial and management reports. FSG reports are defined in a step-by-step approach. Each component of the report is created and may be mixed and matched with any other component. For example, the YTD column set may be linked with the Balance Sheet row set and the Income Statement row set. Simple to complex financial statements may be produced.

The period process in Oracle General Ledger is very simple. All subsystems must transfer all financial transactions for the period and perform the respective subsystem period close process. All journals should be imported, and posted. The current period should be closed and the next period opened. All subsystem reconciliation processes should occur.

SETUP

Exhibit 5.2 details the Oracle General Ledger setup process. These steps represent a typical Oracle General Ledger installation. Each organization may have additional setup steps. Remember, Oracle General Ledger defines the three Cs. The first step is defining the chart of account structure, which was covered in Chapter 4. The Oracle General Ledger steps include defining the calendar (and the currency if not seeded), the set of books, profile values and intercompany accounts. The system controls should be defined to optimize the journal import process. Once the Oracle General Ledger processing environment has been defined, the period may be opened.

GENERAL LEDGER STEP 3.1: CALENDAR

The accounting calendar defines the organization's financial reporting periods (see Exhibit 5.3).

1. From the General Ledger menu → **Setup** → **Financials** → **Calendars** → **Accounting.**
2. Enter the **Calendar** name and **Description.**
3. Enter the period name **Prefix.** The Prefix name will be linked with the last two digits of the Year to create the period Name. For example, a

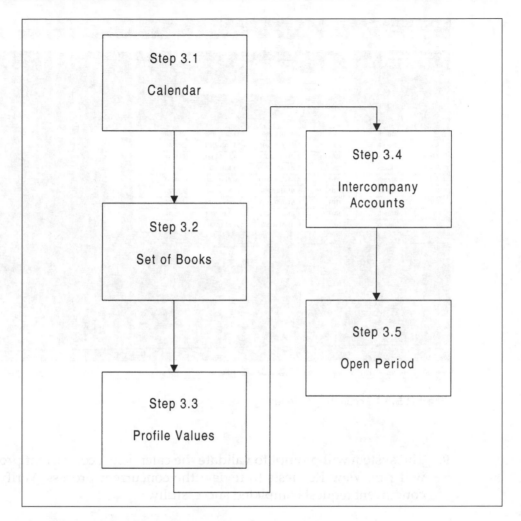

Exhibit 5.2 Oracle General Ledger Setup Steps

Prefix name of JAN and a Year of 2001 will create a period Name of JAN-01.

4. Select the period **Type.** Oracle seeds the Month calendar type. Define other period types in the Calendar Types window.

5. Enter the **Year.**

6. Enter the **Quarter** number and the period **Number.**

7. Enter the **From** and **To** calendar dates.

8. The system automatically creates the period Name.

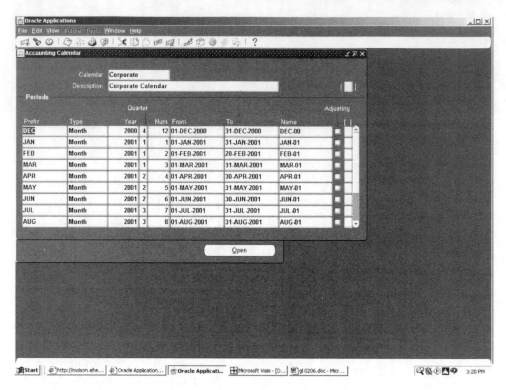

Exhibit 5.3 Accounting Calendar

9. The system will prompt to validate the calendar. A concurrent process will run. View Requests to review the concurrent process. Verify the concurrent request completed successfully.

GENERAL LEDGER STEP 3.2: SET OF BOOKS

The GL Set of Books links the three Cs: the chart of accounts, the calendar, and the functional currency (see Exhibit 5.4).

1. From the General Ledger menu → **Setup** → **Financials** → **Books** → **Define.**
2. Enter the **Set of Books Name,** the Set of Books **Short Name,** and the **Description.** The Set of Books name appears in reports and the short name appears in the window title bar.
3. Select the **Chart of Accounts Accounting Flexfield** structure. Only the

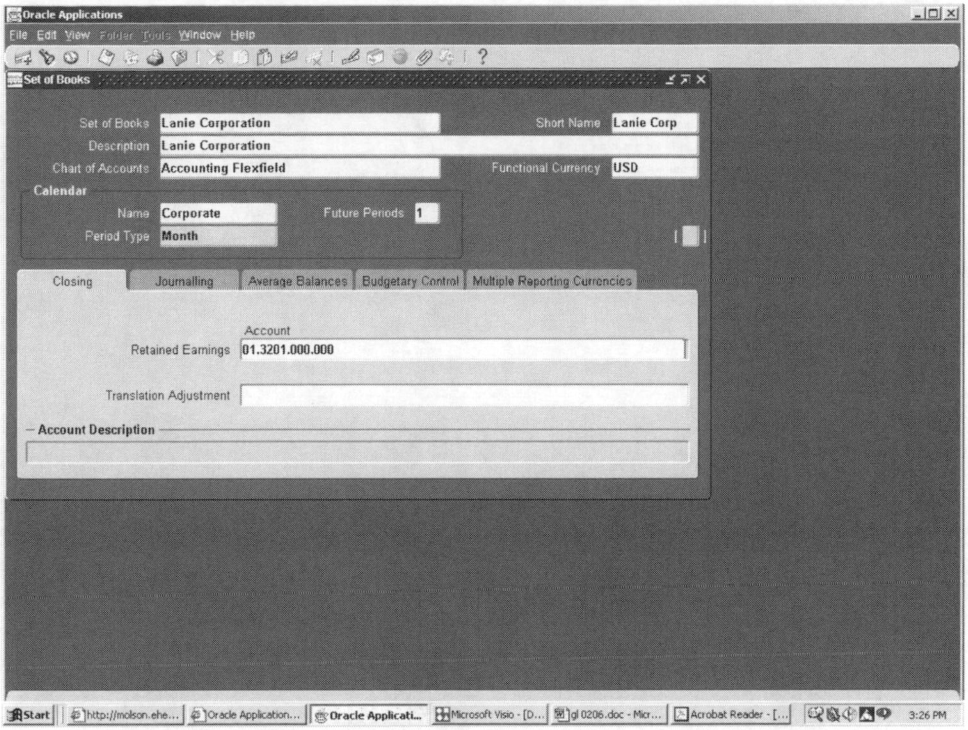

Exhibit 5.4   Set of Books: Closing

successfully compiled accounting flexfield structures are available for selection.

4. Select the **Functional Currency.** Oracle seeds many currencies; define a new currency if necessary.

5. Select the **Calendar Name** from General Ledger Step 3.1.

6. Enter the number of **Future Periods.** The default of 1 is displayed. Typically, one future period is sufficient as future periods allow data entry, but not journal posting.

7. In the Closing tab, enter the **Retained Earnings Account.** This account receives the year-end rollover of income statement accounts.

8. Press the **Journalling** tab.

Enter the GL Set of Books Journal processing parameters such as intercompany and suspense processing options (see Exhibit 5.5).

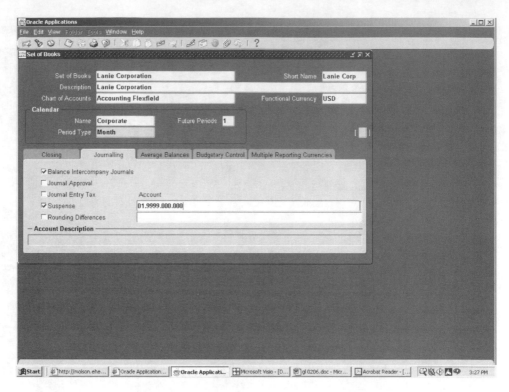

Exhibit 5.5   Set of Books: Journalling

1. Check the **Balance Intercompany Journals** box to have the system automatically balance intercompany balancing entries. The system will display a note to remind you to define the Intercompany account.
2. Check the **Suspense** box to allow out of balance journals to post.
3. Enter the **Suspense Account.** Review the balance in this account and month-end, and prepare correcting journal entries.

GENERAL LEDGER STEP 3.3: PROFILE VALUES

Oracle General Ledger profile values must be set. For example, the GL Set of Books profile value must be set for the new General Ledger responsibility (see Exhibit 5.6).

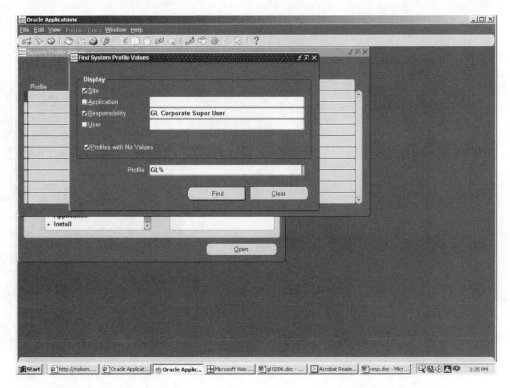

Exhibit 5.6 System Profile

1. From the **File** menu → **Switch Responsibility** → **System Administrator** responsibility.
2. From the System Administrator responsibility →**Profile** → **System.**
3. Check the **Responsibility** box and select the **GL Corporate Super User** responsibility.
4. Enter the **GL% Profile** prefix.
5. Press **Find.**

The GL profile options are displayed (see Exhibit 5.7).

Down arrow to the **GL:Set of Books Name** profile option. Select the **Set of Books Name** under the GL responsibility. The GL:Set of Books Id will be displayed after saving.

Exhibit 5.8 lists some other Oracle General Ledger profile options.

 The General Ledger profile options are discussed in the *Oracle General Ledger User's Guide, Appendix B.*

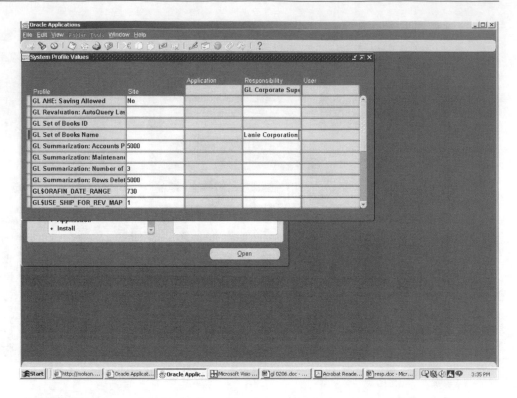

Exhibit 5.7   System Profile: GL Sets of Books

Profile	Use
Profile	*Use*
Sequencing	Defines if journal documents number sequencing is used. Typically used as the journal voucher number.
Currency: Thousands Separator	Defines how amounts in the thousands are displayed.
Currency: Negative Format	Defines how negative amounts are displayed.
FSG	Various FSG profile options may be set.
Journals	Various Journal profile options may be set.

Exhibit 5.8   Oracle General Ledger Profile Values

GENERAL LEDGER STEP 3.4: INTERCOMPANY ACCOUNT

Oracle General Ledger will balance any intercompany journals during posting if enabled in the GL Set of Books window Journalling tab. Unbalanced journals will have additional journal lines created during the journal posting process. Exhibit 5.9 displays the original journal lines and the Oracle General Ledger journal posting program created journal lines.

Determine the intercompany balancing accounts for each journal source and journal category (see Exhibit 5.10).

Journal Lines	Balancing Segments	Debit	Credit
Original journal lines	Company 01	500.00	
	Company 02		500.00
Posting process lines added	Company 02—Due To Account	500.00	
	Company 01—Due From Account		500.00

Exhibit 5.9 Intercompany Journal Balancing

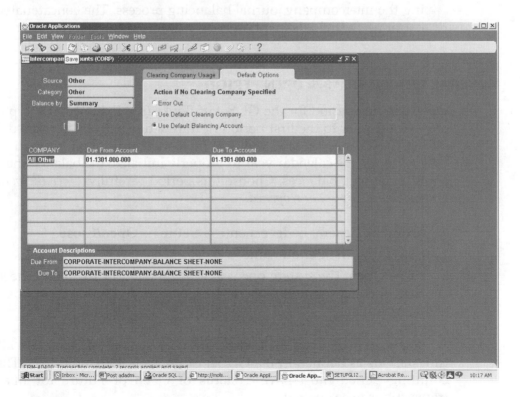

Exhibit 5.10 Intercompany Account

1. From the **File** menu → **Switch Responsibility** → **GL Corporate Super User** responsibility.
2. From the General Ledger menu → **Setup** →**Accounts** → **Intercompany.**
3. Select the journal **Source.**
4. Select the journal **Category.**
5. In the Default Options tab, check the **Use Default Balancing Account** option.
6. Select the **Company** segment value (or balancing segment) to enter the specific intercompany account for the segment value. Otherwise, leave the field blank to have the system create an "All Other" default record.
7. Enter the **Due From Account.** This account is debited as a receivable during the intercompany journal balancing process. The concatenated accounting flexfield description is displayed.
8. Enter the **Due To Account.** This account is credited as a liability during the intercompany journal balancing process. The concatenated accounting flexfield description is displayed.

GENERAL LEDGER STEP 3.5: OPEN PERIOD

Open the first period for the GL Set of Books (see Exhibit 5.11). Typically, one period prior to the first period of transaction activity is opened. This allows the balance sheet accounts to be loaded and rolled forward to the first period in the calendar year to properly initialize the balance sheet account beginning balances. Choose this period carefully. *Once the period is Open, it can't be reset or reopened.*

1. From the General Ledger menu → **Setup** → **Open/Close.**
2. Select the **First Period** name.
3. Press **Open.** The system opens a decision window to double check before opening the first General Ledger period. Press **Yes** to open the first period.

The system displays the first period with a status of Open and all Future periods as defined in the GL Set of Books (see Exhibit 5.12). The accounting period must have a status of Open or Future for financial transactions to be entered.

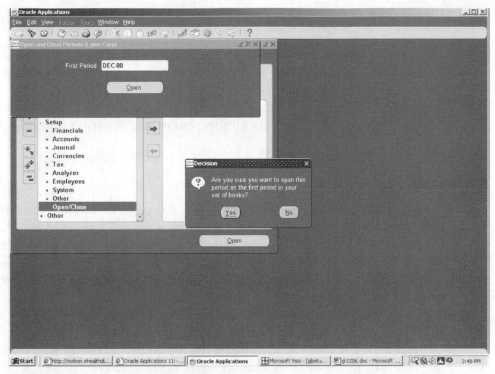

Exhibit 5.11 Open/Close Confirmation

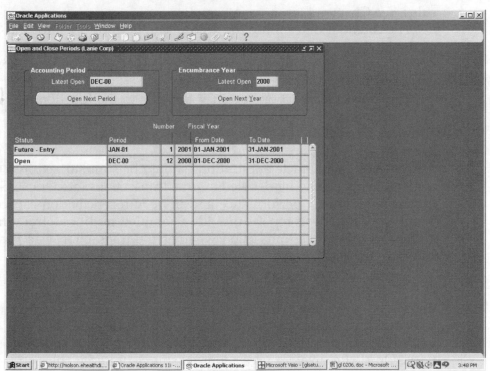

Exhibit 5.12 Oracle General Ledger Business Process Flow

Press **Open Next Period** to open subsequent periods. The system opens a decision window and double checks before starting the concurrent process to open the General Ledger period. Press **Yes.** The system submits a concurrent process to properly populate the GL Balances with the newly opened period's beginning balance and period data.

JOURNALS

Oracle General Ledger provides a variety of journal entry capabilities. Journal entries record the financial transactions to Oracle General Ledger. Journals record the movement between accounts such as depreciation expense or payroll expense. All financial transactions must be created as a journal and posted before the GL balances are updated and available for inquiry and reporting.

Since journal transactions are within a unique GL Set of Books, the three Cs—the chart of accounts, the calendar, and the currency—must be adhered to. The chart of accounts determines the accounting flexfield. The accounting flexfield combination must be enabled, be active within the start and end dates, and have successfully passed the cross-validation rules. See Chapter 4 for more information.

The calendar determines the accounting periods open for the GL Set of Books. Journals may be entered for any open or future enterable period. Journals may only be posted in an open General Ledger accounting period.

The journal transaction currency defaults to the functional GL Set of Books functional currency. Enter any other currency and perform foreign currency translation, or select the currency of STAT to record statistical journal data.

Journals from Oracle applications should be summarized into Oracle General Ledger. Sending detailed journal transactions into Oracle General Ledger may impact performance and impede reconciliation capabilities. The Account Analysis reports provide a complete audit trail from the subsystem to the source transaction whether the transaction was posted in summary or detail.

Oracle General Ledger provides an audit trail to the feeding subsystem via the use of journal sources and journal categories. Oracle Applications seed predefined journal sources and categories. Oracle Payables uses a journal source of Payables and journal categories of Purchase Invoices for expense distribution, and Payments for disbursement distributions. Oracle Receivables uses a journal source of Receivables and journal categories of Sales Invoices, Trade Receipts, Credit Memos, Debit Memos, Miscellaneous Receipts, Adjustments, and Chargebacks.

Journal Business Process

Oracle General Ledger journal methodologies include manual journals, recurring journals, allocation journals, budget journals, and imported journals (see Exhibit 5.13). Manual journals are journals entered when no other subsystem exists to create the journals, for example, a correcting entry. Recurring journals occur periodically and may have fixed or variable amounts. Allocation journals distribute allocation cost pools to various accounts based on usage ratios. Budget journals insert or update budget data. Imported journals are journals created in a subsystem outside Oracle General Ledger, such as conversion journals, but also include Oracle Payables and Oracle Receivables journals.

Journal Architecture

Oracle General Ledger provides three levels of recording journal information: journal batch, journal header, and journal lines (see Exhibit 5.14). The journal header and journal lines are required. The journal batch is automatically created when the journal header is saved.

Originally, Oracle General Ledger required the journal batch. As the

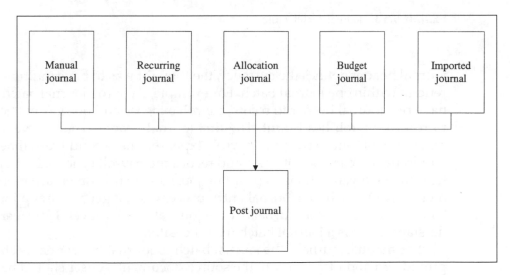

Exhibit 5.13   General Ledger Journal Process

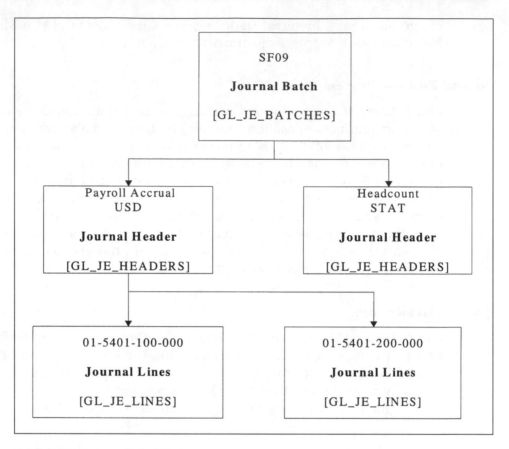

Exhibit 5.14   Journal Architecture

journal header defines the currency, the thought was to have multiple currencies within one journal batch. For example, a payroll journal batch may have one journal header to record payroll expense and one journal header to record payroll headcount. The first journal header would have a currency of USD and record the payroll expense. The second journal header would have a currency of STAT and record the payroll headcount. In practice, many organizations kept a one-journal-batch = one-journal-header mentality. As such, the journal entry process no longer requires a journal batch and users enter journals at the journal header level. However, understand there is a journal batch record created.

For manual journals, the journal batch or journal header name should provide an audit trail back to the source document. A user should be able to take the online batch name and locate the actual source document stored in the Accounting Department's filing cabinet or imaging system. Determine the naming and filing conventions for manual journals and follow the process online with the journal batch or journal header name. For example, the filing convention is by period name, then user initials and user batch number: FEB-01 SF09.

Journal Entry

Enter the manual journal entry header and journal entry lines (see Exhibit 5.15).

1. From the General Ledger menu → **Journals** → **Enter.**
2. The Journal window defaults to a Find window. Press **New Journal** to enter a journal header and journal lines. To retrieve an existing journal entry, enter the search criteria and press OK.

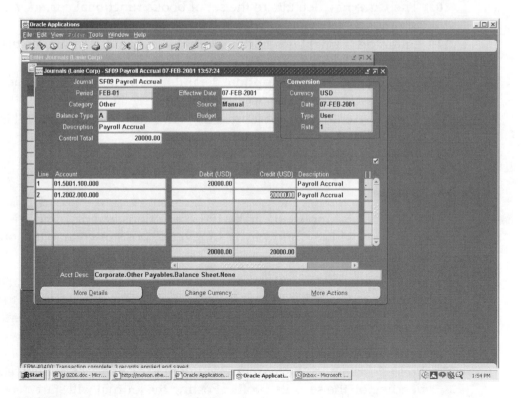

Exhibit 5.15 Journals Enter Window

3. Enter the **Journal** header name following in-house journal naming conventions.

4. The oldest open period will default in the **Period** field. Accept the default or select any open or future period. The system date will display in the Effective Date field.

5. Select the **Category.** The journal category values are predefined but additional journal categories may be defined.

6. The journal Source is Manual and can't be changed. The source of Manual indicates the journal was created online.

7. The Balance Type is Actual and can't be changed. Budget journals will have a Balance Type of B.

8. Enter the journal **Description.** The journal header description will default to the journal line description field.

9. Enter the **Control Total.** If the sum of the journal lines doesn't agree with the control total, a warning message will be displayed when the window is closed.

10. The **Currency** defaults to the set of books functional currency. Enter another currency or STAT to enter a statistical journal.

11. Enter the journal lines starting with the journal **Line** number, the **Account,** the **Debit,** or **Credit** amount

12. The journal line **Description** defaults from the journal header description. Overwrite as necessary.

13. Press ↓ to enter the next journal line. The next line number will increment from the first line number entered.

14. Press **More** Actions.

Journal Maintenance

If the journal is unposted, make the corrections online, otherwise the More Actions window allows you to reverse, post, or change the journal period (see Exhibit 5.16).

1. Press **Reverse Journal** to reverse the journal. A journal must be marked reversed before the Reverse Journal Form will create the reversed journal. The system will prompt for the period to reverse to. The system will submit a concurrent request to create the reversed journal. Post the reversal journal as any other journal.

2. Press **Post** to post the journal. Posting may or may not be allowed depending on the security profile. Posting the journal will start a concurrent process. A request id window will open. The journal status will

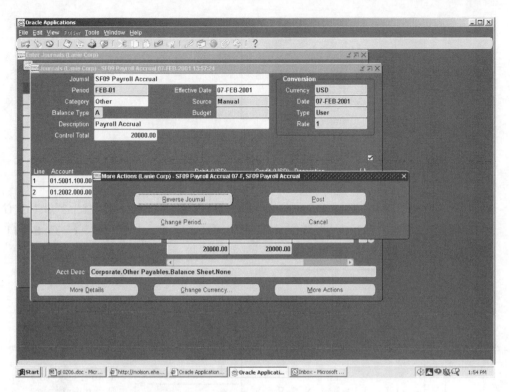

Exhibit 5.16 Journal More Actions Window

change to Selected for Posting. When the concurrent job successfully completes, the journal status will change to Posted and the GL balances will be updated.

3. Press **Change Period** to change the journal period from one period to another.

Journal Posting

The journal posting selects the journal entry to process and updates the appropriate GL balances. When the journal entry is first created, the journal status is Unposted (see Exhibit 5.17).

The journal status changes to Selected for Posting during the journal selection and posting process. After the posting process is successful, the journal status will change to Posted. A journal entry may go to error status for a number of reasons. For example, the accounting flexfield may be in error or the calendar period may not be open. An Error status indicates the journal was selected and rejected by the posting process. All errors

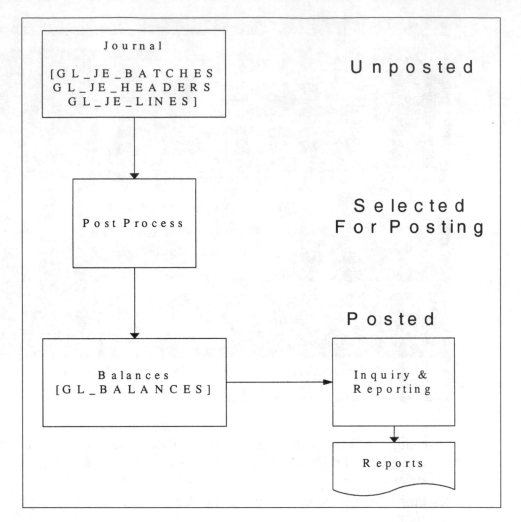

Exhibit 5.17   Journal Post Process

must be corrected before the journal may be posted and available for GL balances inquiry and reporting.

 Review the *Oracle General Ledger User Guide*, Correcting Batch Posting Errors section for a complete list of error codes.

1. From the General Ledger menu → **Journals** → **Post**.
2. Enter the search criteria for the journals to be posted. To retrieve all unposted journals, leave the search criteria blank.

3. Press **Find.**

4. All journals matching the search criteria will be displayed (see Exhibit 5.18).

5. Check the **Posting** box to indicate the journal is to be posted. The system will highlight the record.

6. Press the **Post** button to initiate the journal posting concurrent process. The journal status will change to Selected for Posting. The system will respond with "Your Posting concurrent request id is *n*." Press **OK.** Review the concurrent request to verify the concurrent process completed successfully. View the journal online and verify the status has changed to Posted. Optionally, run the "Journals – General" reports and select Posted for the Posting Status.

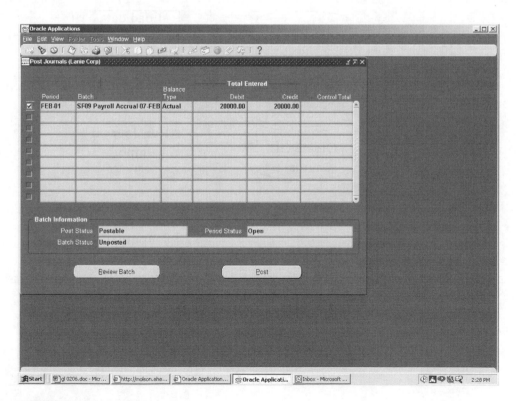

Exhibit 5.18 Journal Post

Journal Import

An overview of a typical journal import process into Oracle General Ledger is depicted in Exhibit 5.19. Oracle General Ledger journal import allows applications to create journal entries.

Oracle applications Application Desktop Integrator (ADI), Oracle Payables, and Oracle Receivables all utilize the journal import process. The journal import process creates standard Oracle General Ledger journals including the journal batch, journal header, and journal line records. In addition, all conversion data from the legacy general ledger system will utilize the journal import process.

Oracle Payables and Oracle Receivables may automatically run the journal import process depending on the respective application options. For example, the Oracle Payables Options Transfer to GL tab determines if the journal import process is automatically run. In Oracle Receivables,

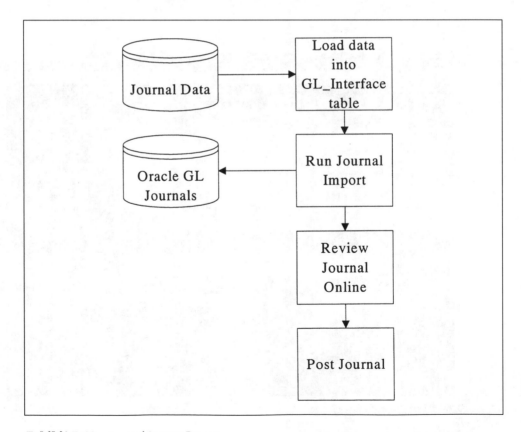

Exhibit 5.19 Journal Import Process

the user defines if the journal import process is automatically run when the GL Interface concurrent process is initiated.

 Review the *Oracle General Ledger User's Guide* for more information on the open journal interface process.

Prior to running the journal import process, the journal data file must be loaded into the Oracle General Ledger GL_INTERFACE table.

1. From the General Ledger menu → **Journals** → **Import** → **Run.**
2. Select the journal **Source** to import (see Exhibit 5.20).
3. The journal import files may be broken into Groups if the file is large. Select the Group Id if applicable.
4. Check the **Post Error to Suspense** box. If GL Set of Books suspense option is enabled and the journal is unbalanced, the system will post the difference to the suspense account.

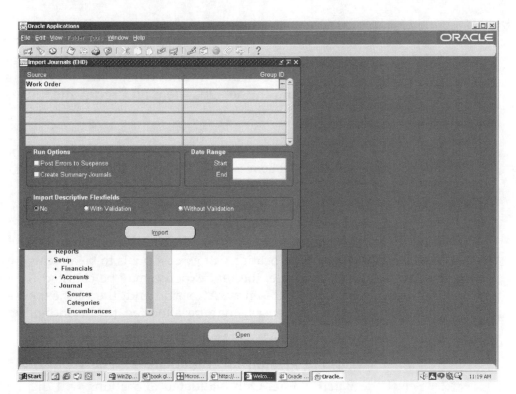

Exhibit 5.20 Journal Import Run

5. Check the **Create Summary Journals** box. This option will summarize the journal by unique accounting flexfield, period, and currency.

6. Press **Import** to initiate the journal import concurrent process. The system opens a decision window to double check before starting the concurrent process. Press **Yes.** The system responds with "Your concurrent request id is *n*." Review the Journal Import Execution report. View the journal online. Optionally, run the "Journals – General" reports which have a report run-time parameter of Unposted journal status.

Journal Import Corrections

Simple journal import errors may be corrected online in the Journals Import Correct window. Query the error record and update the record with the correct data. Rerun the journal import process. Journal import errors can include accounting flexfield validation issues and the period not being open.

Journal Import Deletions

If the errors are so significant and the file should be rerun, navigate to the Journal Import Delete window and delete the journal import source. Correct the errors in the subsystem and rerun the journal import process.

 Do not delete Oracle Payables or Oracle Receivables journal import files or journals as they cannot be recreated!

Mass Allocations

Oracle General Ledger Allocations allow cost pools to be allocated to various accounts. For example, the rent expense may be charged to one account during payables data entry. At period end, the rent expense (and other related facility expenses) may be allocated to the individual cost centers.

1. From the General Ledger menu → **Journals** → **Generate** → **Allocation.**

2. Select the **Batch Name.** Only validated allocations will display (see Exhibit 5.21).

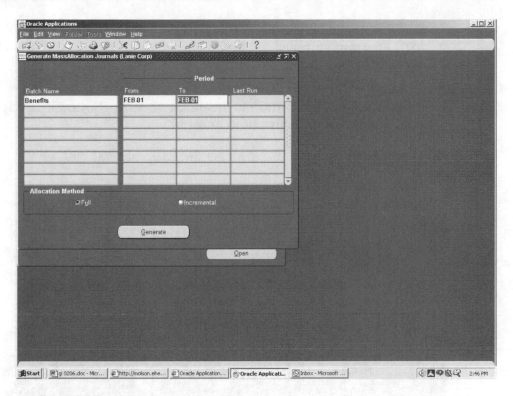

Exhibit 5.21 Generate Mass Allocations

3. Select the **From** and **To** Periods. Once the allocation journal has been created, the From Period will default to the last period run that the allocation was generated.

4. The Last Run date will display if the allocation has been generated previously.

5. Press the **Generate** button to initiate the journal posting concurrent process. Review the concurrent request to verify the allocation journal was created successfully.

Recurring Journals

Recurring journals expedite journal entry by creating either journals with the same account and fixed amounts each period or the same account and variable amounts each period. The variable amounts are entered after the recurring journal has been generated.

1. From the General Ledger menu → **Journals** → **Generate** → **Recurring.**
2. All recurring journals will be displayed (see Exhibit 5.22). Check the **Recurring** box to create the recurring journal.
3. Select the **Period.**
4. Press the **Generate** button to create the recurring journal. The system will display the Concurrent Request Id.

BUDGETS

Oracle General Ledger provides a variety of flexible budget capabilities. Oracle budgets may be used for management reporting purposes to compare actual results to anticipated or budgeted results.

Oracle General Ledger provides a variety of budget data entry

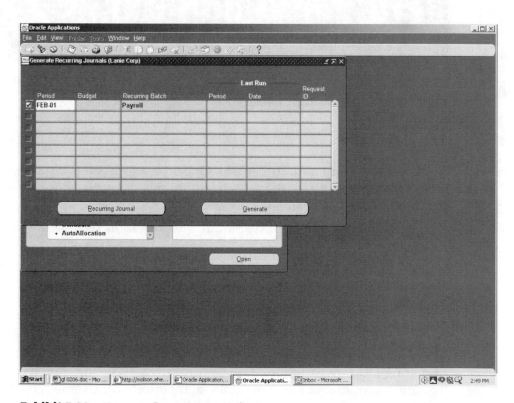

Exhibit 5.22   Generate Recurring Journals

methodologies including online entry and batch load. Online entry capabilities include direct data entry and budget rules or simple budget formulas. In addition, budget amounts may be calculated via mathematical formulas utilizing statistical data. Budgets may be transferred online as well. Users may easily move budgets from one accounting flexfield range to another accounting flexfield range.

Oracle General Ledger budget batch load capabilities include importing budgets via ADI or from another budget subsystem. Oracle General Ledger provides an open budget interface. The chapter on budgeting in the *Oracle General Ledger User Guide* details the open budget interface process.

Budgets and budget variances may be viewed online in Oracle General Ledger or displayed in FSG reports. Budget versus actual comparisons may be viewed online in the GL account inquiry window. Simply enter the budget name and navigate through the windows to view the budget data and actual-to-budget variances. In addition, if the budget balances were created from budget journals, drill-down to the journal detail is available.

Budget Organization

A budget organization defines the accounts to be budgeted at one time. Budget organizations may be divided by cost centers to allow decentralized budget data entry. A budget organization must be defined prior to budget entry (see Exhibit 5.23).

1. From the General Ledger menu → **Budgets** → **Define** → **Organization.**
2. Select the **Budget Organization.**
3. Enter the **Organization** name and **Description.**
4. Enter the **Ordering Segment** sequence. The ordering sequence dictates which segments will be displayed in what order. For example, if the budget organization has the company and cost center segments constant, they may be last in the ordering sequence and account first in the ordering sequence.
5. Press **Ranges** to enter the accounting flexfield ranges for the budget organization.

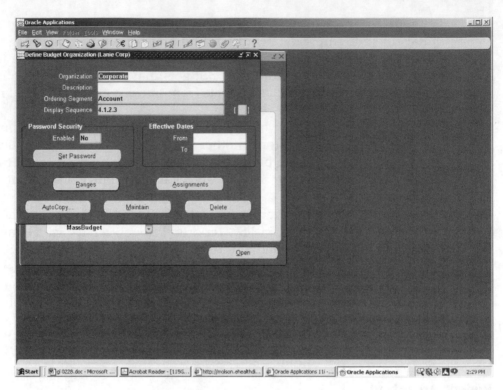

Exhibit 5.23 Budget Organization

Enter the accounting flexfield ranges for the budget organization (see Exhibit 5.24).

1. Enter the **Line** number.
2. Enter the **Low** and **High Accounting Flexfield** ranges for the budget organization.
3. Select the **Type** of **Entered** to manually enter budget amounts. Select the Type of Calculated to use budget formulas.
4. A concurrent request will run. Verify the concurrent request completed successfully and the budget organization was created.

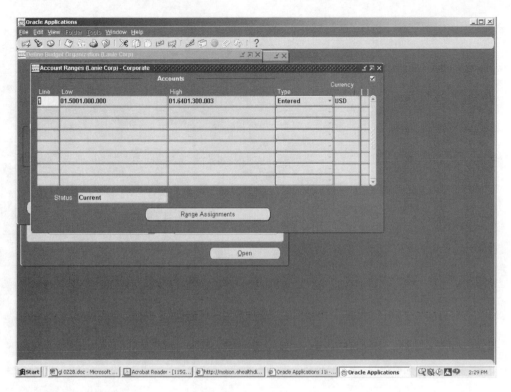

Exhibit 5.24   Budget Organization Ranges

Budget

Define the Budget. Budgets represent the different budget forecasts (see Exhibit 5.25).

1. From the General Ledger menu → **Budgets** → **Define** → **Budget.**
2. Enter the budget **Name** and **Description.** Use a short, yet descriptive name.
3. Select the budget **Status.** Budget statuses include Current, Open, and Frozen. The Current budget status denotes the default budget.
4. In the Budget Periods region, enter the **First** and **Last** budget period fields. Typically, these represent the entire year.

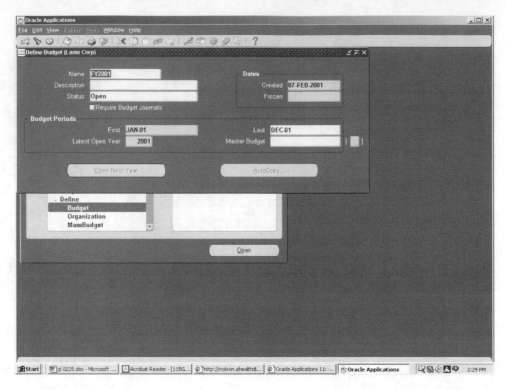

Exhibit 5.25 Budget

5. Press **Open Next Year** to open the budget.

6. A concurrent request will run. View Requests to review the concurrent process. Verify the concurrent request completed successfully.

Budget Entry

Oracle General Ledger provides three modes of online budget data entry:

1. *Worksheet*. One row per accounting flexfield. The user must scroll right to complete the data entry process (see Exhibit 5.26).

2. *Single row*. One row per accounting flexfield. The user enters the budget data, which is word-wrapped in the window (see Exhibit 5.27).

3. *Journal*. One row per accounting flexfield. The user enters the budget data in a journal format (see Exhibit 5.28).

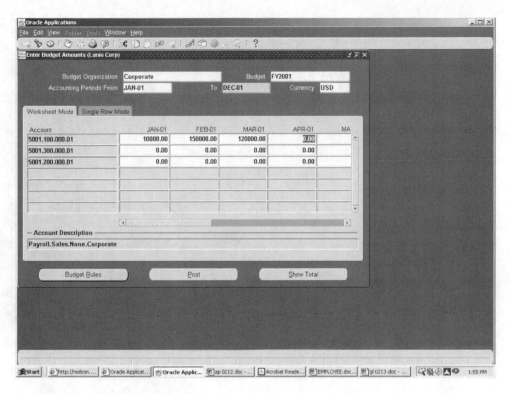

Exhibit 5.26 Budget Entry: Worksheet Mode

Budget entry in worksheet mode displays all accounts and as many amounts as may be displayed in a single row. The eight-step procedure for worksheet mode is:

1. From the General Ledger menu → **Budgets** → **Amounts.**
2. Select the **Budget Organization.**
3. Select the **Budget.**
4. Select the **Accounting Period From.** The Accounting Period To will default.
5. The currency defaults from the set of books functional currency.
6. Place the cursor on the **Account** row and enter the **Low and High** segment value ranges to budget for.
7. Enter the budget data under the appropriate **Period.**
8. Press **Post** when complete with budget entry. The system will display a message confirming the budget update process. Press **Yes.**

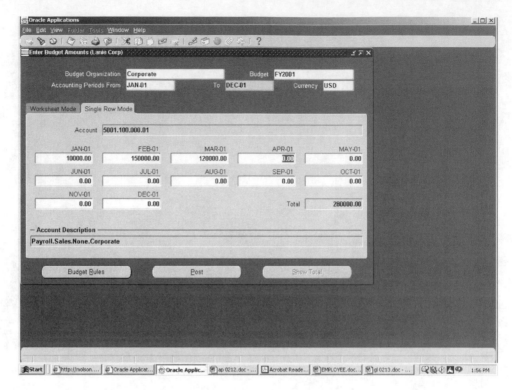

Exhibit 5.27   Budget Entry: Single-Row Mode

Review the concurrent request to verify the budget data was created successfully.

Budget entry in single-row mode displays one account and all amounts.

1. From the General Ledger menu → **Budgets** → **Amounts.**
2. Select the **Budget Organization.**
3. Select the **Budget.**
4. Select the **Accounting Period From.** The Accounting Period To will default.
5. The currency defaults from the set of books functional currency.
6. Place the cursor on the **Account** and enter the **Low and High** segment value ranges.
7. Enter the **Period** budget data.

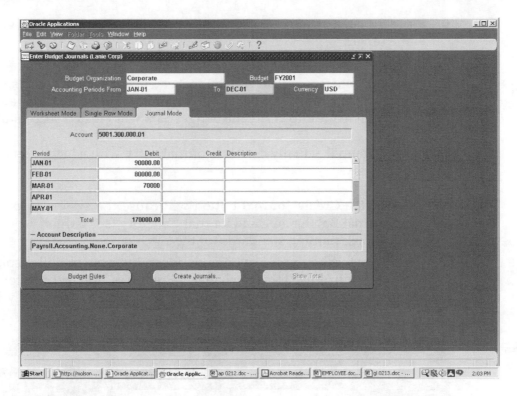

Exhibit 5.28 Budget Journals—Journal Mode

8. Press **Post** when complete with budget entry. The system will display a message confirming the budget update process. Press **Yes.** Review the concurrent request to verify the budget data was created successfully.

Budget entry in journal mode displays one account with amounts displayed down the window.

1. From the General Ledger menu → **Budgets** → **Journals.**
2. Select the **Budget Organization.**
3. Select the **Budget.**
4. Select the **Accounting Period From.** The Accounting Period To will default.
5. The currency defaults from the set of books functional currency.

6. Place the cursor on the **Account** and enter the **Low and High** segment value ranges.

7. Enter the **Period** budget data.

8. Press **Post** when complete with budget entry. The system will display a message confirming the budget update process. Press **Yes.** Review the concurrent request to verify the budget data was created successfully.

The budget journal actually creates a journal entry with a batch name and journal category.

1. Pressing the **Create Journal** button will cause the system to prompt for a **Journal Batch** name and journal **Category** (see Exhibit 5.29). Follow in-house naming standards for the batch name.

2. Press **Done.** When you leave the window, the system will display a message confirming to save changes. Press **Yes.** Review the concurrent request to verify the budget journal was created successfully. Post

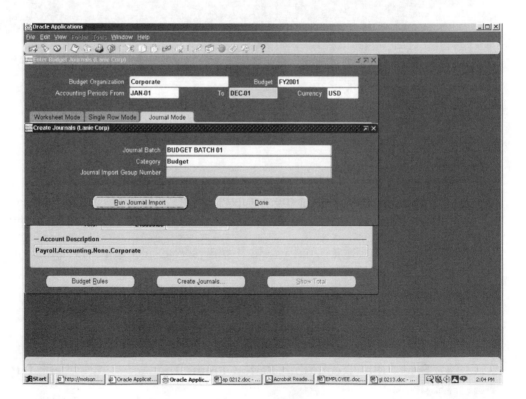

Exhibit 5.29   Budget Journals—Create Journal

the budget journal as you would any other journal. The Oracle General Ledger period status of Open or Future is irrelevant to post a budget journal.

Budgeting mass maintenance capabilities are available (see Exhibit 5.30).

1. From the General Ledger menu → **Budgets** → **Transfer.**
2. Select the **Budget.**
3. Enter a **Batch Name.** Follow in-house naming standards for the batch name.
4. The currency defaults to the set of books functional currency.
5. Select the **From Budget Organization** and **Account** to move budgets from.
6. Select the **To Budget Organization** and **Account** to move budgets to.

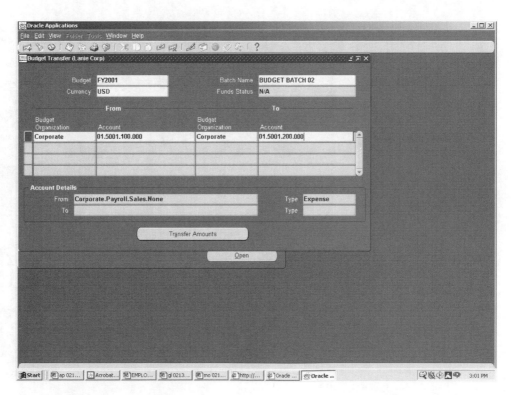

Exhibit 5.30 Budget Transfer

7. Press **Transfer Amounts.**

1. Select the **Period** to transfer (see Exhibit 5.31).
2. Enter a **Percent** or **Amount** to transfer.
3. The From Account Old Balance displays the amount to be transferred.
4. The To Account Old Balance displays the original budget amount.
5. When you close the window, the budget transfer concurrent process starts. Review the concurrent request to verify the budget journal was created successfully.

INQUIRY AND REPORTING

Oracle General Ledger provides extensive online and reporting capabilities. The account inquiry displays the posted balances, navigates to the journal details, navigates to the Oracle application subsystem which cre-

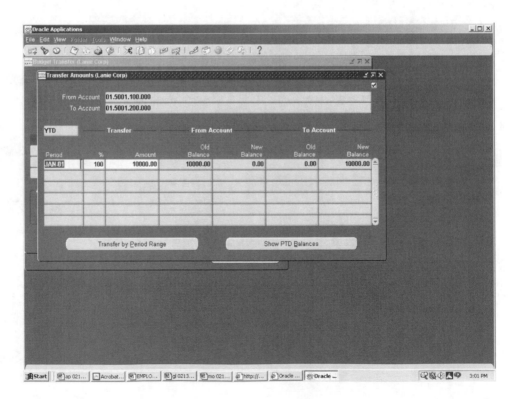

Exhibit 5.31   Budget Transfer Amounts

ated the journal, and optionally displays the detail T-account and journal entry transactions (see Exhibit 5.32).

The account inquiry window starts by selecting the GL Set of Books three Cs: the chart of accounts, the calendar period, and the currency. Once the GL Set of Books selection criteria is entered, the GL account balances are displayed by period. Account balances include actuals, budgets, and encumbrances. The journals which comprise the balance may be reviewed. If the journal source is Oracle Payables or Oracle Receivables, the account inquiry form can zoom to the subsystem transaction.

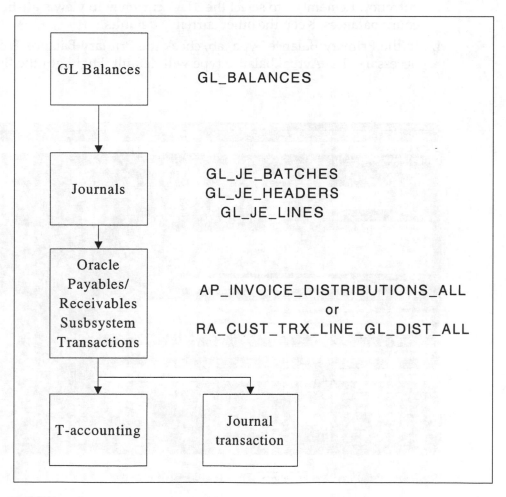

Exhibit 5.32 Inquiry Process

In addition, the T-accounting and actual balanced journal transaction may be displayed.

The Oracle General Ledger account inquiry window is displayed in Exhibit 5.33.

1. From the General Ledger menu → **Inquiry** → **Account.**

2. The Accounting Period To and From will default to the latest open GL period. Select the **From** period. The period name will default in the To period field. Select the **To** period name. Typically, the From and To fields represent the entire GL Set of Books calendar for the year.

3. The Currency field displays the default GL Set of Books functional currency. Remember to select the STAT currency to view statistical account balances. Keep the other currency defaults.

4. In the Primary Balance Type tab, check the Primary Balance Types as necessary. The Actual balance type will default. Highlight the Budget

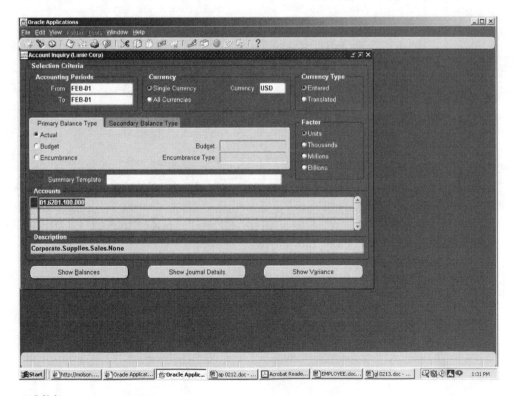

Exhibit 5.33 Account Inquiry

circle and select the Budget to be displayed if performing actual to budget variance calculations.

5. Enter the **Accounts.** For each accounting flexfield segment, enter the accounting flexfield low and high segment values range. Use the Low and High values to select a range of values. All accounting flexfields meeting the entered range criteria are displayed.

6. Press **Show Balances** to view the posted balance amounts for the selected accounting flexfield record.

> Use the < and > symbols to select an accounting flexfield range. For example, to view cost centers 501 through 599, enter > 500 and < 600.

1. The posted Oracle General Ledger PTD and YTD balances for the accounting flexfield are displayed (see Exhibit 5.34).

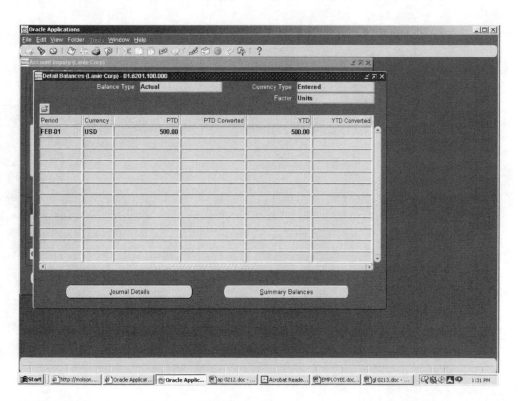

Exhibit 5.34   Account Inquiry—Balances

2. Press **Journal Details** to view the journal entry data which comprise the GL balance amount for each applicable period.

Journal batch, journal header, and journal line data are displayed in Exhibit 5.35.

If the journal was created from Oracle Payables or Oracle Receivables, the user may drill-down from the journal entry to the subsystem's actual transaction that created the journal. Press **Drilldown.**

The Oracle Payables invoice header data is displayed in Exhibit 5.36.

Press **Show Transaction Accounting** to view the journal entry lines created from the transaction.

The Oracle Payables journal lines for the invoice transaction are displayed in Exhibit 5.37.

Press **T Accounts** to view the T-accounts for the transaction. The T Accounts options window opens. Within the options window, select either **T Accounts** to view the T-accounts graphical representation of the financial

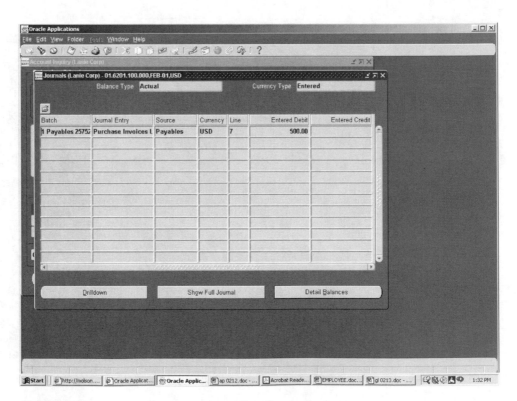

Exhibit 5.35   Account Inquiry—Journal Details

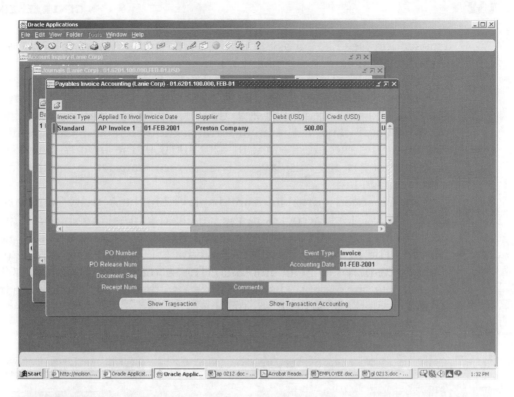

Exhibit 5.36   Account Inquiry—Drill-down

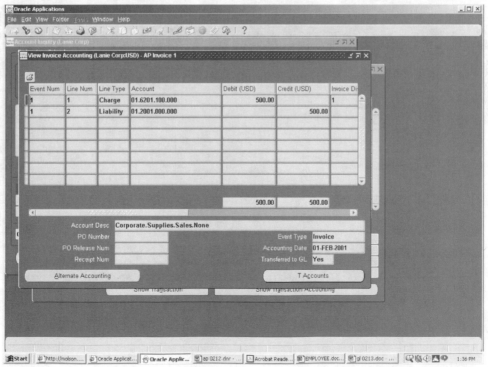

Exhibit 5.37   Account Inquiry—Show Transaction Accounting

transaction (see Exhibit 5.38) or press **Activity Summary** to view the balanced journal entry (see Exhibit 5.39).

The graphical representation of the T-accounts for the journal line is displayed (see Exhibit 5.38). Both accounts in the balanced journal are shown. The first account 01.2001.000.000, the Accounts Payable liability account, is displayed. The invoice transaction created a $500 credit journal line. The second account 01.6201.100.000, the invoice line expense distribution, is also displayed. The invoice transaction created a $500 debit journal line.

The balanced journal lines are displayed in the Activity Summary (see Exhibit 5.39). Both accounts in the balanced journal are shown. The first account 01.2001.000.000, the Accounts Payable liability account, is displayed. The invoice transaction created a $500 credit journal line (scroll right to display the credit amounts). The second account 01.6201.100.000, the invoice line expense distribution, is also displayed. The invoice transaction created a $500 debit journal line.

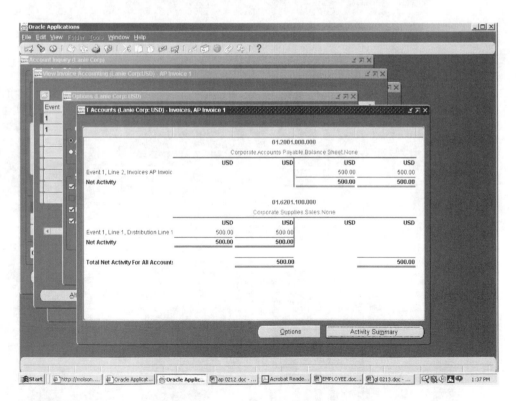

Exhibit 5.38   Account Inquiry—T-Accounts

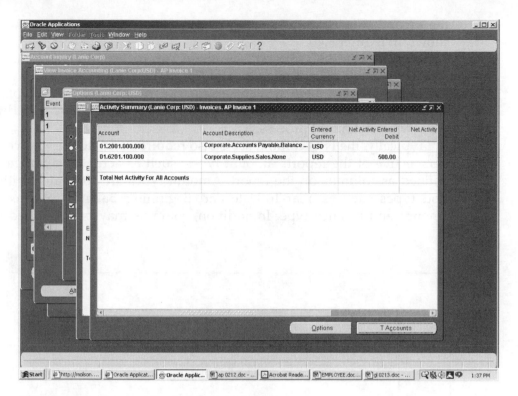

Exhibit 5.39　Account Inquiry—Activity Summary

Reporting

Oracle General Ledger provides standard General Ledger financial reports. In addition, Oracle General Ledger provides a financial report writer tool called the Financial Statement Generator (FSG). FSG produces user-defined financial reports. Users define the report format, including the layout and contents of the report. FSG produces financial reports from posted GL balances including actuals, budgets, and encumbrances. Sample FSG reports include financial statements such as a Balance Sheet, an Income Statement, or a Department Budget and Actual Comparison report.

Financial Statement Generator Architecture

To understand the components of an FSG report, think of a financial statement as a relational database table or a spreadsheet made of rows and columns. An FSG report has three dimensions. The rows of the report comprise the first dimension. The columns of the report comprise the second dimension. The page breaks create the third dimension as shown in Exhibit 5.40.

Typically, the FSG row set is required and defines the horizontal perspective of the report. Row set data elements include row headings and the accounting flexfields, which make up the row amounts, are displayed. Calculations such as subtotals and grand totals may also be included in the row set definition process.

Typically, the FSG column set is also required and defines the vertical perspective of the report. Amount types, such as actual and budget, are defined as columns on the report. Amount types are combined with period types such as Year-To-Date and Beginning Balance to reflect the amount and balance type. In addition, columns may be formatted with

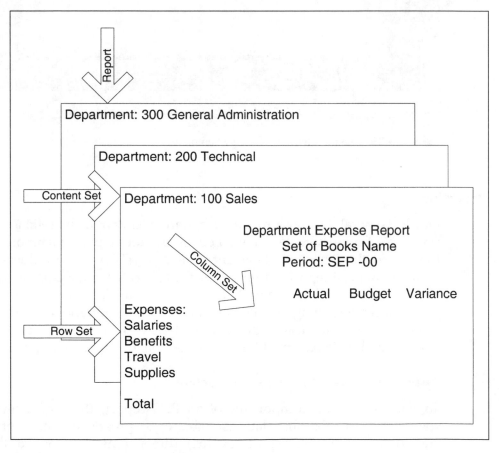

Exhibit 5.40   FSG Reports Architecture

display size, rounding, and decimal precision. Calculations such as subtotals and totals of columns may also be performed.

The FSG content set is optional, but typically used. The content set represents the data content of the report and where page breaks occur. The FSG report component allows the user to link the individual FSG components into an FSG report. In addition, a report set may be defined which is a compilation of individual reports. For example, a period-end report set may include all individual period-end reports, such as the Balance Sheet and Income Statement reports.

Financial Statement Generator Report

1. From the General Ledger menu → **Reports** → **Request** → **Financial.**
2. Select the **Report** (see Exhibit 5.41). If the report hasn't been defined, press Define Ad Hoc Report to request the individual FSG components.

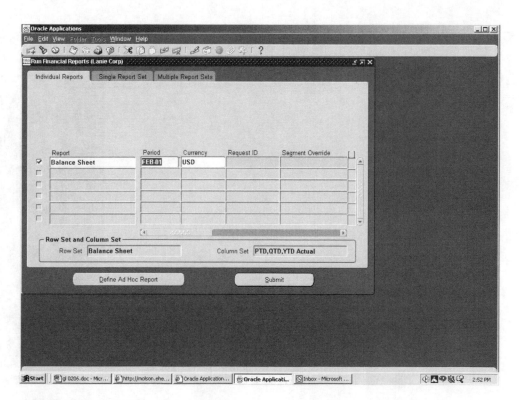

Exhibit 5.41 FSG Report Request

3. Select the **Period.** This is the reporting period.

4. The Currency defaults to the set of books functional currency.

5. Optionally, enter a segment override value to run the report just for the override segment value. For example, entering a segment override value of 01 would produce the FSG report for company 01 only.

6. Press **Submit** to initiate the concurrent process. Review the concurrent requests to verify the FSG report completed successfully.

 All Ad Hoc reports create a record and the Concurrent Program Delete Ad-Hoc Reports program should be run periodically.

A sample FSG report is displayed in Exhibit 5.42. The row set defined the lines of the report and the column set defined the Year-To-Date column.

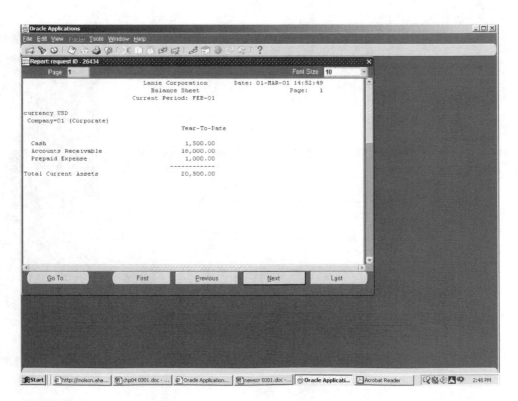

Exhibit 5.42   FSG Sample Report

Standard General Ledger Report

Oracle General Ledger provides a variety of standard General Ledger reports and listings. All reports and listings are run as an Oracle Standard Report Submission (SRS) concurrent request as shown in Exhibit 5.43.

1. From the General Ledger menu → **Reports** → **Request** → **Standard.**
2. Select the **Report.**
3. Select the report **Parameters.**
4. Press **Submit** to initiate the concurrent process. The system will display the concurrent request number. Review the concurrent request to view the report online.

A sample Oracle General Ledger standard report is displayed in Exhibit 5.44. Exhibit 5.45 lists other common Oracle General Ledger reports, listings, and other concurrent processes.

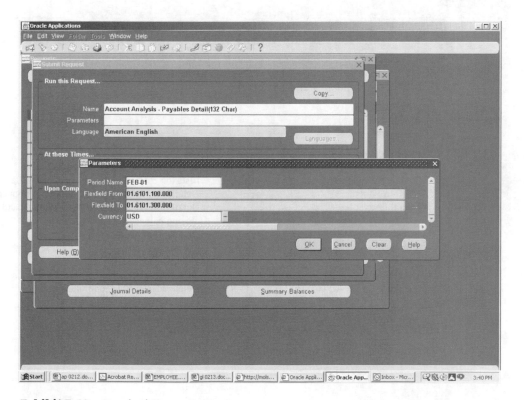

Exhibit 5.43 Standard Report Request

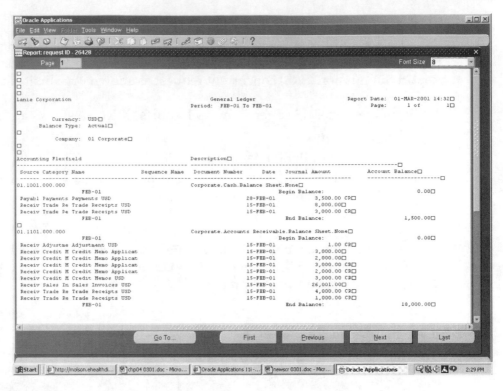

Exhibit 5.44 Standard Report Sample

Oracle General Ledger Report	Description
Accounts Analysis	Details the analysis of GL accounts
Chart of Accounts	Lists the chart of accounts segment values
FSG Components	Details the individual FSG report components
General Ledger	Details the beginning balance, journals and closing balance for GL accounts
Journals	Details journal entries
Optimizer	Creates the accounting flexfield segment indexes
Trial Balance	Details the organization's GL Trial Balance
Program – Delete Ad Hoc (FSG) reports	Delete ad-hoc FSG reports

Exhibit 5.45 Oracle General Ledger Standard Reports

PERIOD-END PROCESS

All journals should be entered and posted before closing a period. Oracle Payables and Oracle Receivables should perform their respective period end processes before closing the Oracle General Ledger period. Opening a period in Oracle General Ledger creates a concurrent process, which opens the period and calculates the beginning balances for the period.

When Oracle General Ledger opens the first period in a new year, the balance sheet accounts are rolled forward and the income statement accounts are closed to the retained earnings account as defined in the GL Set of Books. The year-end close process is transparent to the user. If a prior year journal is entered and posted, the proper roll-forward process will occur.

The closing screen is shown in Exhibit 5.46.

1.   From the General Ledger menu → **Setup** → **Open/Close.**

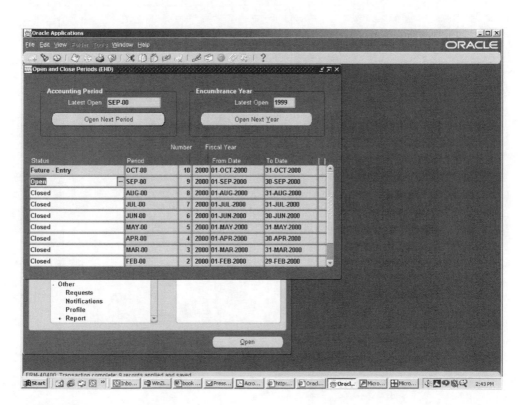

Exhibit 5.46   Close Period

CHAPTER 6

Multi-Org

OVERVIEW

Oracle Applications multiple-organization (multi-org) functionality allows each organization to define its respective operating practices independent of the Oracle applications instance. Organization parameters such as the GL Set of Books, the application system options, the customer site and supplier site definitions, and security may be defined specific to the organization. As an Oracle applications organization may or may not equate to the physical organization, the team needs to understand the capabilities and constraints within a multi-org environment before defining the multi-org structure into production.

SETUP

The multi-org setup step includes defining the organizations, the responsibilities, and the organization profile values. In addition, the DBA runs a program to build the multi-org infrastructure (see Exhibit 6.1).

Setting up Oracle Applications in a multi-org structure is optional but recommended. The full functionality of multi-org should be understood prior to determining whether the multi-org environment is applicable.

 Refer to the *Multiple Organizations in Oracle Applications* documentation for more information.

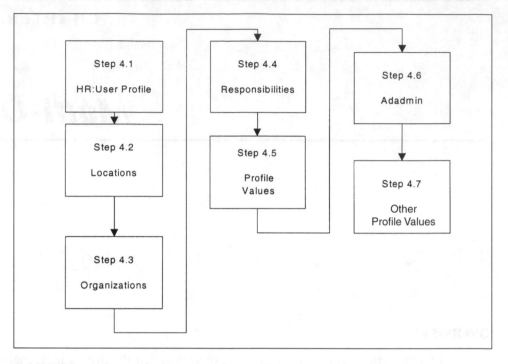

Exhibit 6.1   Multi-Org Setup Steps

MULTI-ORG STEP 4.1: HUMAN RESOURCES USER PROFILE

The Human Resources user type profile value must be defined (see Exhibit 6.2).

1. From the **File** menu → **Switch Responsibility** →**System Administrator.**
2. From the System Administrator menu → **Profiles** →**System.**
3. Check the **Responsibility** box and select the **Responsibility.**
4. Enter the **Profile** value parameter **HR:User%.**
5. Press **Find.**

 All the required multi-org windows are in the seeded Receivables Manager responsibility.

Select the **HR:User Type** profile option for the seeded Receivables responsibility (see Exhibit 6.3).

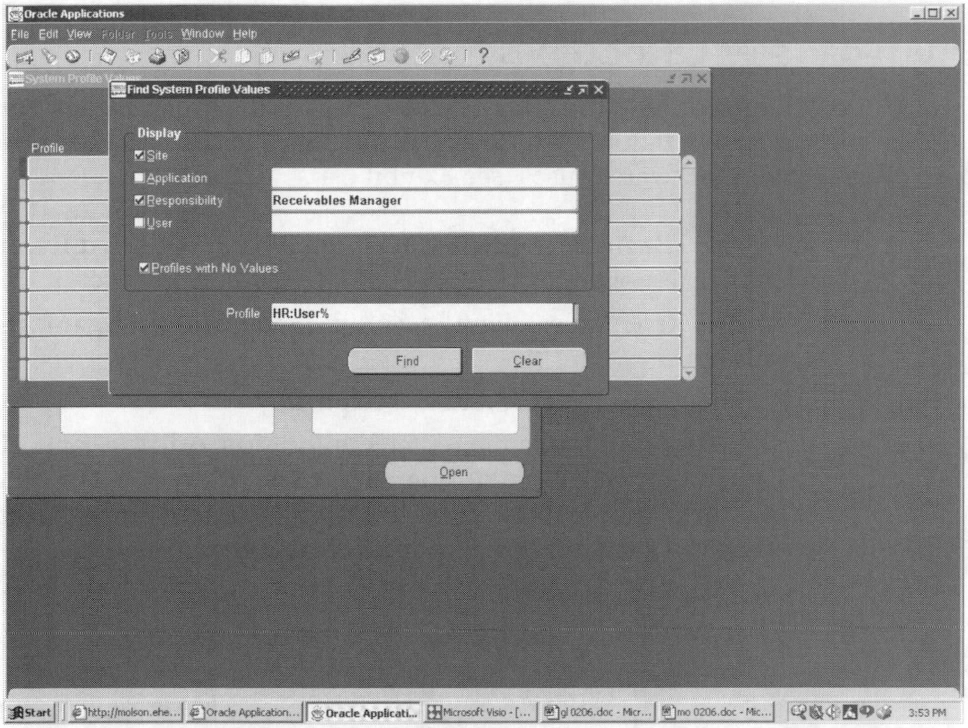

Exhibit 6.2 Human Resources: User Profile Find

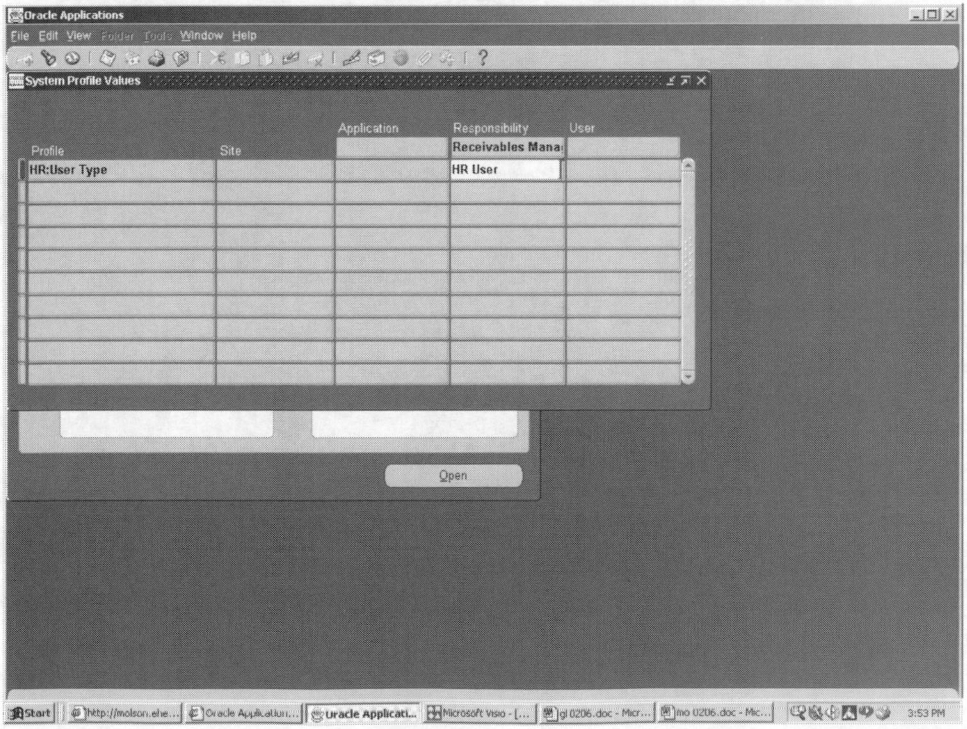

Exhibit 6.3 Human Resources: User Profile Definition

MULTI-ORG STEP 4.2: LOCATIONS

Locations represent the physical addresses for the organization. For example, an organization's locations may include headquarters, field offices, and inventory warehouses (see Exhibit 6.4).

1. From the **File** menu → **Switch Responsibility** → seeded **Receivables Manager** responsibility.
2. From the Receivables menu → **Setup** → **System** → **Organizations** → **Locations.**
3. Enter the location **Name** and **Description.**
4. In the Address Details tab, enter the location **Address** data. The address window will open during data entry. Address data includes the organization name on address line 1 and the remaining lines for the street, city, state, and postal code address data.

Repeat for all locations.

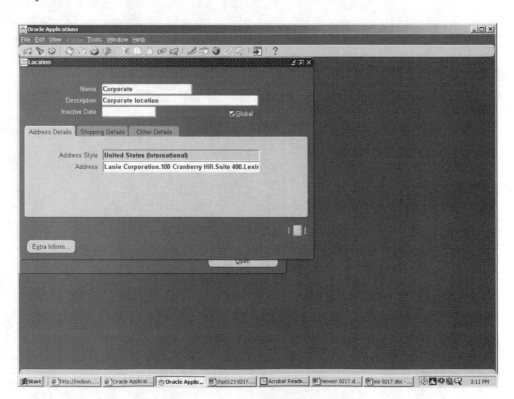

Exhibit 6.4 Location Definition

MULTI-ORG STEP 4.3: ORGANIZATIONS

Oracle application multi-org structure must be defined from the business group level down to the operating unit level and the inventory org level if using Oracle Inventory (see Exhibit 6.5).

Refer to the multi-org design as described in Chapter 1. Start at the top of the organization and work down the organizational structure. The Business Group org must be defined before the GRE/Legal Entity org, which must be defined before the Operating Unit org. If using Oracle Inventory capabilities, the Inventory org must be defined after the Operating Unit org.

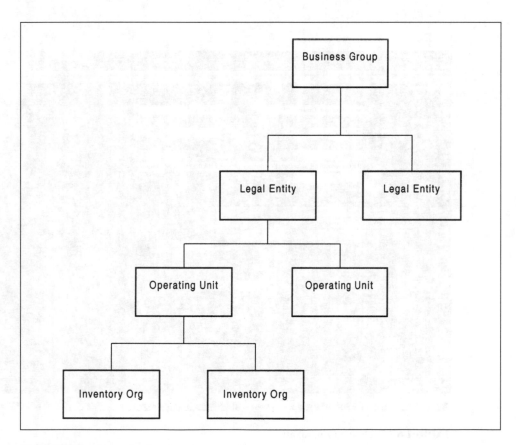

Exhibit 6.5 Organization Levels

Business Group

1. From the Receivables menu → **Setup** → **System** → **Organizations** → **Organizations.**

2. Press **Find (B)** to display all Organizations.

3. Oracle applications seeds the **Setup Business Group,** which is displayed. Use this seeded org as the Business Group if possible (see Exhibit 6.6).

4. Select the **Location.**

5. In the Organization Classification region, select the org levels and define the respective org level parameters. The HR Organization is displayed by default. Enter the GRE/Legal Entity level, then the Operating Unit level and, if necessary, the Inventory Org level.

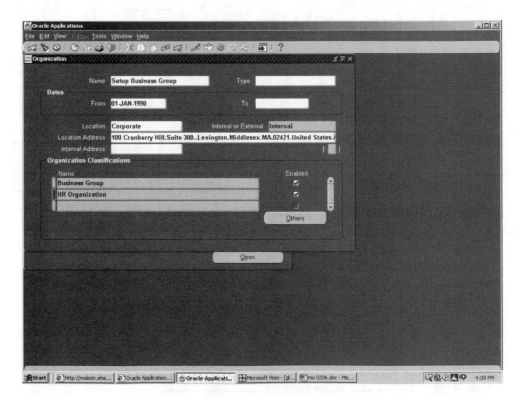

Exhibit 6.6   Define Organizations

GRE/Legal Entity

Typically, the GRE/Legal Entity equals a GL Set of Books. A legal entity represents the level for financial and tax reporting.

1. Highlight the **GRE/Legal Entity** record (see Exhibit 6.7).
2. Check the **Enabled** box at the GRE/Legal Entity record.
3. Press <u>Others</u> to enter the organization parameters for the GRE/Legal Entity org level.

The Employer Identification sets the taxpayer id.

1. Enter **Employer Identification** in the GRE/Legal Entity window (see Exhibit 6.8).
2. Press <u>OK</u>.

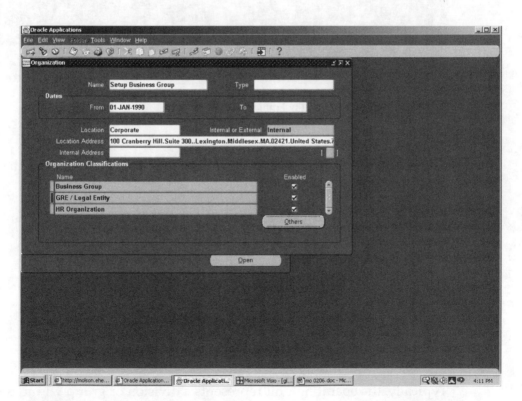

Exhibit 6.7 GRE/Legal Entity

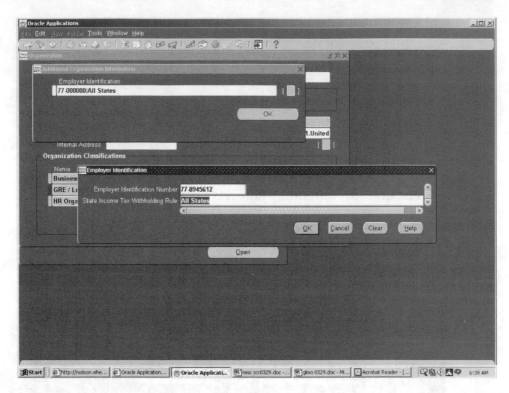

Exhibit 6.8   GRE/Legal Entity Employer Identification

The Set of Books links the chart of accounts, the calendar, and the currency to the legal entity.

1. Select **Legal Entity Accounting** in the GRE/Legal Entity parameters window.
2. Press **OK.**
3. Press tab to open the window.
4. Select the (GL) **Set of Books** name (see Exhibit 6.9).
5. Press **OK.**

Operating Unit

Typically, the operating unit represents a division or group within the GL Set of Books. The operating unit defines the Oracle applications processing environment and security may be enabled at this level.

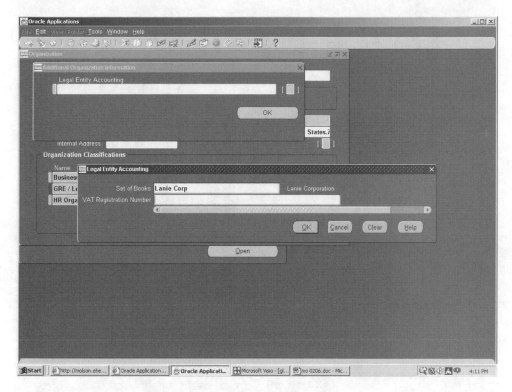

Exhibit 6.9   GRE/Legal Entity Set of Books

1. Select the **Operating Unit** org level (see Exhibit 6.10).
2. Check the **Enabled** box at the Operating Unit record.
3. Press **Others** to enter the organization parameters for the Operating Unit.

The operating unit represents the organization within Oracle Payables and Oracle Receivables.

1. Select the (GRE)/**Legal Entity** organization.
2. Press tab to open the window.
3. Select the (GL) **Set of Books** (see Exhibit 6.11).
4. Press **OK.**

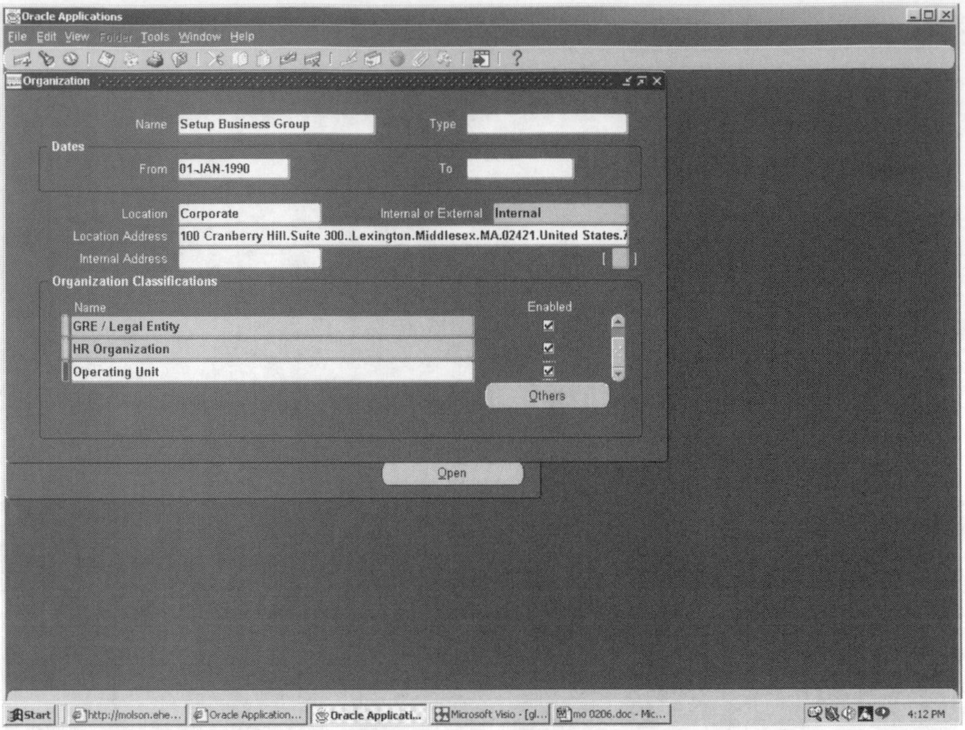

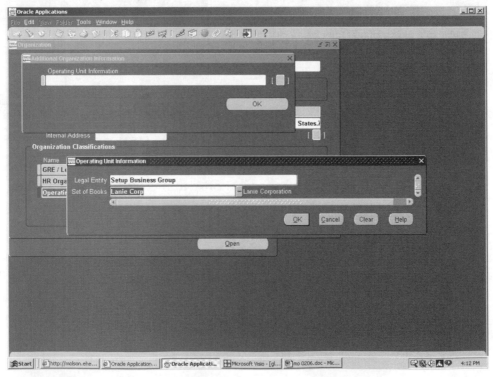

Exhibit 6.10 Operating Unit

Exhibit 6.11 Operating Unit Information

Inventory Org

If using Oracle Inventory capabilities, define the Inventory Org and respective parameters as well. Remember Oracle manufacturing applications use inventory capabilities, as does Oracle Purchasing for receiving functions. Typically, an inventory org represents a warehouse or logical collection of inventory items.

 Refer to *Multiple Organizations in Oracle Applications* for more information.

MULTI-ORG STEP 4.4: RESPONSIBILITIES

Define the new multi-org responsibilities for the various Oracle Applications to be implemented (see Exhibit 6.12).

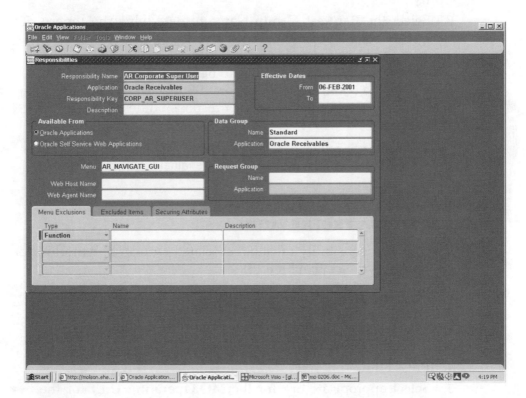

Exhibit 6.12   Define Responsibility

1. From the **File** menu → **Switch Responsibility** → **System Administrator** responsibility.
2. From the System Administrator menu → **Security** → **Responsibility** → **Define.**
3. Enter a **Responsibility Name.** The name should reflect the application, the user access, and the GL Set of Books characteristics. For example, AR Corporate Super User indicates the application is Oracle Receivables, the GL Set of Books is Corporate, and the user access is full.
4. Select the **Application.**
5. Enter a unique **Responsibility Key.**
6. Select a **Data Group.** Typically, the Data Group Name is Standard.
7. Select the **Data Group Application** for the Data Group. Typically, the application is the same as the application responsibility.
8. Select the **Menu** to display when the user signs on to the responsibility.
9. Select the **Request Group Name** to determine the reports. The Request Group Application is displayed.

Repeat for all responsibilities to be defined in the multi-org environment. For the book, the AP Corporate Super User, AR Corporate Super User, and GL Corporate Super User responsibilities were defined.

 Link the new multi-org responsibilities to the user names and disable the seeded responsibilities used during the initial setup process.

MULTI-ORG STEP 4.5: PROFILE VALUES

Each new responsibility must be associated with an MO (multi-org) operating unit level (see Exhibit 6.13).

1. From the System Administrator menu → **Profile** → **System.**
2. Check the appropriate **Display** profile level box.
3. Enter the **MO% Profile** value to query.
4. Press **Find.**
5. Select appropriate org for the **MO:Operating Unit** for the **new Responsibility.**

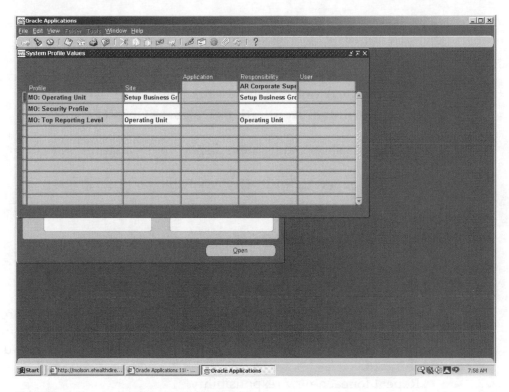

Exhibit 6.13   System Profile Values Definition

6. Select the appropriate **MO:Top Reporting Level** for the **new Responsibility.**

    Repeat for each new multi-org responsibility.

   Remember to set the MO:Operating Unit profile value at the site level to allow adadmin to run successfully.

MULTI-ORG STEP 4.6: ADADMIN

Oracle applications provide an Oracle Applications set of utilities known as adadmin. One function of the adadmin process is to build the multi-org infrastructure. This process updates the application software and maintains the installed system.

Review the *Oracle Applications, Maintaining Oracle Application Release 11i* manual for more information.

1. The DBA or System Administrator must run the Multi-Org convert option in the AutoInstall utility adadmin.
2. Select **1 Maintain Applications Database Objects** menu.

Exhibit 6.14 shows the system display of the adadmin menu.

1. Select **8 Convert to Multi-Org** (see Exhibit 6.15).
2. Monitor the adadmin process.

 Review the Multi-Org Validation report for errors.

MULTI-ORG STEP 4.7: OTHER PROFILE VALUES

After the adadmin process is complete, a variety of other multi-org profile options must be defined. Select the appropriate profile option for each new multi-org responsibility. The profile options are included in Exhibit 6.16.

Repeat for each new responsibility.

 Refer to the *Multiple Organizations in Oracle Applications* documentation for more information as the profile names and options change periodically.

```
 AD Administration Main Menu
 -----------------------------------------------------

    1.   Maintain Applications Database Objects menu

    2.   Maintain Applications Files menu

    3.   Exit AD Administration



 Enter your choice : 1
```

Exhibit 6.14 adadmin Menu

```
                    Maintain Applications Database Objects
        ----------------------------------------------------

        1.    Validate APPS schema(s)

        2.    Compile APPS schema(s)

        3.    Recreate grants and synonyms for APPS schema(s)

        6.    Compile flexfield data in AOL tables

        6.    Maintain multi-lingual tables

        6.    Check DUAL table

        7.    Convert to Multiple Reporting Currencies

        8.    Convert to MultiOrg

        9.    Return to Main Menu

    Enter your choice : 8
```

Exhibit 6.15   adadmin Multi-Org Option

Profile Option	*Profile Value*
HR:Business Group	Setup Business Group
HR:User Type	HR User
GL: Set of Books Name	Select the appropriate set of books
INV: Intercompany Currency Conversion	Corporate
Tax: Allow Override of Tax Code	Yes
Tax: Invoice Freight as Revenue	No
Sequential Numbering	Not Used

Exhibit 6.16   Multi-Org Profile Values

CHAPTER 7

Payables

OVERVIEW

This chapter describes using Oracle Payables to track suppliers, supplier invoices, and supplier payments. Suppliers include vendors, contractors, and employees. Supplier invoices can include standard invoices, credit memos, invoices matched to a purchase order, invoices imported from another system, prepayments, and employee expenses. Supplier payments can include checks and electronic funds transfers (EFT).

Oracle Payables provides the standard supplier, invoice, and payment processes. In addition, Oracle Payables provides state-of-the-art payables capabilities with procurement card and electronic data interchange (EDI) functionality. Furthermore, Oracle's web applications allow users outside of Oracle applications to enter their data. For example, a user may enter an expense report through a web browser using Oracle's Self Service applications.

Oracle Payables is fully integrated with Oracle General Ledger. The GL Set of Books defines the accounting environment. In addition, all Oracle Payables financial transactions create journal entries to Oracle General Ledger with full audit trail capabilities regardless of the summarization level. Online inquiry includes drill-down from the Oracle General Ledger journal entry to the Oracle Payables invoice distribution with full T-accounts and journal entry transaction distribution display capabilities.

Oracle Payables is fully integrated with Oracle Human Resources and Oracle Projects. If the employee expense report processing occurs in Oracle Projects or Oracle Payables, the employee information is shared with Oracle Human Resources. The employee information such as the default expense account may be defined.

Oracle Payables is fully integrated with Oracle Purchasing. All supplier, purchase order, and receipt data are shared between Oracle Purchasing and Oracle Payables. Typically, to ensure an organization is not charged more than the agreed-to business terms and conditions, a purchase order (and/or receipt) is matched with the supplier invoice.

Oracle Payables is fully integrated with Oracle Cash Management. The bank reconciliation process occurs in Oracle Cash Management from the Oracle Payables disbursement data. In addition, the cash requirements from Oracle Payables are available. Cash inflows are created from cash forecasts from Oracle Receivables to complete the cash management perspective.

Oracle Payables is fully integrated with Oracle Fixed Assets. All supplier invoices to an asset account are forwarded to Oracle Fixed Assets for processing into capital assets. In addition, an invoice to an expense distribution may also be marked and forwarded. A full audit trail from the capital asset back to the original invoice is provided.

The typical Oracle Payables business process flow is setup, suppliers, invoices and payments, inquiry and reporting, and period-end processing (see Exhibit 7.1).

The Oracles Payables business flow is setup, supplier entry, invoice entry, payments or disbursements generation, inquiry and reporting, and period-end processing. Each organization must define its specific operating environment.

First, the Oracle Payables environment must be defined. Suppliers must be defined before an invoice may be entered. Likewise, an invoice must be entered and approved before a payment may be created or entered. Both transactions create journal entries to Oracle General Ledger.

SETUP

Oracle Payables provide default data values to speed data entry. These default values cascade from the Financials or Payables Options to the invoices and payments (see Exhibit 7.2). For example, the payment terms default from the Financial Options, which cascade down to the supplier level, which cascade down to the supplier site level. The terms will then cascade to the invoice batch and invoice header. The terms may be overridden at any level during the data entry process.

Careful consideration of the most commonly used data values must oc-

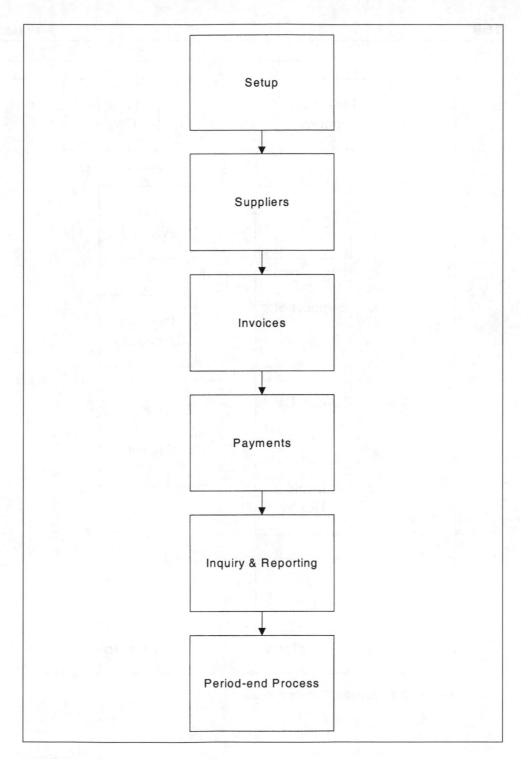

Exhibit 7.1 Payables Business Process Flow

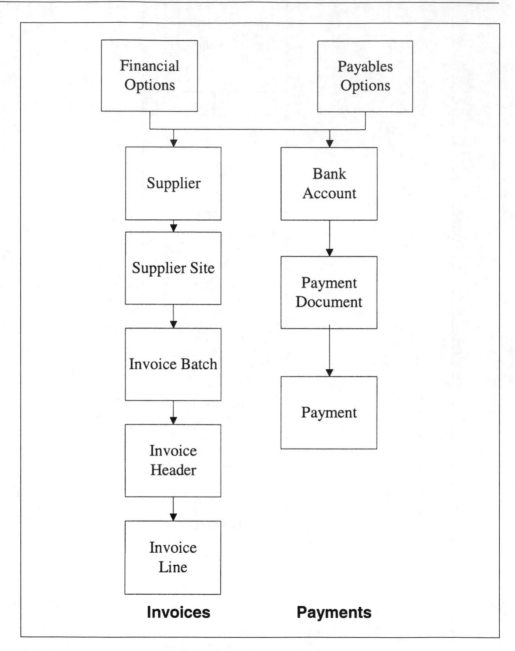

Exhibit 7.2   Payables Defaults Cascade

cur during the Oracle Payables system definition process. Exhibit 7.3 lists the most common default data elements. The most commonly set defaults are the accounts, particularly the liability account. In addition, the multi-org environment may determine the default level value. For example, in a multi-org environment, the liability account is not set at the supplier level; only the supplier site level as the parameter is organization-specific.

 Review the *Oracle Payables User Guide,* Appendix E, for the complete hierarchy list. The list details invoice, payment, and account defaults.

Defining the Oracle Payables environment is a relatively simple process (see Exhibit 7.4). Oracle Payables is set up at the operating unit level in a multi-org environment. Therefore, each organization may define its specific Oracle Payables environment. The Oracle Payables setup steps listed in Exhibit 7.4 presumes Oracle General Ledger *and* the multi-org environment have been defined.

The Oracle Payables setup process includes defining the lookup codes, selecting the GL Set of Books, defining the profile values, defining the payment terms, and the bank accounts. Financial and payables processing options must also be defined. If employee expenses are to be entered, the default employee expense report template should be defined. The tax reporting entity should be defined. The last step is to open the period for Payables processing.

Level	*Default Values*
Financial Options	• Liability account
	• Prepayment account
	• Discount taken account
	• Payment method
	• Terms
Payables Options	• GL date
	• Pay group
	• Pay through date
	• Terms date
Supplier	• Terms
Supplier Site	• Liability account
	• Terms
Invoice Batch	• Liability account
	• Terms
	• GL date

Exhibit 7.3 Payables Default Data Elements

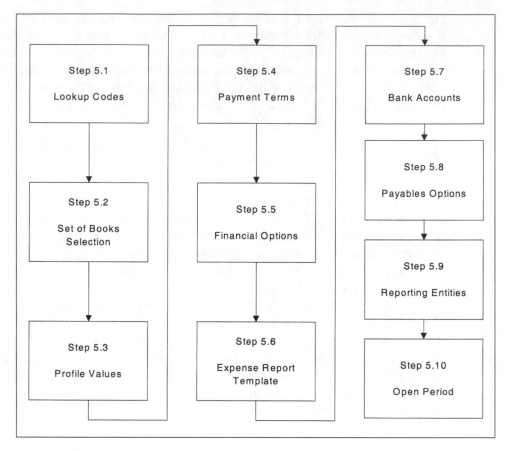

Exhibit 7.4   Setting Up Payables

PAYABLES STEP 5.1: LOOKUP CODES

Oracle Payables lookup codes allow user-defined data values (see Exhibit 7.5). These data values are displayed in the List of Values list for selection during data entry. The Pay Group lookup code allows disbursement runs to be segregated by Pay Group. For example, one payment run may be for employee expense reports and another payment run may be for supplier invoices.

Other common Lookup Types defined include:

- Vendor Types
- FOB
- Freight Terms

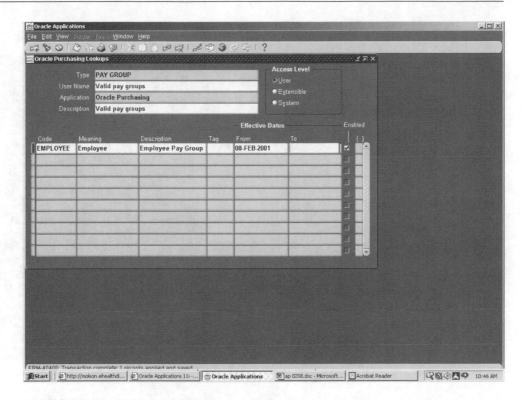

Exhibit 7.5   Payables Purchasing Lookup Codes

The four-step procedure is:

1. From the **File** menu → **Switch Responsibility** → **AP Corporate Super User.**
2. From the Payables menu → **Setup** → **Lookups** → **Purchasing.**
3. Query the lookup **Type.**
4. Enter the lookup **Code, Meaning,** and **Description** fields.

PAYABLES STEP 5.2: SELECT SET OF BOOKS

Each Oracle Payables instance must be linked to an Oracle General Ledger Set of Books. The multi-org definition process linked the new Payables responsibility to the Set of Books. In addition, Oracle Payables setup process includes selecting the GL Set of Books (see Exhibit 7.6). This ensures the proper accounting flexfield, calendar, and currency values are

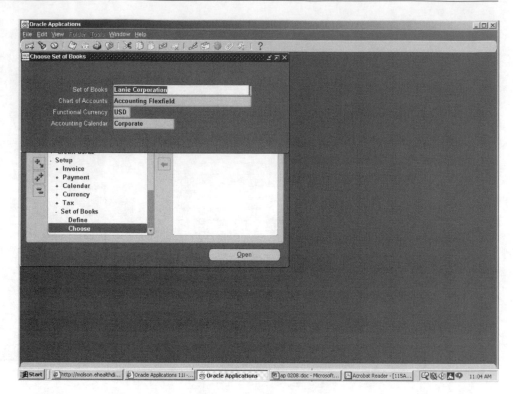

Exhibit 7.6   Select Set of Books

displayed during data entry, and the Payables financial transactions flow to the proper Oracle General Ledger Set of Books.

1. From the Payables menu → **Setup** → **Set of Books** → **Choose.**
2. Select the **Set of Books.** The Chart of Accounts, Functional Currency, and Accounting Calendar are displayed.

PAYABLES STEP 5.3: PROFILE VALUES

Typically, the System Administrator sets the initial profile value settings (see Exhibit 7.7). The user may change individual settings as he/she sees fit. However, the many Oracle profile options can only be set by the System Administrator. The message "(Profile) Item is protected against update" indicates the profile value may not be changed by the user.

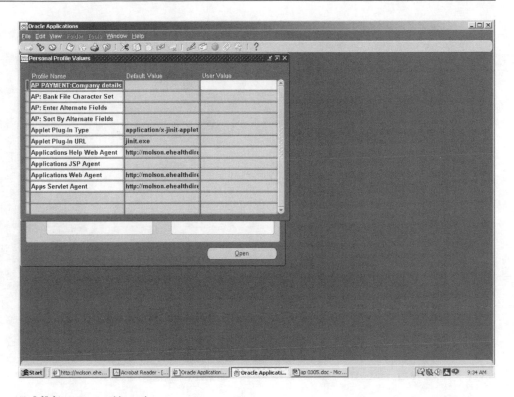

Exhibit 7.7   Profile Values

1. From the Payables menu → **Other** → **Profile.**
2. Enter the **AP%** Profile value to query.
3. Press **Find.**
4. Enter the profile value at the appropriate level.

 All Oracle Payable profile values not defined in the multi-org profile definition process are optional.

PAYABLES STEP 5.4: PAYMENT TERMS

The Payment Terms define when the invoice is due for payment (see Exhibit 7.8).

1. From the Payables menu → **Setup** → **Invoice** → **Payment Terms.**
2. Enter the payment term **Name** and **Description.**

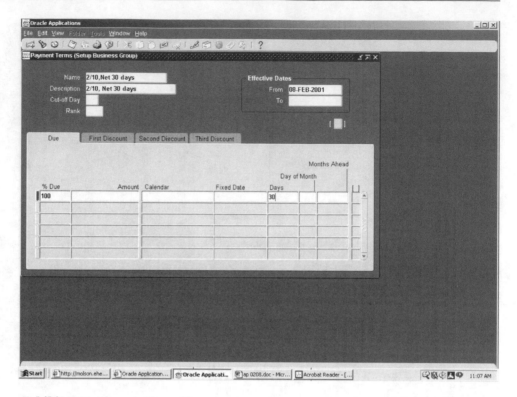

Exhibit 7.8   Payment Terms: Due

3. Enter the **% Due** or **Amount.**

4. Enter the number of **Days** to be added to determine the invoice due date.

5. Press the **First Discount** tab to enter the discount percent or amount.

Enter the discount **% Amount** and the number of discount **Days** (see Exhibit 7.9).

PAYABLES STEP 5.5: FINANCIAL OPTIONS

The Oracle Payables Financial Options set the accounting, supplier, encumbrance, tax, and human resource system parameters. The Accounting option defines the default accounting flexfields for Oracle Payables finan-

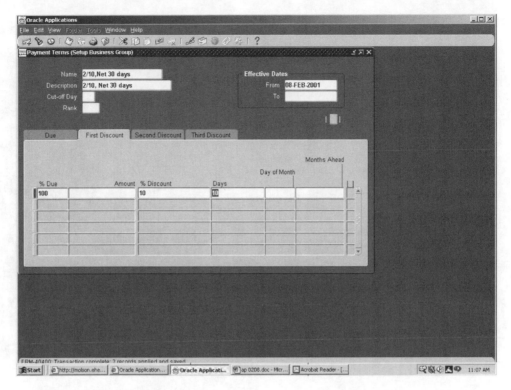

Exhibit 7.9 Payment Terms: Discount

cial transactions which create Oracle General Ledger journal entries (see Exhibit 7.10).

1. From the Payables menu → **Setup** → **Options** → **Financials.**
2. In the GL Accounts tab, enter the accounting flexfields for:
   - The accounts payable **Liability** account credited in an invoice transaction and debited in a disbursement transaction or a credit memo transaction
   - The **Prepayment** account debited in a prepayment transaction
   - The **Discount Taken** account credited in disbursement transaction
   - The **PO Rate Variance Gain and Loss** accounts. These are required whether Oracle Purchasing is implemented.
3. Press the **Supplier-Entry** tab.

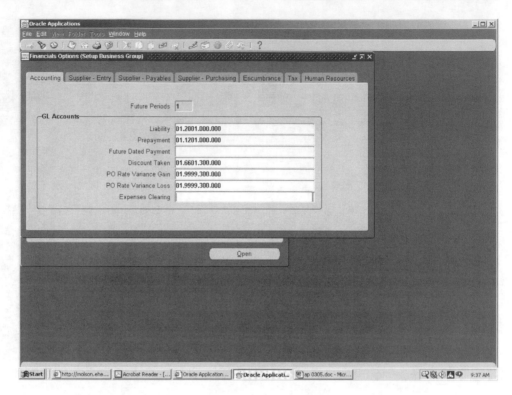

Exhibit 7.10   Financial Options: Accounting

The Supplier-Entry options define the supplier numbering scheme and the default matching option (see Exhibit 7.11).

1. Select the Supplier Numbering **Entry** parameter. Supplier numbers can be either automatically generated or manually entered.

2. Select the Supplier Number **Type.** Select Numeric if alphabetic characters are not allowed.

3. Enter the Next Automatic Number if Automatic supplier numbering has been enabled.

4. Press the **Supplier - Payables** tab.

The Supplier-Payables options define the default payment terms and payment method. The ability to always take the supplier discount may also be defined (see Exhibit 7.12).

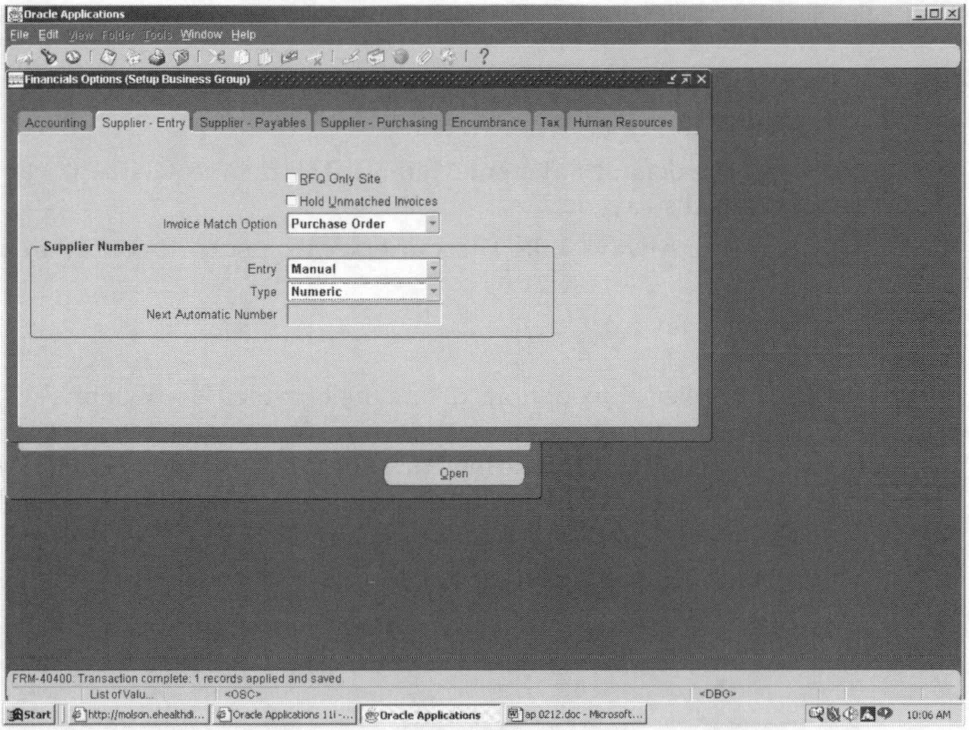

Exhibit 7.11   Financial Options: Supplier–Entry

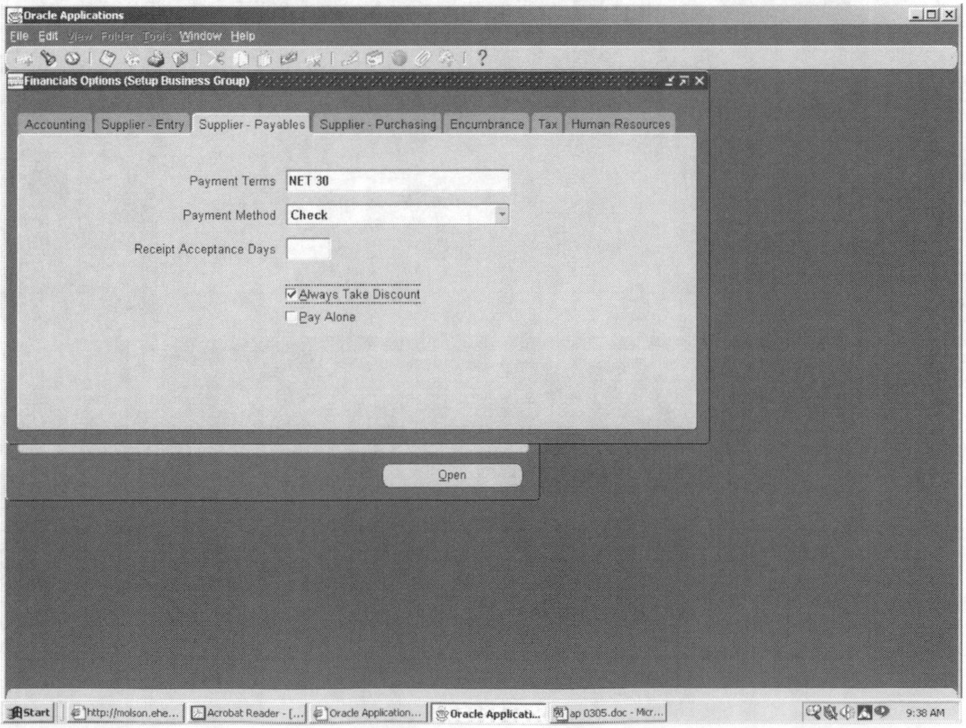

Exhibit 7.12   Financial Options: Supplier–Payables

1. Select the default **Payment Terms** from the previously defined payment terms in step 5.4.

2. Select the default **Payment Method.** The default Payment Method of Check is displayed.

3. Check the **Always Take Discount** box to ensure discounts are always taken.

4. Press the **Tax** tab.

   The Supplier – Tax options define the tax rules (see Exhibit 7.13).

1. Select the default **Rounding Rule** for tax calculations. The field is required regardless of the organization's use of Oracle Payables tax functionality.

2. Press the **Human Resources** tab.

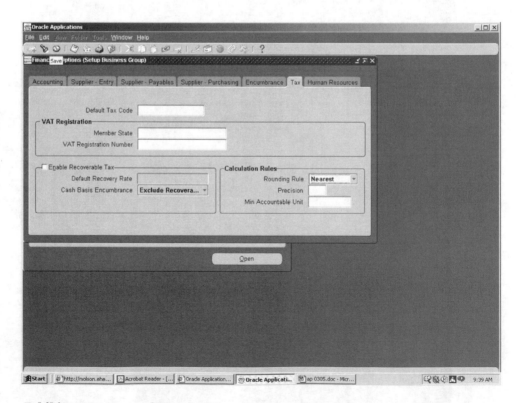

Exhibit 7.13   Financial Options: Tax

The Human Resources option defines the employee numbering scheme and the employee address for disbursements (see Exhibit 7.14).

1. The Business Group is displayed from the HR:Business Group system profile option set by the System Administrator during multi-org definition process. See Chapter 6 for more information.

2. Select the default employee **Expense Reimbursement Address.** The default of Home is displayed. Alternatively, select the Office address.

3. Enter the Employee Numbering **Method** of either Manual or Automatic.

4. Enter the **Next Automatic Number** if the Automatic Method was selected.

 Review the remaining Financial Options tabs for other setup data values.

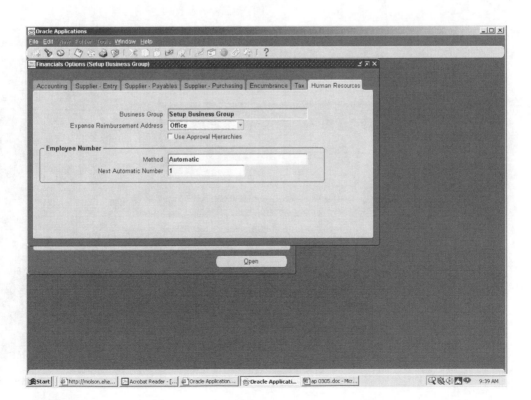

Exhibit 7.14   Financial Options: Human Resources

PAYABLES STEP 5.6: EXPENSE REPORT TEMPLATE

Employee expense report templates must be defined prior to entering employee expense reports. Typically, the expense report templates define the organization's expense report formats. For example, an organization may have two expense report formats: an employee travel expense report format and an employee relocation expense report format. The expense report template details the specific expense report type with the individual expense report line items (see Exhibit 7.15).

1. From the Payables menu → **Setup** → **Invoice** → **Expense Report Templates.**
2. Enter the **Template Name and Description.**
3. Enter the **Expense Item.**
4. Scroll right to enter the default **GL Account** segment values. Not all segment value defaults may be set. The defaults may be overridden

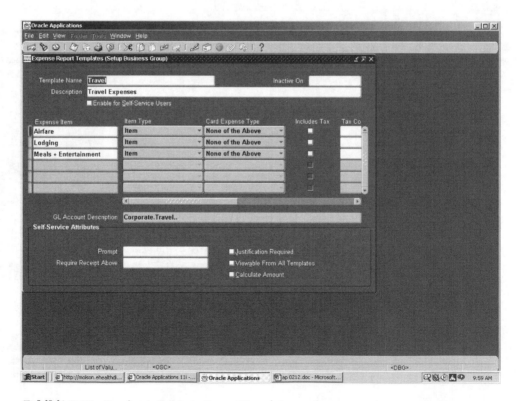

Exhibit 7.15   Employee Expense Report Template

with the "Default Expense Account" assigned to the employee in the Purchase Order Information tab in the define employee window.

Repeat for all expense report line items.

PAYABLES STEP 5.7: BANK ACCOUNTS

The Oracle Payables disbursement bank and bank accounts must be defined. In addition, the supplier bank and bank account data may be defined for EFT (see Exhibit 7.16).

1. From the Payables menu → **Setup** → **Payment** → **Banks**
2. Enter the **Bank Name,** the **Bank Branch Name**, and the **Bank Number.**
3. Select the Institution. The default Bank is displayed.

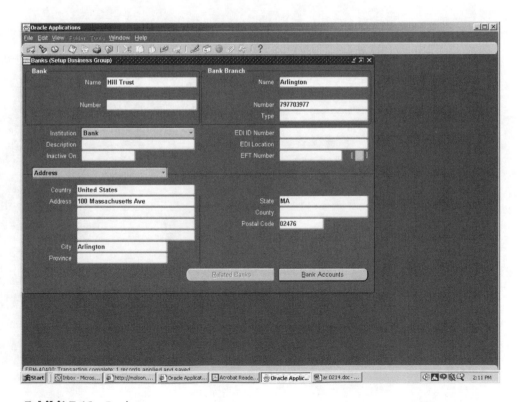

Exhibit 7.16 Banks

4. Enter the **Address** data including **Country, Address, City, State,** and **Postal Code** data.
5. Press **B**ank Accounts.

The GL accounts define the cash account credited during the disbursement process. Other accounts for bank processing may be defined as well (see Exhibit 7.17).

1. Enter the **Bank Account Name.**
2. Enter the **Bank Account Use.** The default Internal is displayed. Use Supplier to denote the bank account as a supplier bank account.
3. Enter the **Bank Account Number.**
4. Enter the **Bank Account Currency.**

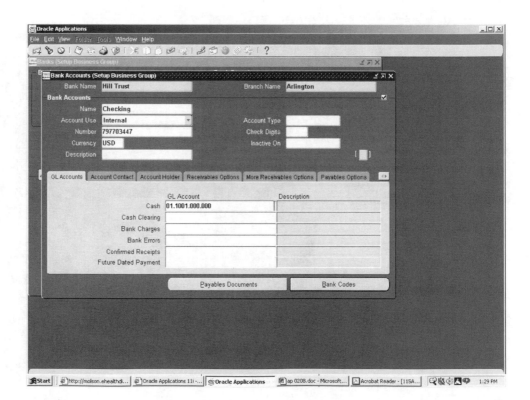

Exhibit 7.17   Bank Accounts: GL Accounts

5. In the GL Accounts tab, enter the **Cash** accounting flexfield. The Cash account will be credited during the disbursement journal creation process.

6. Press **P̲ayables Documents.**

Enter the different disbursement document types for the bank account, including manual and automated check formats (see Exhibit 7.18). Automated check formats can include checks and EFT disbursements.

1. Enter the **Document Name.**
2. Select the **Disbursement Type.**
3. Select the **Payment Format.** Confirm the payment format program with technical personnel.
4. Press the **Additional Information** tab.

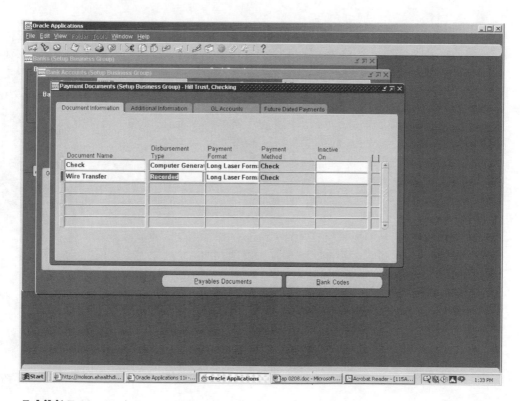

Exhibit 7.18   Bank Accounts: Document Information

The payment documents represent the different disbursement methods and their respective numbering schemes.

1. Enter the **Last Document Used** number for the bank account document (see Exhibit 7.19).
2. Enter the **Last Available** number for the bank account document.

 If using an impact printer, define the number of setup checks. These checks are used for alignment and will be voided during the disbursement run process.

PAYABLES STEP 5.8: PAYABLES OPTIONS

The Payables options define the accounting method, the transfer to General Ledger parameters, invoice, tax, expense report, and payment defaults (see Exhibit 7.20). The Accounting Method defines the primary

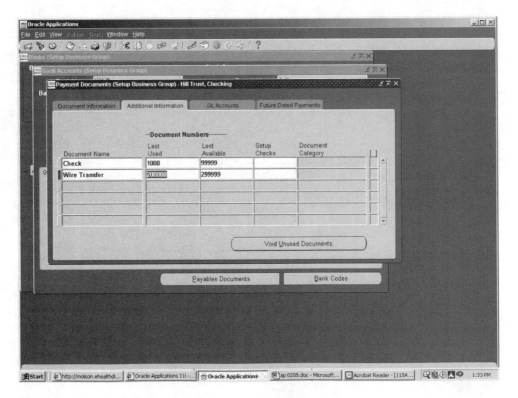

Exhibit 7.19   Bank Accounts: Additional Information

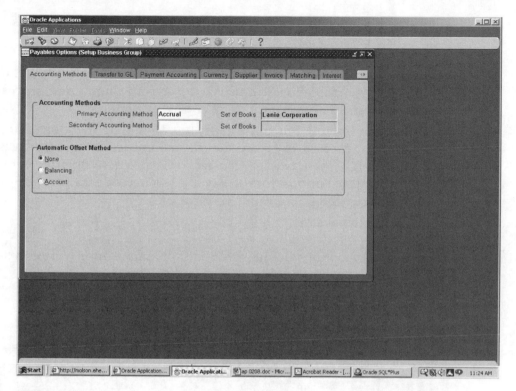

Exhibit 7.20   Payables Options: Accounting Method

accounting method. Typically, organizations record under the accrual method which states financial transactions are recorded when they occur, not when the cash is disbursed.

1. From the Payables menu → **Setup** → **Options** → **Payables.**

2. In the Accounting Methods region, select the **Primary Accounting Method.** The default Accrual is displayed. The Set of Books is displayed.

3. Press the **Transfer to GL** tab.

The Transfer to GL options define the journal entry summarization level to Oracle General Ledger. To maximize system performance, journals should be summarized by the accounting period. Oracle applications online inquiry and reporting capabilities provide a complete and detailed audit trail of the summarized journals. Also, the set journal import to run automatically after the Oracle Payables financial transactions has been created (see Exhibit 7.21).

1. In the Transfer to GL Interface region, select the Transfer to GL Interface option. Enable the **Summarize by Accounting Period** processing option to create summary journal entries by period.

2. Check the **Submit Journal Import** box to initiate the journal import concurrent process to create the journal entries after the successful completion of the Payables transfer to GL process. Otherwise, manually run journal import for the Payables source. See the journal import section in Chapter 5 for more information.

3. Press the **Invoice** tab.

The Invoice options define batch control, online approval processing, and GL accounting date defaults (see Exhibit 7.22).

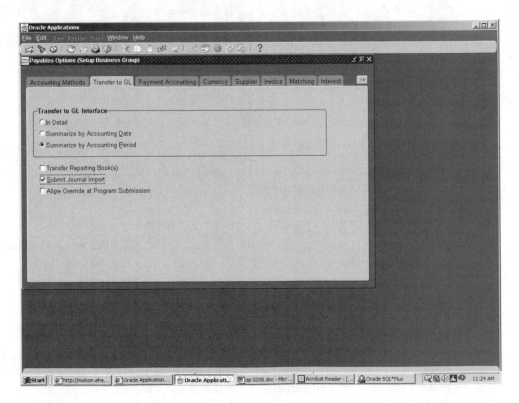

Exhibit 7.21   Payables Options: Transfer to GL

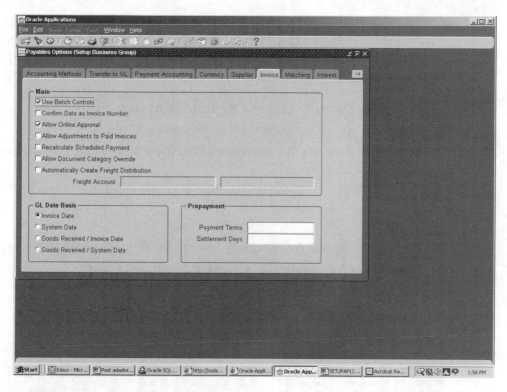

Exhibit 7.22   Payables Options: Invoice

1. In the Main region, check the **Use Batch Control** box to batch invoice. Check the Online Approval box to allow invoices to be approved online.

2. Uncheck the **Confirm Date as Invoice Number** box.

3. Check the **Allow Online Approval** box to allow invoices to be approved online.

4. Check the **Allow Adjustments to Paid Invoices** box to allow invoice adjustments after the invoice has been paid.

5. Check the **Invoice Date** GL Date Basis option.

6. Press the **Expense Report** tab.

 There are more tabs than are displayed at once. Use the ← → tab to move between blocks.

The Expense Report options define the default employee expense report template, employee payment terms, and employee pay group. Also, the default to create suppliers records automatically from employee records may be selected (see Exhibit 7.23).

1. Select the **Default (Expense Report) Template.**
2. Select the default expense report **Payment Terms.**
3. Select the default expense report **Pay Group.** Typically, employees are a separate pay group.
4. Enter a **Payment Priority** number. Enter the default value of 99. The pay group and the payment priority may be selected during a disbursement.
5. Check the **Apply Advances** box to apply advances to expense reports.
6. Check the **Automatically Create Employee as Supplier** box to auto-

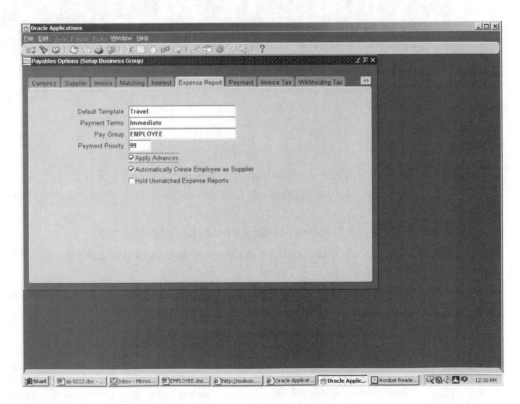

Exhibit 7.23   Payables Options: Expense Report Tab

matically create supplier records from the employee records during the Payables expense report import process.

 Review the remaining Payables Options tabs for other setup data values.

PAYABLES 5.9: REPORTING ENTITIES

Reporting entities define the organization's 1099 reporting groups (see Exhibit 7.24).

1. From the Payables menu → **Setup** → **Tax** → **Reporting Entities.**
2. Select the organization **Name.**
3. Enter the **Tax ID Number.** The data is reported as the Federal Tax Identifier on 1099 forms.
4. Select the **Location.**

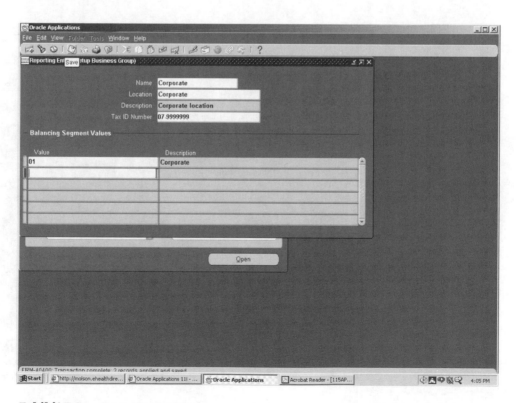

Exhibit 7.24   Reporting Entities

5. Select the **Company** balancing segment values which report 1099 information under this ID.

PAYABLES STEP 5.10: OPEN PERIOD

The Oracle Payables periods are displayed from the GL Set of Books calendar. Oracle Payables periods may be opened and closed independent of the other applications, including Oracle General Ledger (see Exhibit 7.25).

1. From the Payables menu → **Accounting** → **Control Payables Periods.**
2. Select **Open** in the Period Status field to allow Payables processing for the first period.

Multiple periods may be Open at once; however, the Accounts Payable personnel must carefully watch the GL Date defaults created

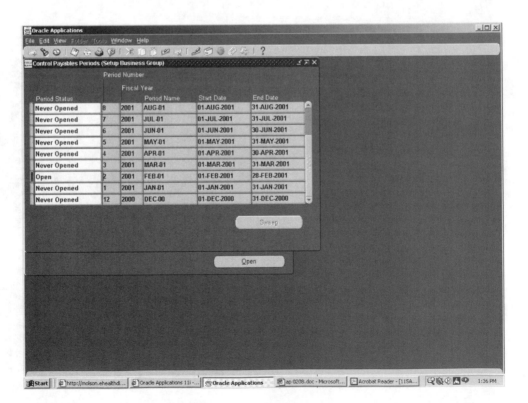

Exhibit 7.25   Control Payables Periods

from the Payables Options GL Date Basis parameter. One period should be open at a time to ensure financial transactions are recorded to the proper accounting period and to assist the reconciliation process.

SUPPLIERS

Oracle Payables utilizes supplier and supplier sites to define the supplier name and address information. Oracle Payables supplier records minimally have two components; a supplier record and a supplier site record. The supplier record defines the supplier name and is shared across all organizations. The supplier site record defines the address data and is specific by organization in a multi-org environment. Optionally, the third supplier component is the supplier contact.

Oracle Payables supports a one-supplier-to-many-supplier-sites architecture. This relational database architecture allows one supplier record to have one or more supplier site records, hence a one-to-many relationship. Understanding and utilizing the one-supplier-to-many-supplier-sites concept is critical for all Oracle applications to run as efficiently and effectively as possible. Strict in-house naming standards for supplier name and site identification, supplier verification procedures, and supplier data entry procedures will improve the Oracle Payables system and the organization's business processes.

Either the Purchasing department or the Payables department takes the responsibility to define the supplier and supplier site records. Each organization is different. Sometimes, the Purchasing department likes to control the supplier entry, as suppliers are required for purchase orders. Sometimes, the Payables department likes to control the supplier entry, as suppliers are required for invoices, even if not matched to a purchase order. Regardless, a thorough supplier verification and supplier data entry process must be defined and followed.

Supplier and supplier site records may be converted or imported. A review of the active supplier and address records in the legacy system. The number of records should determine if the supplier conversion process is a manual process or an automated process. Both conversion strategies require users to clean the data. The current supplier must be extracted and the users must review the data. The one-supplier-to-many-supplier-site architecture must be established and duplicates must be eliminated. In addition, consistent in-house naming standards must be applied. The supplier data may then be entered manually or automatically via a conversion program. Unfortunately, there is no delivered supplier open interface, so one must be written in-house or delivered by a consulting organization. In addition to converting supplier and supplier site data, the project team must understand the Financials and Payables options default values, as the appropriate database id values must be populated during the load program. For example, the payment terms defaults from the Financial Options to the supplier records; therefore, the payment terms id must be incorporated into the supplier load program.

Supplier Architecture

An Oracle applications supplier record consists of three records: the supplier record, the supplier site record, and the supplier site contact (see Exhibit 7.26.) The supplier record defines the supplier name, number, and optionally, taxpayer information. Suppliers are shared across organizations. The supplier site defines the address and site-specific information such as the accounting flexfield defaults, payment defaults, and tax defaults in a multi-org environment. The supplier sites are specific to an operating level organization. The supplier site contact data contains the supplier's personnel information for business discussion purposes.

Prior to entering a supplier, perform in-house supplier verification procedures. These may include contacting the supplier to confirm name, address, and tax status prior to data entry (see Exhibit 7.27).

1. From the Payables menu → **Suppliers** → **Entry.**
2. Enter the **Supplier Name.** Follow in-house naming standards such as last name, first name.
3. The Payables Options set the supplier numbering methodology. If auto-numbering has been selected, the **Supplier Number** field will be blank and a unique number will be generated when the record is saved. If manual-numbering has been enabled, enter a unique Supplier Number. Duplicates are not allowed.
4. If the supplier requires 1099 tax reporting, enter the Tax Payer ID number. Otherwise, skip this field.
5. Press the **Payment** tab.

The Payment Tab is displayed in Exhibit 7.28.

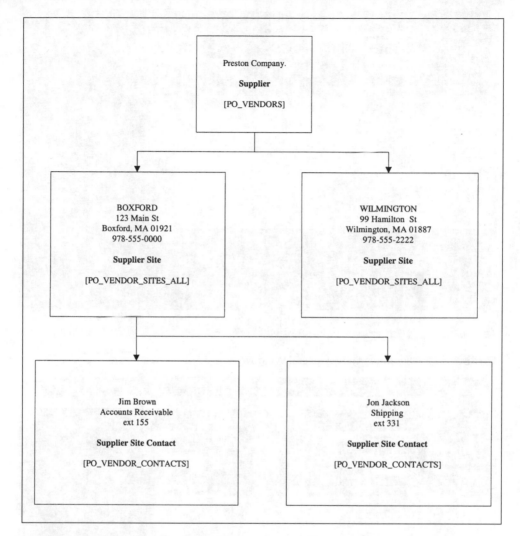

Exhibit 7.26 Supplier Site Architecture

1. Enter the default payment **Terms** as defined in setup Accounts Payable Step 5.4.

2. Press the **Tax Reporting** tab if the supplier is 1099 reportable.

The Tax Reporting parameters define the 1099 reporting for the supplier (see Exhibit 7.29). Skip this step if 1099 reporting is not required for the supplier.

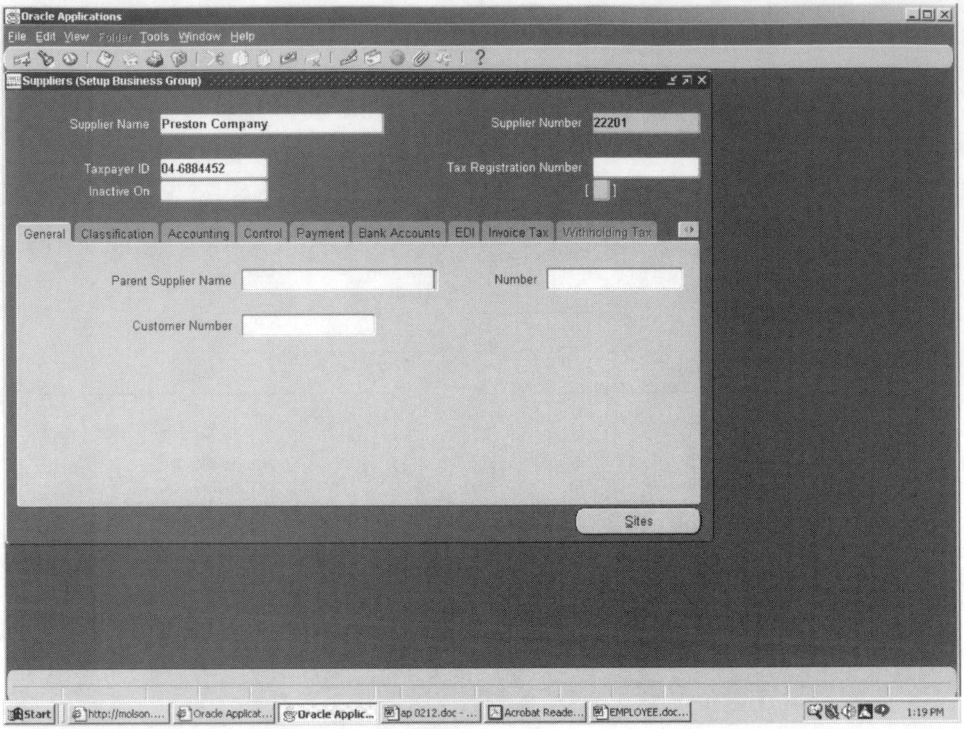

Exhibit 7.27 Suppliers Entry: General Window

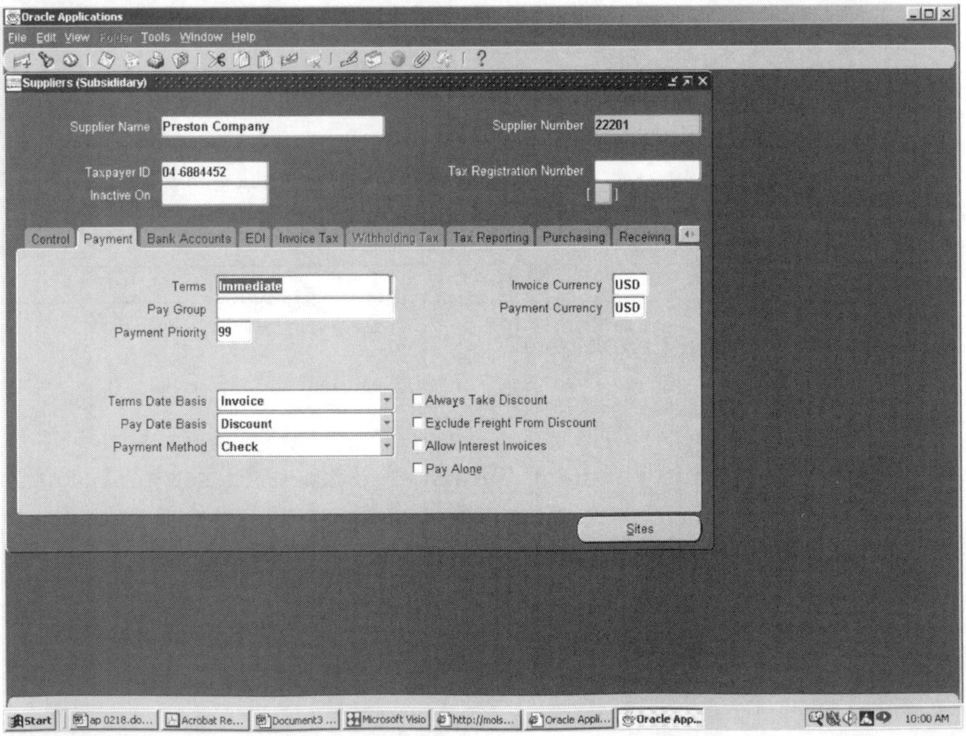

Exhibit 7.28 Suppliers: Payment Window

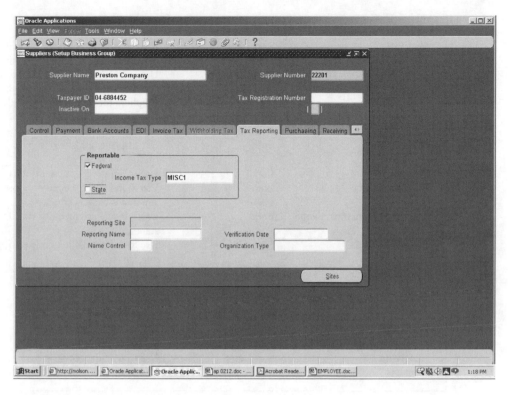

Exhibit 7.29 Suppliers Entry: Tax Reporting

1. Check the **Federal Reportable** box to indicate the supplier is 1099.
2. Select the **Income Tax Type.** The valid 1099 reporting types are displayed.
3. The Reporting Site data will be displayed once the unique supplier tax reporting site is defined.
4. Enter the Reporting Name if different than the Supplier Name.
5. Press **Sites.**

The supplier and supplier sites share a number of the same parameters; therefore, the windows are almost identical. See Exhibit 7.30 for a list of all the supplier and supplier site windows.

Data default values entered at the supplier level will cascade to the supplier site level during the initial data entry process.

Optional Windows	Supplier/Site Level	Use
General	Both	Use to cross-reference the supplier number to the customer number.
Classification	Supplier	Use to link employee records to a supplier record. Also use to classify suppliers for reporting purposes.
Accounting	Both if single org Site only if multi-org	Use to default accounting distributions.
Control	Both	Use to place holds and invoice limits.
Payment	Both	Use to default payment options.
Bank Accounts	Both	Use to pay electronically via the supplier's bank account.
Electronic Data Interchange	Both	Use to pay electronically via EDI standards.
Invoice Tax	Both	Use to default the tax code during invoice entry.
Withholding Tax	Both	Use to default the withholding options during invoice entry.
Tax Reporting	Both	Use to identify tax reporting information.
Purchasing	Both	Use to default purchasing parameters.
Receiving	Supplier	Use to default receiving parameters.
Contacts	Site	Use to enter contact information.

Exhibit 7.30   Supplier/Suppliers Sites Windows

 Once a site has been established, changing the supplier data value will not change the supplier site level values. Each site must be modified individually after initial setup.

Supplier Sites

The supplier site record defines the supplier address and site uses (see Exhibit 7.31).

1. Enter the **Site Name** using in-house naming conventions. Typically, the City field is also used as the site name for quick reference during invoice data entry. Duplicate Site Names are not allowed.

2. Enter the **Address** data using as many as four address lines, such as street address, building number, suite number, and so on. If entering a two-party check, enter the second payee on the first address line.

3. Enter the **City, State,** and **Postal Code.**

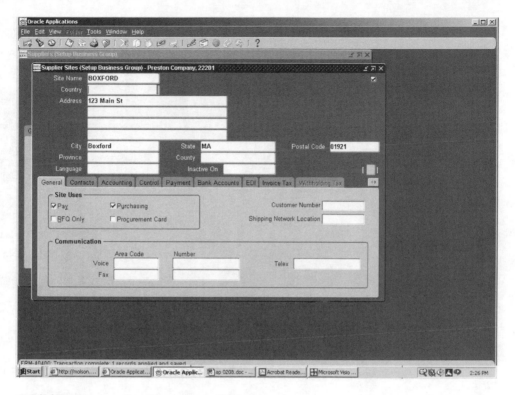

Exhibit 7.31   Suppliers Sites: General Window

4. In the General tab, check the **Pay** box to allow disbursement to the site. One Pay site per supplier is required. Multiple pay sites are allowed.

5. Enter the site's **Area Code** and phone **Number** for Voice and Fax communications.

6. Press the **Tax Reporting** tab.

Select one supplier site as the Income Tax Reporting site (see Exhibit 7.32).

Check the **Income Tax Reporting Site** box to indicate this address is reported for 1099 tax reporting. If the supplier is not a 1099 supplier, skip this step.

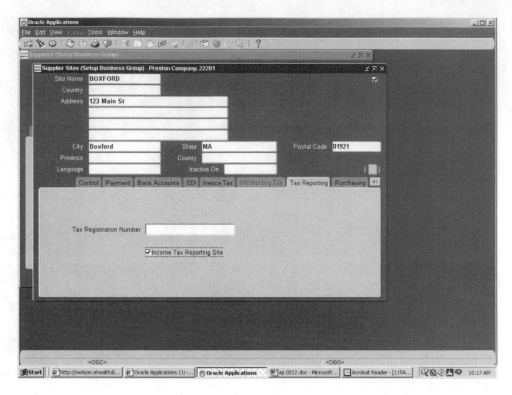

Exhibit 7.32   Suppliers Sites: Tax Reporting

INVOICES

Oracle Payables is the last application in the procurement cycle. Oracle Payables records an organization's expenditures and payments for goods and services. Oracle Payables invoice types include:

- Invoices
- Credit memos
- Invoices to match to purchase orders and/or receipts
- Invoices for prepayments or advances
- Invoices for employee expense reports
- Recurring invoices
- Imported invoices from another system

Oracle Payables provides a variety of data entry capabilities. Oracle Payables provides the Invoice Workbench and the Invoice Gateway. The Invoice Workbench is the standard online data entry process. The Invoice Gateway allows heads-down data entry. The data is really being entered in a payables interface table that must be imported to create an invoice transaction.

Other invoice records may be imported as well. Oracle Payables does provide an open invoice interface, which populates the appropriate invoice tables. In earlier releases of Oracle Payables, the invoice import populated the employee expense report tables. Review the *Oracle Payables User Guide* for more information.

All invoices must run through the invoice approval process. The invoice approval process validates tax, accounting, and other payables data elements. An invoice that is successful through the invoice approval process will be available for payment and journal entry creation. An invoice may be placed on hold if the invoice approval process fails. An invoice on hold must be released prior to disbursement and possibly prior to being transferred to a General Ledger journal.

The Oracle Payables invoice business process consists of entering an invoice transaction, approving the invoice transaction, and optionally, maintaining the invoice transaction (see Exhibit 7.33). Oracle Payables provides a variety of transaction types including invoices, credit memos, prepayments, and employee expense reports. Recurring invoices may also be defined. Optionally, if Oracle Purchasing is installed, invoices may be matched to purchase orders and receipts in a paperless processing environment.

Typically, the Oracle Payables invoice architecture consists of invoice batches, invoice headers, and invoice line distributions (see Exhibit 7.34). The Payables invoice batch records the control count and total invoice amounts. The invoice header records the supplier, invoice number, and invoice amount. The invoice line distributions record the specific line item including price and quantities. In addition, the invoice line distribution records the expense accounting flexfield accounts.

Invoice Entry

Typically, the invoices should be grouped and divided into batches of 25 invoices. Add all the invoice transaction amounts in the batch. Note the count and dollar total of the batch (see Exhibit 7.35).

1. From the Payables menu → **Invoices** → **Entry** → **Invoice Batches.**
2. Enter the **Batch Name,** following in-house naming conventions.

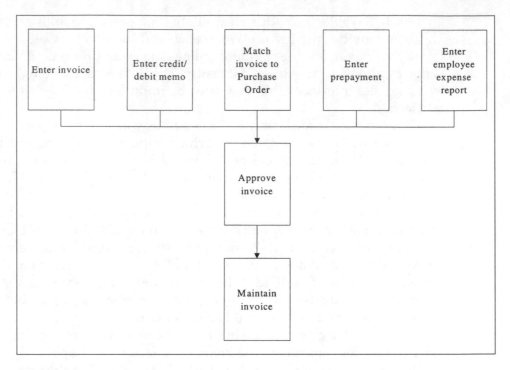

Exhibit 7.33 Invoice Business Process

3. Enter the total number of invoices for the batch in the **Control Count** field.

4. Enter total invoice amount for the batch in the **Control Amount** field.

5. The next few fields display the difference between the control count and amount, and the actual count and amount entered. A warning will appear if the window is closed prior to the counts and amounts agreeing. The user may still exit the window, but the out-of-balance batch must be addressed.

6. All other batch level fields will default from the Financial and Payables options. Scroll right to override these fields. A sample of fields includes: Payment Terms, Pay Group, GL Date, and Liability account.

7. Press **Invoices** to enter invoices in the batch.

8. When done entering the invoice batch, return to the batch and press **Approve 1** to approve all invoices in the batch.

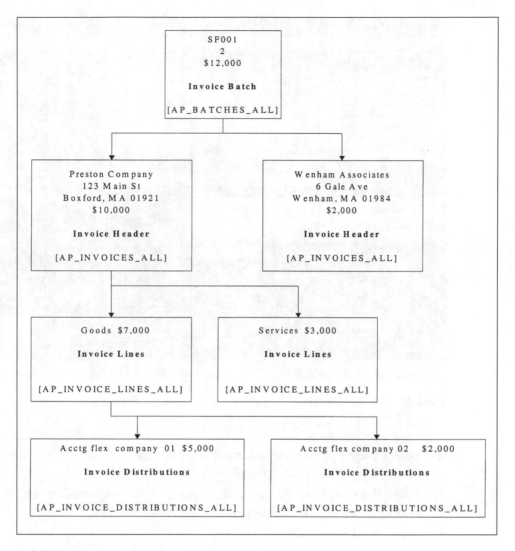

Exhibit 7.34 Payables Invoice Architecture

The invoice header data entry includes the supplier, invoice date, and invoice amount information (see Exhibit 7.36).

1. The system defaults the **Invoice Type** to Standard if not overridden in the invoice batch. Other invoice types include: Credit Memo, Debit Memo, Prepayment, Expense Report, PO Default, Quick Match, and Mixed.

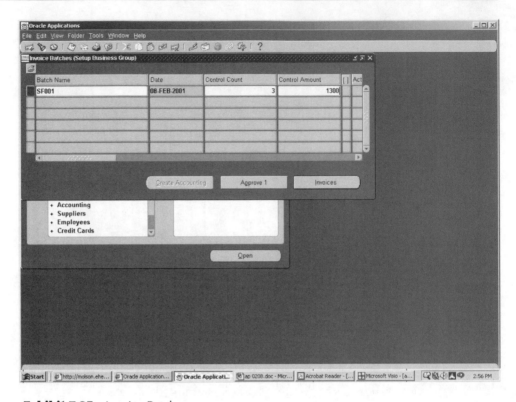

Exhibit 7.35 Invoice Batch

2. Select the **Supplier.** An enabled supplier must exist for invoice entry. The supplier number is displayed.

3. Enter the supplier **Site** name or select an enabled supplier site. If there is only one pay site, the system will default the site.

4. Enter the **Invoice Date.**

5. Enter the **Invoice Number.** Duplicate invoice numbers for the same supplier aren't allowed. Follow in-house numbering standards for invoices without an invoice number, such as utility bills. Only the first 10 characters appear on the invoice number section of the standard remittance advice. Therefore, continue the invoice number in the description field if necessary to continue the display of the invoice number on the disbursement advice or check stub.

6. Enter the total **Invoice Amount.**

7. Press **Distributions** button to enter the invoice accounting flexfield distribution.

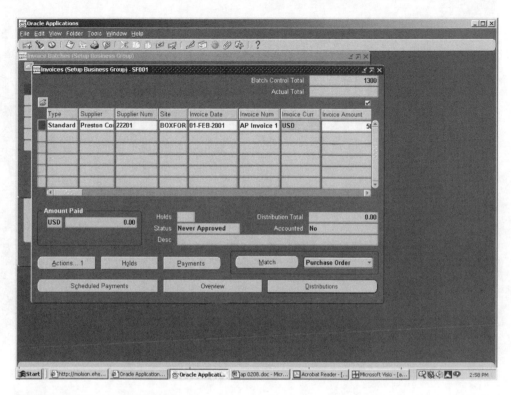

Exhibit 7.36   Invoice Header

The invoice line distribution data entry includes the line amount and GL account (see Exhibit 7.37).

1. The system assigns the line **Num**bers starting with line 1.
2. The system defaults to the invoice **Type** of Item. Tax, Freight, and Miscellaneous are other valid selections.
3. Enter the invoice line distribution **Amount.**
4. Enter the expense **Account** accounting flexfield for the invoice line distribution.

 To enter 1099 invoice data, note the income tax type will default from the supplier and supplier site records. Select an income tax type if different during invoice line distribution data entry process.

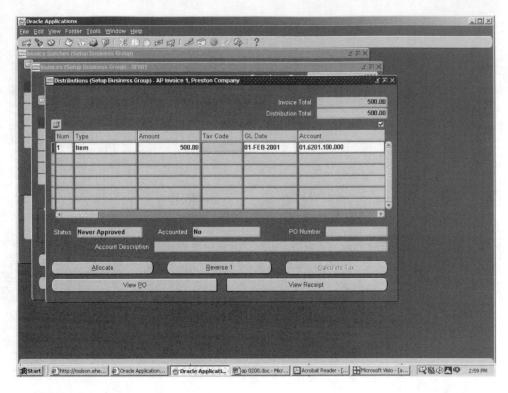

Exhibit 7.37 Invoice Distributions

Invoice Approval

Invoices must be approved before they will be available for payment and journal processing. The Invoice Approval process validates accounting flexfields, period status, taxes, and matching parameters. The invoice approval process may place the invoice on system hold.

System hold conditions include account errors, matching errors, or invoice amount errors. System holds are released automatically when the hold condition is no longer true. For example, if the invoice distribution doesn't agree with the invoice header amount, the invoice will have a Distribution Variance hold placed. To correct the hold condition, either the invoice line distribution amounts must be changed or the invoice header amount must be changed. The Distribution Variance system hold will not be released until the condition is corrected. All invoices must be reapproved after corrections or modifications have been entered. Use Oracle Payables standard reports to monitor invoices on hold and perform corrections regularly. Also, the invoice approval process may run automatically at regularly scheduled times throughout the day.

In addition, user holds may be placed on an invoice. User holds must be released manually. These holds may include waiting for acceptance by the authorizing party. Other user-defined holds include awaiting authorized signatures or exceeds signature authority. The user hold release process provides a full audit trail of the release reason and the release date.

 A complete list of invoice hold codes may be found in the *Oracle Payables User's Guide*, Appendix J.

To Approve an Individual Invoice Online

Press the **Actions . . . 1** button to approve the highlighted invoice (see Exhibit 7.38).

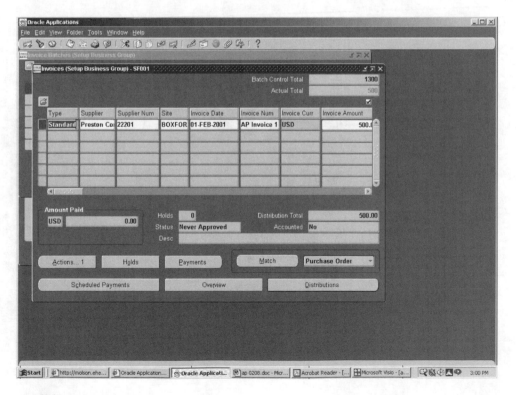

Exhibit 7.38 Invoice Approval

The Payables Invoice Options determine if invoices may be approved online.

1. Check the **Approve** box to approve the selected invoice (see Exhibit 7.39).

2. Check the Approve Related Invoices box to approve an invoice matched to a credit memo.

3. Press **OK** to run the invoice approval process.

If the invoice approval process is successful, the invoice will have a status of Approved. If the system has placed the invoice on hold, the invoice status will be Needs Reapproval. The system condition causing the hold will remain until the condition is corrected and the approval process has successfully completed.

Invoices with the invoice header amount unequal to the sum of the in-

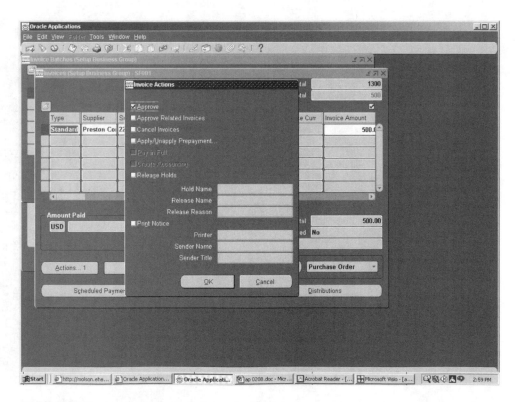

Exhibit 7.39   Invoice Approval: Select Invoice

voice line distribution amounts will be placed on Dist(ribution) Variance system hold (see Exhibit 7.40).

Press **Holds** to view the invoice hold condition.

The system displays all Hold Names (see Exhibit 7.41).

Dist Variance is an Oracle Payables system hold. Either change the invoice line distribution amounts or change the invoice header amount. If an invoice is on Dist Variance hold, the invoice will not create a journal entry to Oracle General Ledger. In addition, the invoice will not be selected during a disbursement run.

Invoice Maintenance

Oracle Payables invoice may or may not be maintained given the invoice status. If an invoice is paid or posted to Oracle General Ledger, invoice maintenance may or may be available.

Samples of invoice maintenance may include:

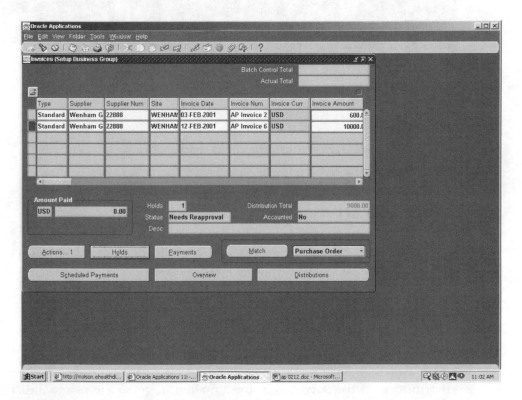

Exhibit 7.40   Invoice System Hold: Distribution Variance

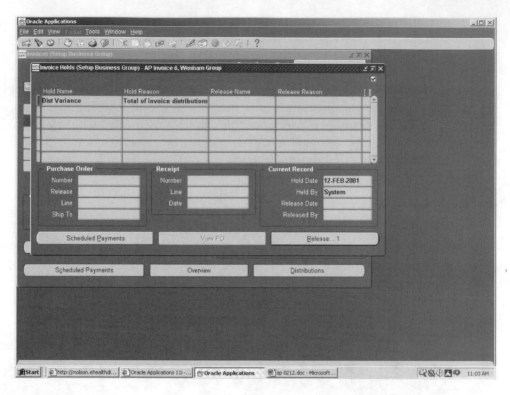

Exhibit 7.41 Invoice System Hold

- Changing the accounting flexfield distribution
- Changing the invoice date
- Changing the invoice to match to another purchase order
- Canceling an invoice

 Review the *Oracle Accounts Payable User Guide,* Invoice Adjustment charts in the Invoices chapter for the complete list.

Invoice Distribution Correction

If the invoice has not been posted to General Ledger, simply query the invoice. Delete the original invoice distribution and enter the correct invoice distribution. If the invoice has been posted, reverse the original distribution and enter the correct distribution (see Exhibit 7.42).

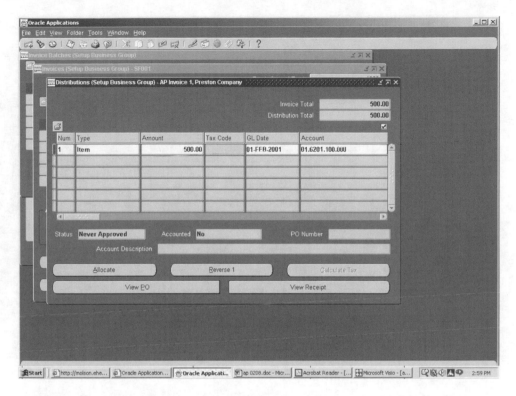

Exhibit 7.42   Reverse Accounting Flexfield Distribution

1. From the Payables menu → **Invoices** → **Entry** → **Invoices**.
2. Query the invoice.
3. Press **Reverse 1**. The system will reverse the original accounting flexfield distribution.
4. Enter the corrected accounting flexfield distribution. The journal entry created will be:

    Dr New distribution
        Cr Original distribution

 The Payables Options Allow Paid Invoice Adjustments will dictate if a paid invoice line distribution may be reversed.

1. From the Payables menu → **Invoices** → **Entry** → **Invoices**.
2. Query the invoice (see Exhibit 7.43).

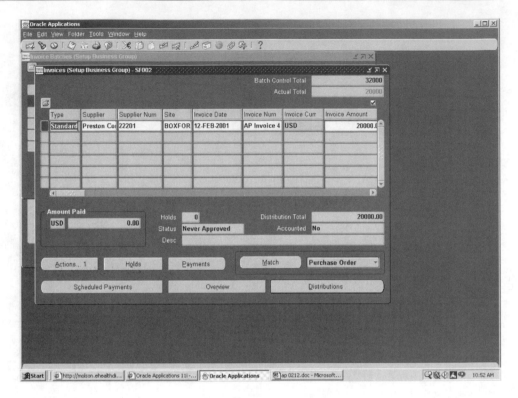

Exhibit 7.43   Payment Schedule Modification: Invoice Header

3. Press **S̲cheduled Payments** to modify the invoice due date calculated by default from the invoice payment terms.

Enter the revised Due Date (see Exhibit 7.44).

CREDIT MEMOS

The Oracle Payables business process includes credit transactions against invoices. For example, items purchased may be returned and a credit memo transaction generated. Oracle Payables provides users with both credit memos and debit memos, though most will only use credit memos.

Both credit memos and debit memos represent a reduction of the invoice liability and are entered as a negative invoice. From an Oracle Payables perspective, credit memos are received from the supplier and represent a negative invoice. From an Oracle Payables perspective,

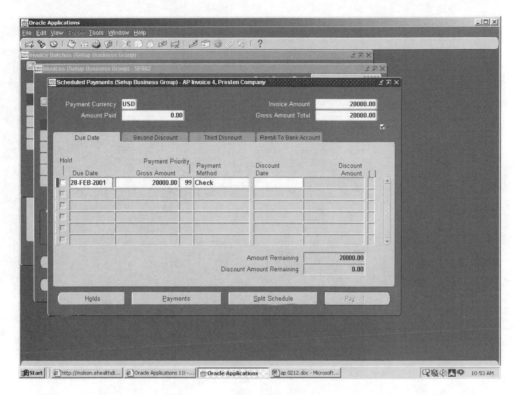

Exhibit 7.44 Payment Schedule Modification: Due Date

debit memos are generated in-house and sent to the supplier for credit. Both credit memos and debit memos should be applied to the original invoice and are netted with invoices during the payment process to determine the payment due. Since credit and debit memos are just another invoice type, the invoice business process and invoice architecture remain the same.

Typically, only Oracle Payables credit memos are used. The credit memo entry is the same as the invoice entry process with two exceptions. First, the credit memo transaction amounts are entered as a negative amount. Second, the credit memo transaction may be linked to the original invoice transaction. The Oracle General Ledger journal process works identically for credit memos, but with the accounts reversed.

Separate the credit memo transactions into their own invoice batch (see Exhibit 7.45). Enter a credit memo transaction just as an invoice transaction, except with negative amounts. In addition, credit memos may be matched to an invoice.

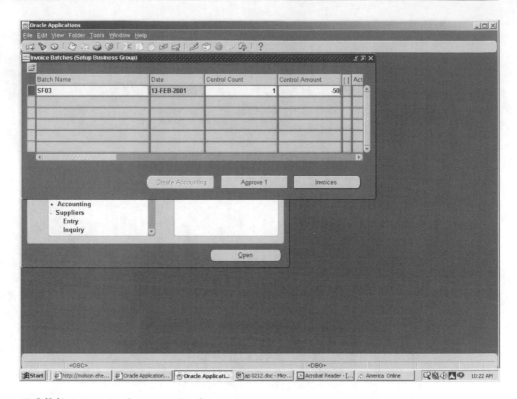

Exhibit 7.45 Credit Memo Batch

1. From the Payables menu → **Invoices** → **Entry** → **Invoice Batches.**
2. Enter the **Batch Name,** using in-house naming conventions.
3. The system defaults to today's date.
4. Enter the **Control Count** for the batch.
5. Enter the **Control Amount** for the batch as a negative amount.

The invoice header data entry includes the supplier, invoice date, and invoice amount information (see Exhibit 7.46).

1. Select the invoice type of **Credit Memo** to default during data entry.
2. Enter the **Supplier Name.** The supplier number is displayed.
3. Select an enabled supplier **Site.** If there is only one pay site, the system will default the supplier site.
4. Enter the credit memo **Date.**

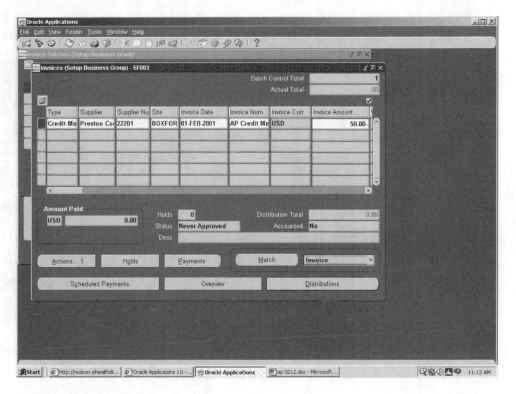

Exhibit 7.46 Credit Memo Header

5. Enter the credit memo **Number.** Duplicate credit memo numbers for the same supplier aren't allowed. Follow in-house numbering standards for credit memos without a credit memo number, such as the original invoice number with a CM suffix.

6. Enter a negative credit memo **Amount.** Credit memo amounts must be a negative amount.

7. If applicable, select **Invoice,** then press **Match** to relate the credit memo to the invoice.

Enter the **Invoice Number** or other search criteria to match to the credit memo (see Exhibit 7.47). Then press **Find.**

1. Check the **Match** box.

2. Enter a negative **Credit Amount** (see Exhibit 7.48).

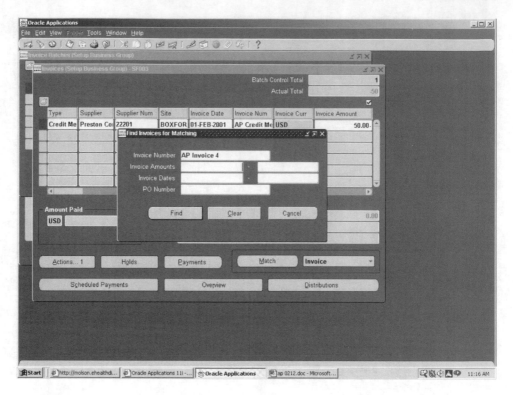

Exhibit 7.47 Credit Memo Match to an Invoice

3. At the invoice header level, press the **Actions. . . 1** button and check the **Approve** and **Approve Related Invoices** boxes.

4. Press **OK.**

MATCHING TO PURCHASING

Oracle applications provide online electronic matching capabilities. Oracle Purchasing and Oracle Payables share the purchase order, receipt, and invoice data. The purchase order dictates the quantity and price a supplier is permitted to invoice. In addition, the purchase order accounting flexfield distributions default into the invoice line distribution accounting flexfields.

The invoice approval process verifies the quantity invoiced is less than or equal to the purchase order and receiving price/amount plus tolerance. The purchase order when entered indicates the type of matching to occur. Valid options include:

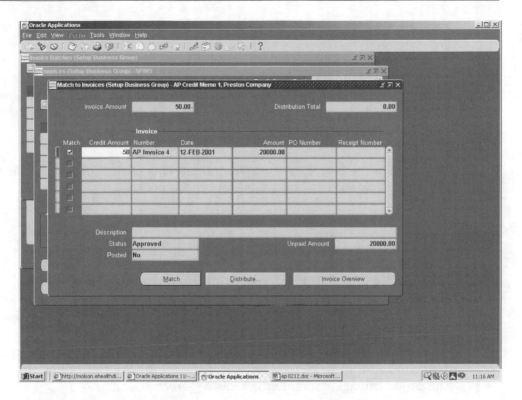

Exhibit 7.48 Credit Memo Match to an Invoice: Credit Amount

- Two-way match—purchase order and invoice. Typically used for services.

- Three-way match—purchase order, receiver, and invoice. Typically used for goods. Most common type of matching option.

- Four-way match—purchase order, receiver, inspection, and invoice. Typically used for expensive or complex goods which must be reviewed prior to acceptance.

The procurement business process includes matching the purchase order to the receipt to the invoice to ensure the price and quantity are per terms and conditions. The matching process used to occur with paper. For example, the purchase order white copy went to the supplier, the green copy went in Purchasing files, the pink copy went to Receiving, and the yellow copy went to Accounts Payable. As the goods arrived at the different business areas, each area would manually update its copy and forward it to the Accounts Payable department. The invoice would be paid only after all the copies had been manually matched by the Accounts Payable personnel.

The Oracle applications matching process occurs electronically. When an invoice is entered, it is matched to the purchase order and receipt. If the invoice matches, the invoice is available for payment. If the invoice doesn't match, the system places the invoice on system hold until the hold condition has been corrected.

 Review the *Oracle Payables User's Guide* for more information on matching as Oracle Purchasing is out of scope in this book.

PREPAYMENTS

Another Oracle Payables invoice type is prepayments. Prepayments are advances against future invoices to either an employee or a supplier. Temporary advances are expected to be applied to an expense report or invoice. Typically, a travel advance is an example of a temporary advance. A permanent advance is not expected to be applied to an invoice.

The Prepayment account default is set during the Financials Options definition and may be overridden at the supplier or supplier site level. The prepayment General Ledger journal created is:

Dr Prepayment accounting flexfield
    Cr Liability accounting flexfield

During expense report data entry, the system will display a message indicating the employee has outstanding prepayments. Either apply the prepayment to the expense report or ignore the message and continue data entry. If the prepayment is applied, the journal entry created will reverse the original prepayment entry.

Employee Entry as Supplier

If the employee has not been automatically created as a supplier record during a previous employee expense import, the employee must be created as a supplier record (see Exhibit 7.49).

1. Enter the supplier record as any other supplier record.
2. Press the **Classification** tab to link the employee record to the supplier record.

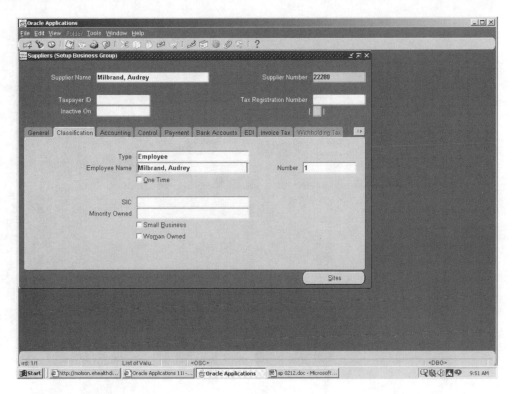

Exhibit 7.49 Employee Supplier

3. Select **Type.**
4. Select the **Employee Name.**

 The Payables Expense Report Options dictate the employee numbering scheme.

The employee supplier must have a supplier site record (see Exhibit 7.50).

1. Enter the **Site Name** using in-house naming conventions. Typically, the City field is also used as the site name for quick reference during invoice data entry. Duplicate Site Names are not allowed.

2. Enter the **Address** data using as many as four address lines.

3. Enter the **City, State,** and **Postal Code.**

4. In the General tab, check the **Pay** box to allow disbursement to the site. One Pay site per employee is required.

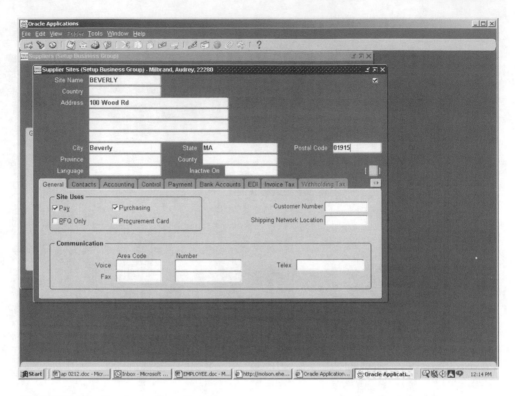

Exhibit 7.50   Employee Supplier Site

Prepayment Entry

Once the employee has been defined as a supplier, the prepayment invoice entry process may commence (see Exhibit 7.51).

Follow the normal invoice entry process, but select an Invoice type of **Prepayment.** Then enter the remaining data elements just as with any other Oracle Payables invoice transaction.

EMPLOYEE EXPENSE REPORT

Employee expenses may be entered directly into Oracle Payables or may be imported from another system. Oracle's Self Service and Oracle Projects are two examples of employee expenses imported into Oracle Payables.

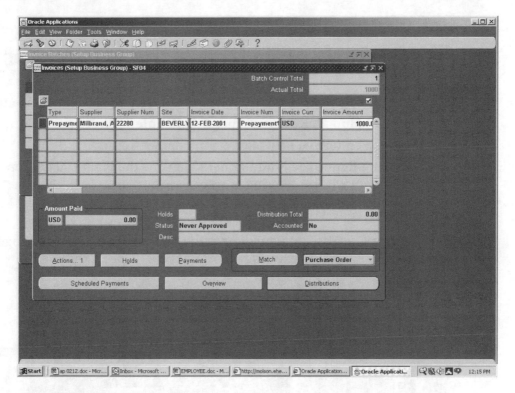

Exhibit 7.51   Prepayment Entry

An employee record must be defined prior to entering an expense report. If Human Resources is installed, switch to a Human Resources responsibility and define the employee. Set the employee default expense accounts in the Employee Assignment window. Employees must be assigned to the proper organization as defined in the multi-org setup process.

Once an employee expense report is entered, a concurrent process converts the expense report into an invoice. In addition, the employee records may automatically create the corresponding supplier records. Some organizations enter employee expenses directly into the invoice windows to avoid the additional processing step.

 All Oracle Human Resource key flexfields including the Job, Position, and Group flexfields must be defined and compiled prior to entering employees.

Employee Entry

If Oracle Human Resources is installed, switch to an Oracle Human Resources responsibility (see Exhibit 7.52).

1. From the **File** menu → **Switch Responsibility** → **US HRMS Manager.**
2. From the Human Resources menu → **People** → **Enter and Maintain.**
3. Enter the employee **Last Name, First** name.
4. Leave the **Employee Number** field blank as the Financial Options dictate if employee numbering is automatic or manual.
5. Press **Assignment.**

The employee assignment defines the default expense accounting flexfield to be used during expense report data entry (see Exhibit 7.53).

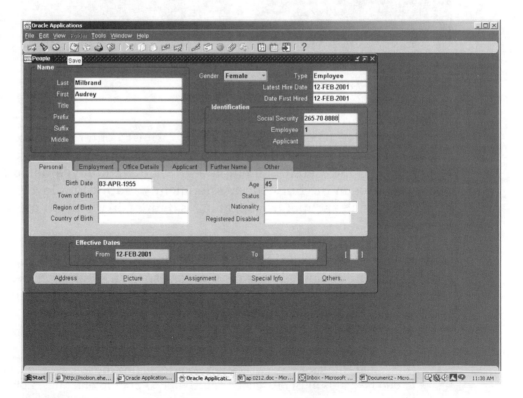

Exhibit 7.52 Employee

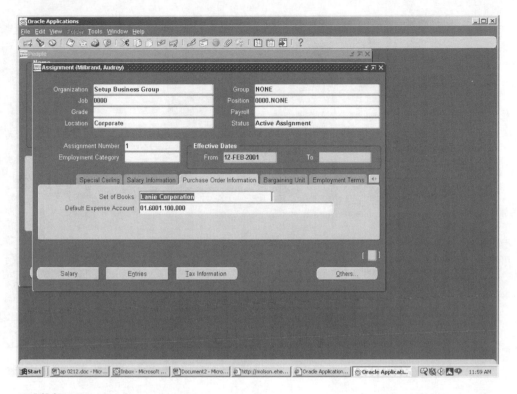

Exhibit 7.53 Employee Assignment

1. Select the employee **Organization.** The Set of Books displays from the Organization.
2. Select the **Group, Job,** and **Position** flexfield values.
3. Enter the employee's **Default Expense Account.**

 After defining the employee record, link the employee record to the supplier record. In the Classifications tab, select Employee as the Type and select the employee in the Employee Name field.

Employee Expense Report Entry

Once the employee data has been entered, the expense report may be entered (see Exhibit 7.54).

1. From the **File** menu → **Switch Responsibility**→ **AP Corporate Super User.**

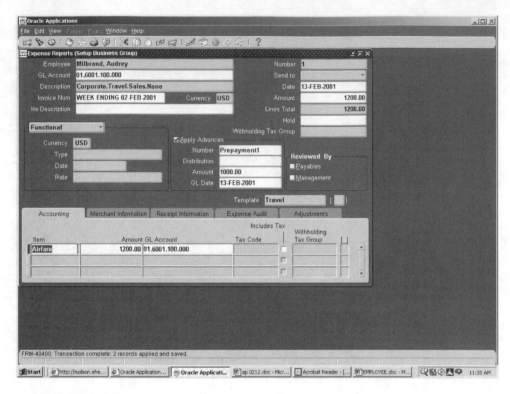

Exhibit 7.54   Enter Expense Report

2. From the Payables menu → **Invoices** → **Expense Report.**
3. Select the **Employee Name** or Number.
4. Enter the **GL Account** if not displayed.
5. Enter the expense report **Date.**
6. Enter the **Invoice Number.** Make sure it is unique.
7. Enter the expense report **Amount.**
8. Enter the expense report **Description.**
9. The default expense report Template is displayed. Override if necessary.
10. Check the Apply Advances box to apply a prepayment. Select the prepayment transaction.
11. Select the expense report template line **Item.**
12. Enter the Item **Amount.**
13. Enter the **GL Account** if the default is incorrect.

All employee expense reports must be processed by the Payables **Invoice Import** concurrent program. Supplier records will be created from the employee records and invoices will be created from the employee expense reports (see Exhibit 7.55).

1. From the Payables menu **Other→ Requests→ Run.**
2. Select **Payables** Invoice Import.
3. Enter an invoice **Batch Name.**
4. Enter **Yes** to summarize the report.
5. Press **OK.**
6. A concurrent process will create Oracle Payables invoices. Verify the concurrent process completed successfully. Review the invoice batch online.

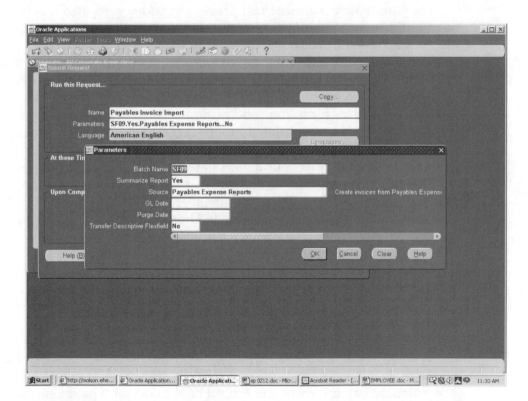

Exhibit 7.55 Employee Expense Report Invoice Import

RECURRING INVOICE

Oracle Payables recurring invoices are invoices that remain the same for some period of time. For example, the rent invoice amount remains the same and occurs every month. These invoice types are considered recurring.

Oracle Payables requires that a special calendar be defined for recurring invoices. In addition, recurring invoices require that the expense accounting flexfields be fixed or constant. Therefore, many organizations process recurring invoices directly through the standard invoice data entry process.

PAYMENTS

The Oracle Payables payment business process includes remitting payments to the supplier invoices. Oracle Payables provides a variety of payment methods including automated payment runs, electronic funds transfers (EFT), and manual payments. Manual payments can include manual checks and wire transfers.

The automated payment run process includes selecting invoices for payment, formatting and printing the payments, and confirming the payments were produced satisfactorily. Only approved invoices will be selected for payment based on the invoice due date and the payment run *pay through date* parameter. After system selects the invoices for the payment run, the user may modify the payment run if necessary. The payments are ready for formatting and printing. The formatting step prepares the payment in the appropriate format, such as check or an EFT file. After the payments have been formatted and printed, the payment records must be updated in the confirmation step.

Manual payments reflect checks which didn't go through the automated payment process. These disbursements have been made outside of Oracle Payables and must be entered in Oracle Payables to reflect the payment and reduce the organization's liability.

Typically, the Oracle Payables automated payment process occurs in three steps (see Exhibit 7.56). The first payment run step selects the invoices for payment. Optionally, the selected invoices may be modified. The next payment run step formats and prints the payments. The last payment run step confirms the payments were produced properly and records the payment transactions.

Typically, the Oracle Payables payment architecture consists of payment batches, checks, and invoices paid by the check (see Exhibit 7.57). The payment batch records the control count and total payment amount. The check records the supplier and check amount. The invoice records the transaction being paid.

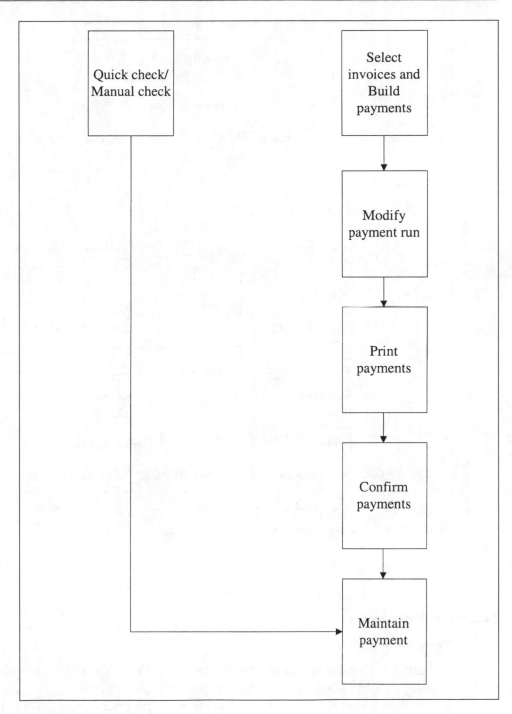

Exhibit 7.56 Payment Business Flow

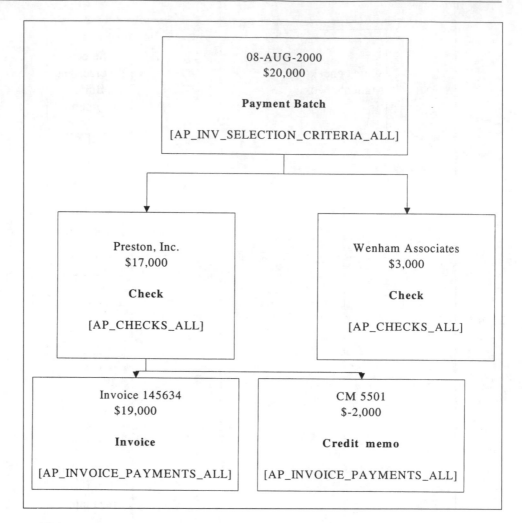

Exhibit 7.57   Payment Architecture

Automatic Payments

Payment Selection

Automatic payments allow Oracle Payables to maximize cash by only paying invoices based on the due date and system options.

Follow in-house procedures for creating payment runs (see Exhibit 7.58).

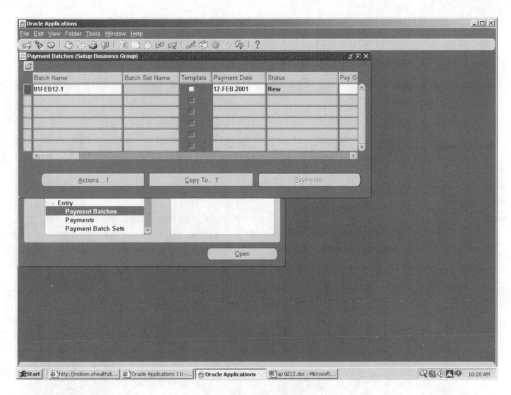

Exhibit 7.58 Payment Batch

1. From the Payables menu → **Payments** → **Entry** → **Payment Batches.**

2. Follow in-house naming standards and enter a payment **Batch Name.**

3. The Payment Date will default to today's date.

4. The Bank Account will default from the Payables options. Change if necessary.

5. Enter the payment **Document** type. The system responds with a "reserving payment document" message.

6. Additional fields can be displayed and modified by scrolling to the right. Common fields to change include Pay Group and Pay Through Date.

7. Press the **Actions . . . 1** button to start the payment run process.

 Once a Bank Account and Document are selected in a payment run, the bank account and document may not be selected until the current payment run is confirmed or cancelled.

1. Check the **Select Invoices** box to select invoices for the payment run (see Exhibit 7.59).

2. Check the **Build Payments** box to build the payment run.

3. Check the **Print Preliminary Register** box to print the Preliminary Register report.

4. A concurrent job will be created for each Payment Batch Action box. Review the concurrent requests and ensure all ran successfully. If the Preliminary Payment Register is correct, skip to Payment Printing and Formatting.

 Perform in-house payment verification procedures. Verify the first document number shown on the report is the next check number on the Preliminary Payment Register. Identify any missing payments that should be included with payment run and modify the payment run only if necessary.

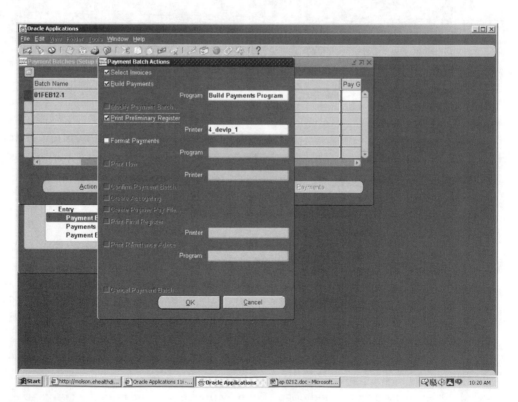

Exhibit 7.59   Payment Batch Select and Build

Payment Modification

Payment run modification is optional. Payment modifications include a new invoice may be entered into the payment run, the selected payment amount may be changed to reflect a partial payment, or an invoice may be deselected from the payment run.

1. Query the payment **Batch Name.** Notice the status has changed to Built (see Exhibit 7.60).

2. Press the **Payments** button to modify the invoices or invoice amounts selected for payment.

The system will display the invoices selected for payment (see Exhibit 7.61). The invoices selected may be modified in the payment run. To deselect an invoice from the payment run, follow these three steps.

1. To modify the payment run, select the **Invoice Number** to alter.

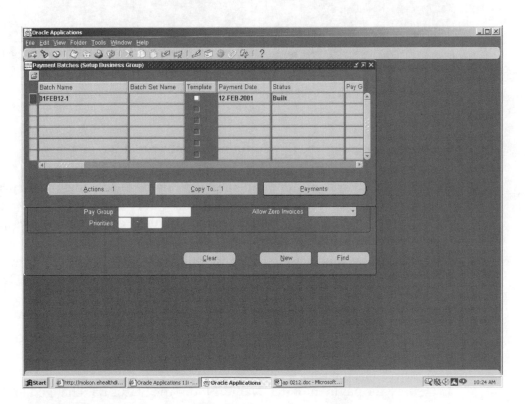

Exhibit 7.60   Payment Batch Modification

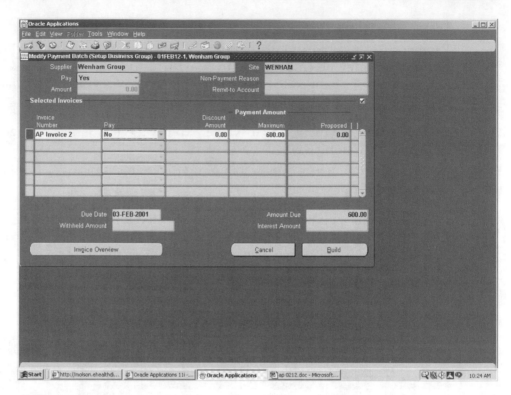

Exhibit 7.61 Payment Modification

2. Select **No** under the Pay column to remove the disbursement from the check run.

3. Press **Build.** The system will submit a new Build Payment concurrent request. The disbursement batch status will be Rebuilding. The status will not change until the concurrent request completes successfully and the batch has been requeried.

Other modifications include changing the payment amount or adding additional invoices to the batch.

Payment Printing and Formatting

Payment printing and formatting are the second required step (see Exhibit 7.62).

1. Query the payment **Batch Name.** Notice the Status has changed to Built.

2. Press **Actions . . . 1** to format the payments.

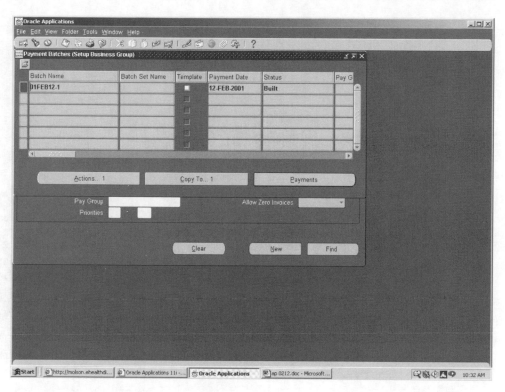

Exhibit 7.62 Payment Printing and Formatting

Select the print and format actions (see Exhibit 7.63).

1. Check the **Format Payments** box.
2. Check the **Print Now** box if printing checks. Have the check stock loaded in the printer.
3. Select the **Printer**.
4. Press **OK**. A concurrent process will run. Review the concurrent request.

 Optionally, the Select, Build, and Format programs may be run together.

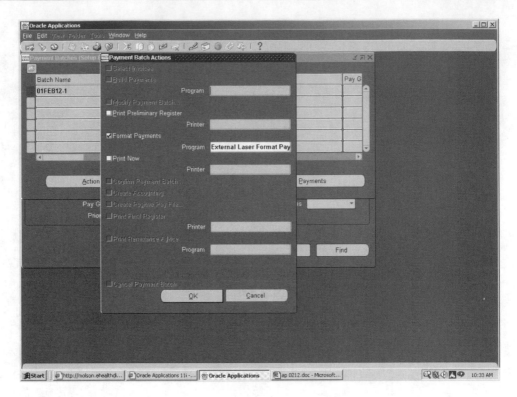

Exhibit 7.63 Payment Batch Printing and Formatting: Actions

Payment Confirmation

The payment confirmation process updates the invoice as paid. The confirmation step allows the user to correct problems with the payment run if necessary.

1. Query the payment **Batch Name.** Notice the status has changed to Formatted (see Exhibit 7.64).
2. Press **Actions .. 1** to confirm the payments.

In the Payment Actions window,

1. Check the **Confirm Payment Batch** box (see Exhibit 7.65).
2. Optionally, check the Print Final Register box to print a register of the payment run.
3. Press the **OK** button.

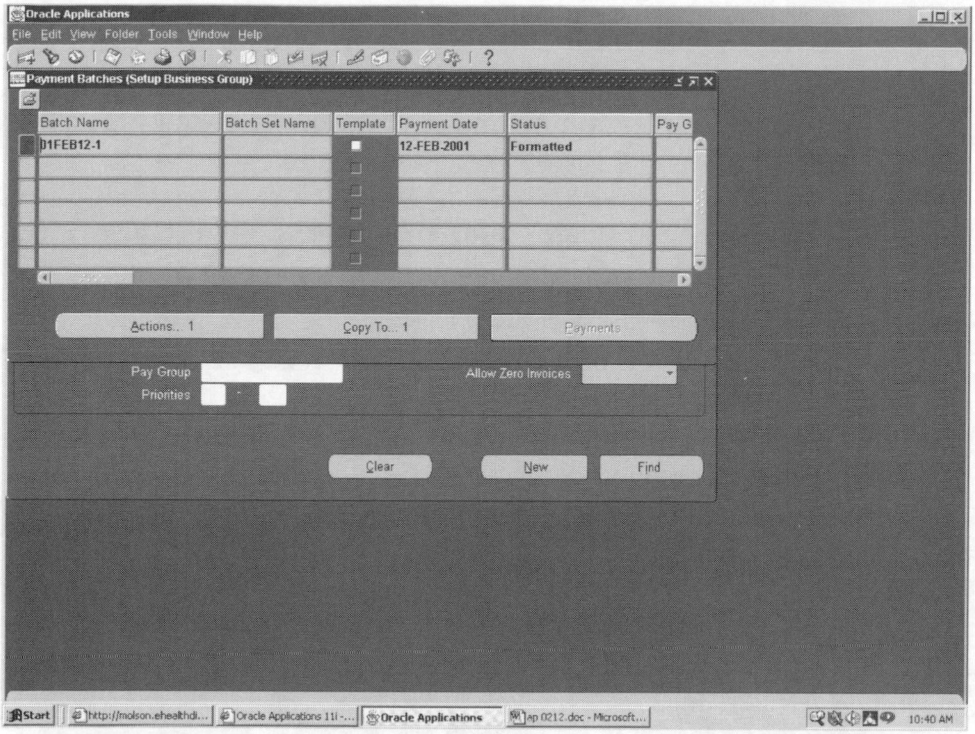

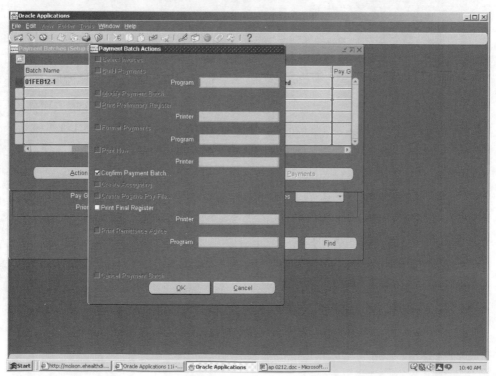

Exhibit 7.64 Payment Batch Confirm: Batch Name

Exhibit 7.65 Confirm Payment Batch

The payment confirmation step ensures the disbursements were properly produced and distributed prior to recording the payment (see Exhibit 7.66).

1. Select the appropriate **Status** to the checks. Valid statuses include:
   - Set Up—records alignment checks for impact printers
   - Printed—records valid checks
   - Skipped—records checks that were not made and skipped due to a printer malfunction
   - Spoiled—records checks that were made and ruined due to a printer malfunction
2. Populate the **From** and **To** fields with the check numbers associated with each Status.

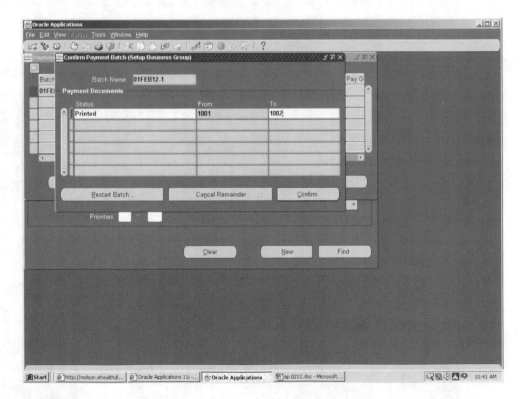

Exhibit 7.66   Payment Confirmation

Typically, if checks didn't print properly, two options are available. First, the payment run may record the partial run and cancel the remaining checks. Invoices without checks will be created in the next payment run.
Alternatively, the payment run may record the partial run and restart printing the remaining checks. If restarting the payment run, enter the next available document number. Checks will not print automatically when a payment batch is restarted. Confirm the payment run as normal.

Payment Cancellation

The batch must not have completed the payment cycle to be canceled.

1. Query the payment **Batch Name** (see Exhibit 7.67).
2. Press the **A**ctions . . . **1** button.

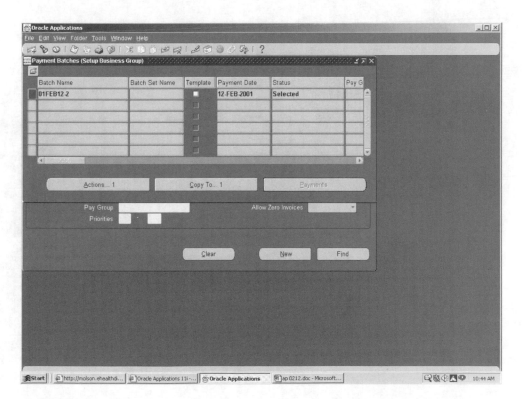

Exhibit 7.67   Payment Run Cancel

In the Payment Actions window,

1. Uncheck any boxes checked by Oracle Payables.

2. Check the **Cancel Payment Batch** box to cancel the payment batch (see Exhibit 7.68).

3. Press the **OK** button to cancel the payment run. Requery the payment batch and verify the status has changed to Cancelled. All invoices selected for payment will be available for selection in future payment runs.

Manual Payments

1. From the Payables menu → **Payments** → **Entry** → **Payments.**

2. The QuickCheck payment method defaults as the Payment Type. Select QuickCheck to print an online check. Select **Manual** to enter a payment already processed, such as a manual check or a wire transfer (see Exhibit 7.69).

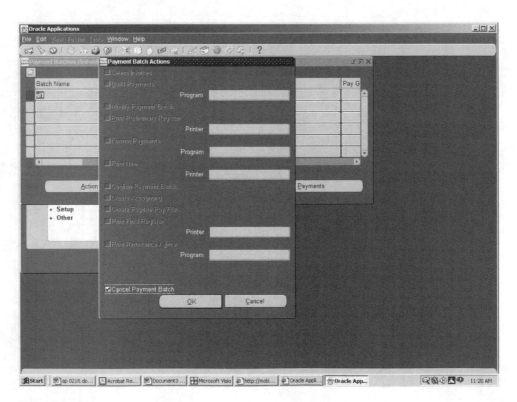

Exhibit 7.68   Payment Cancel

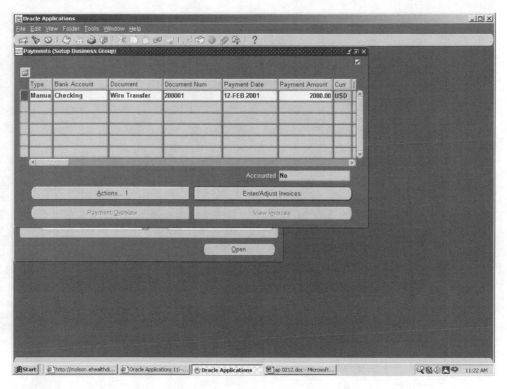

Exhibit 7.69 Manual Payment

3. Select the **Bank Account.**

4. Select the **Document** type.

5. The system will display and reserve the next document number if this is a QuickCheck. Accept the number or enter a valid payment number. If this is a Manual Check Type, enter the **Document Number.**

6. The system date will appear as Payment Date.

7. Enter the **Payment Amount.**

8. Scroll right to select the **Supplier** and **Supplier Site.**

9. Press **Enter/Adjust Invoices** to select the invoices to be paid.

 Only approved invoices may be selected for payment.

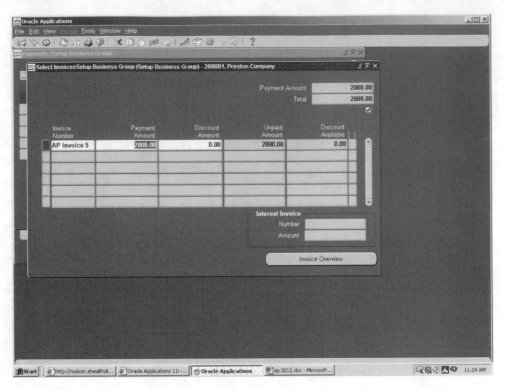

Exhibit 7.70   Manual Payment: Approved Invoices

The invoices approved for payment will display (see Exhibit 7.70).

1. Select the **Invoice Number.**
2. Select the **Payment Amount.**
3. Continue until all invoices for payment are selected.

Payment Void

1. From the Payables menu → **Payments** → **Entry** → **Payments.**
2. Query the payments.
3. Enter the payment search criteria, such as the payment **Number** (see Exhibit 7.71).
4. Press **Find.**

The payment records matching the search criteria are displayed.

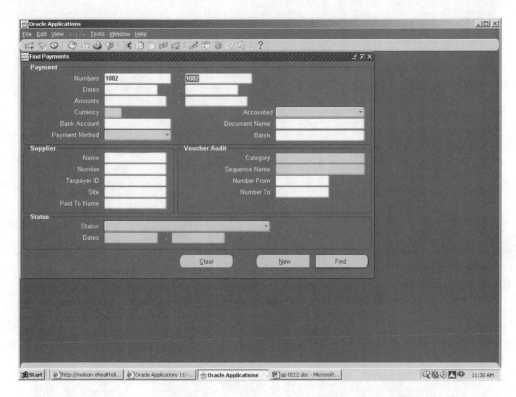

Exhibit 7.71 Payment Search Criteria

1. The system will display the payment record (see Exhibit 7.72).
2. Press **Actions . . . 1.**

Once the payment has been selected, the void action must be performed.

1. Check the **Void** box to void the payment (see Exhibit 7.73).
2. Enter the void **Date,** the **GL Date.**
3. Select the **Invoice Action.** Valid actions include:
   - **None** to open the invoice for payment
   - Hold to put the invoice on hold
   - Cancel to cancel the invoice
4. Press **OK** to void the payment. The system will confirm the void disbursement.

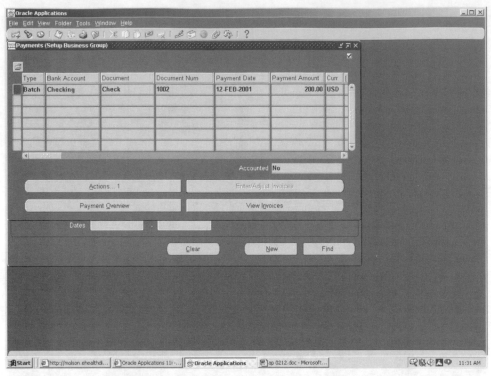

Exhibit 7.72 View Payment Record

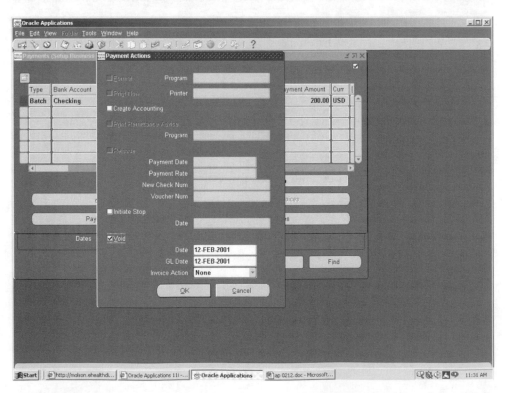

Exhibit 7.73 Payment Void

The system will reverse the original payment journal and create the following journal:

Dr Cash accounting flexfield
    Cr Liability accounting flexfield

INQUIRY AND REPORTING

Supplier Inquiry

Oracle Payables provides robust and thorough inquiry and reporting capabilities. A complete cradle-to-grave audit trail is provided via a variety of inquiry windows and standard reports.

1. From the Payables menu → **Suppliers** → **Inquiry**.
2. Enter the search criteria (see Exhibit 7.74).

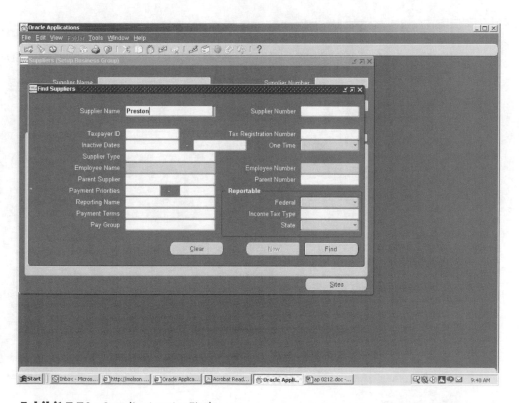

Exhibit 7.74 Supplier Inquiry Find

3. Press **Find**.

4. The supplier data is displayed as in the Supplier window in Exhibit 7.27 shown earlier in this chapter.

5. Press **Sites**.

6. The supplier site data is displayed as in the Supplier Site window shown earlier in Exhibit 7.31.

Invoice Inquiry

1. From the Payables menu → **Invoices** → **Inquiry** → **Invoices**.

2. Enter the search parameters (see Exhibit 7.75).

3. Press **Find**.

The invoices matching the search criteria are displayed (see Exhibit 7.76). Press **Overview** to display the invoice details.

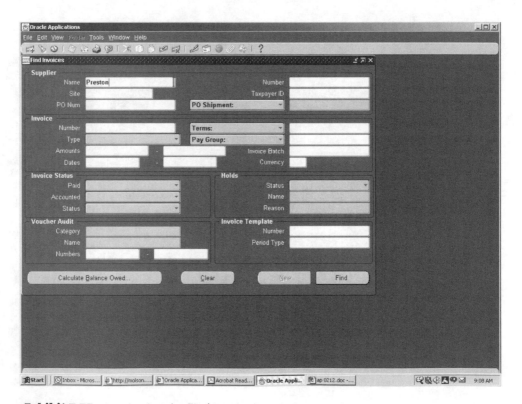

Exhibit 7.75   Invoice Inquiry Find Invoices

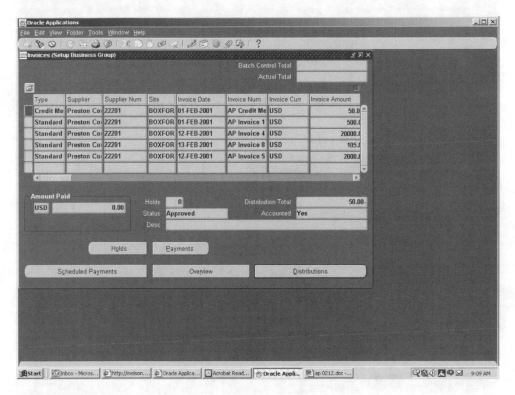

Exhibit 7.76 Invoice Inquiry Search Results

The invoice details, including the payment information, are displayed (see Exhibit 7.77).

Payment Inquiry

Review the payment information (see Exhibit 7.78).

1. From the Payables menu → **Payments** → **Inquiry** → **Payments.**
2. Enter the search criteria.
3. Press **Find.**

The payment details, including the detail payment information, are displayed (see Exhibit 7.79). Press **Payment Overview.**

The payment information, including the invoice details, is displayed (see Exhibit 7.80).

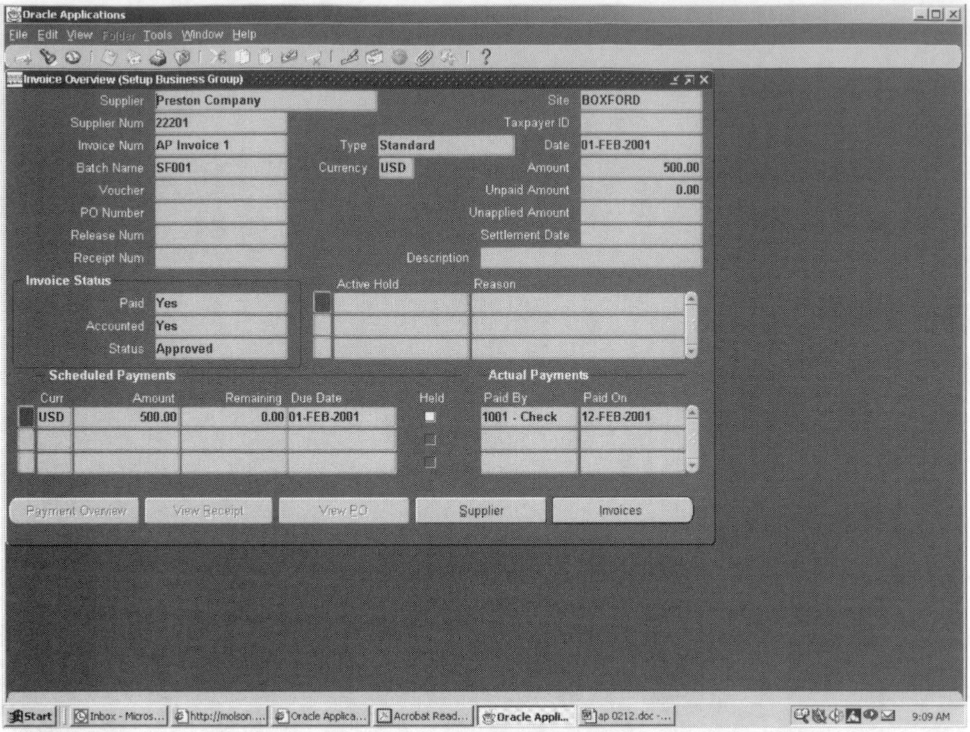

Exhibit 7.77   Invoice Overview

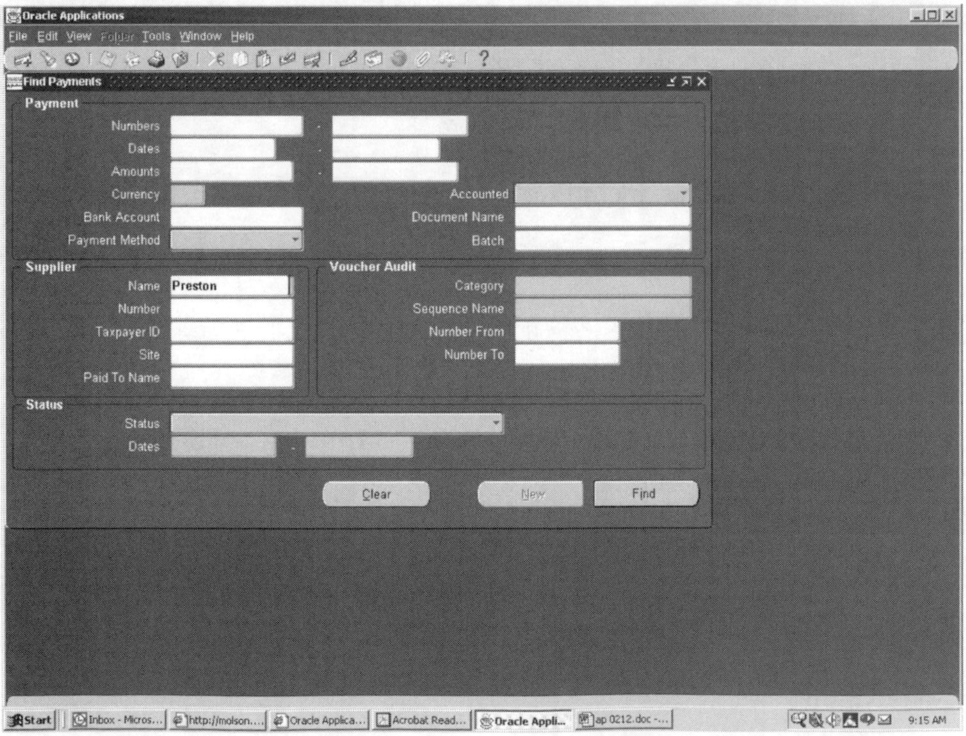

Exhibit 7.78   Payment Batch Inquiry

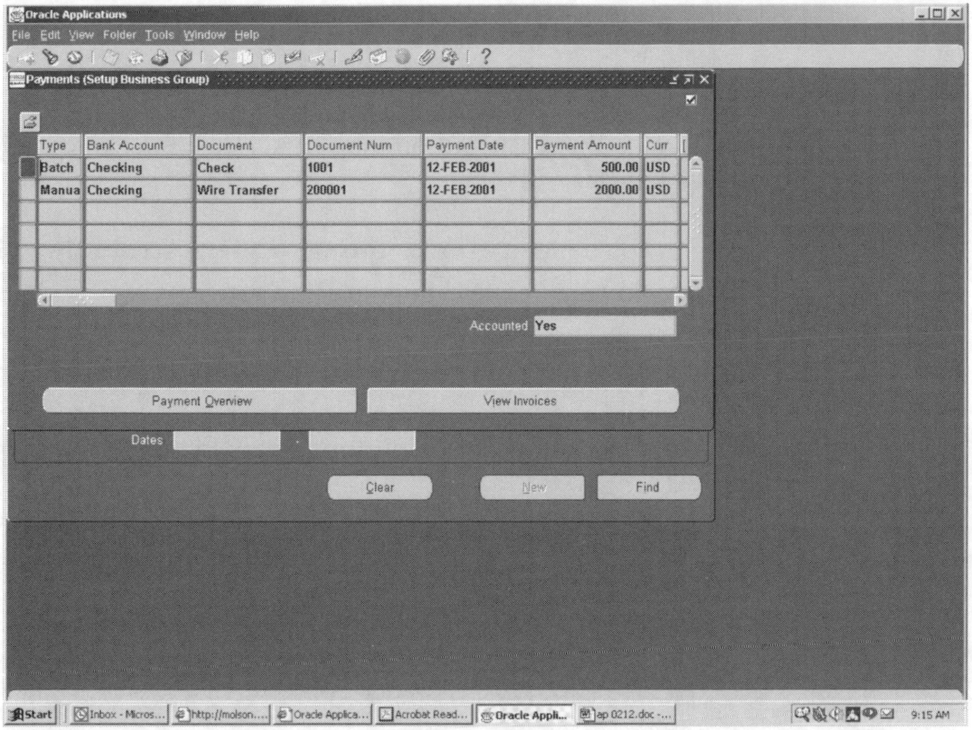

Exhibit 7.79 Payment Details

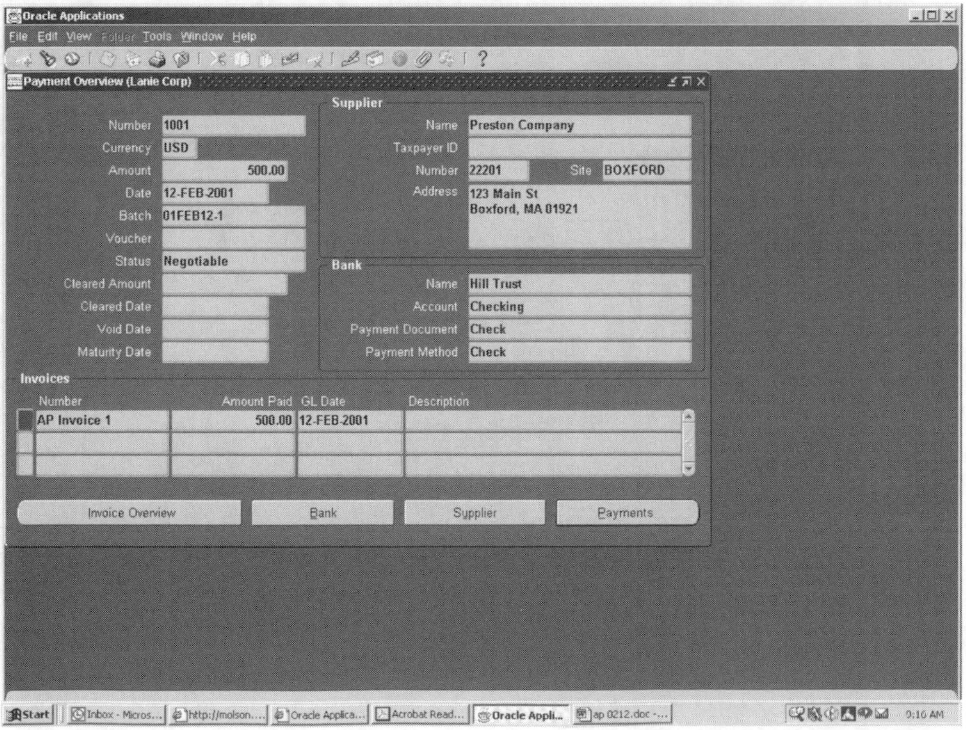

Exhibit 7.80 Payment Overview

Distribution Inquiry

To view the invoice line distribution amounts, enter the accounting flex-field range (see Exhibit 7.81).

1. From the Payables menu → **Accounting** → **View Accounting Lines.**
2. Enter the accounting flexfield **Low** to **High** range.
3. Press **OK.**
4. The system returns to the Find window. Press **Find.**

The invoices expensed to the accounting flexfield ranges are displayed (see Exhibit 7.82).

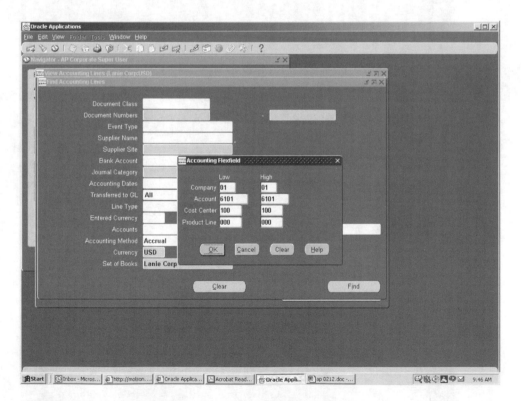

Exhibit 7.81 Invoice Distribution Accounting Inquiry

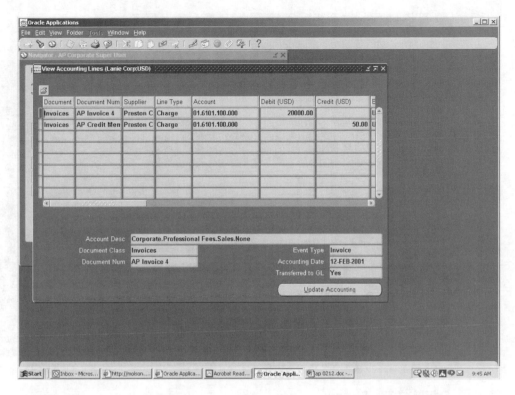

Exhibit 7.82 Invoice Distribution Accounting Invoices

Reports

Oracle Payables utilizes Oracle applications Standard Report Submission for concurrent reports and processes (see Exhibit 7.83).

1. From the Payables menu → **Other** → **Run**
2. Select the Oracle Payables report.
3. Enter the parameters. Press **OK**.
4. The system will display the Submit window. Press **Submit**.
5. The system will display the Concurrent Requests window. Review the report when the concurrent process completes successfully.

Other sample Oracle Payables reports, listings, and concurrent processes are listed in Exhibit 7.84.

Exhibit 7.83 Reports

 See the *Oracle Payables User's Guide* for a complete list of reports, listings, and concurrent processes.

PERIOD PROCESS

Periodically, the Oracle Payables financial transactions should be transferred to Oracle General Ledger. Typically, Oracle Payables journals are transferred to Oracle General Ledger either weekly or at period-end. The Payables Options determine the journal detail level. Typically, Payables journals should be summarized. The Payables Accounts Analysis reports provide a thorough audit trail of the journal transactions. The default posting options are defined in the Payables Options, Transfer to GL window.

The Payables transactions are run through the Payables Accounting concurrent process that transfers the financial transactions into journal entries to Oracle General Ledger. Once the concurrent process is complete,

Oracle Payables Report/Listing/Process	Description
Accounts Payable Trial Balance	Reports the outstanding supplier balances.
Invoice Register	Report displays invoice information.
Payment Register	Report displays payment information.
Void Payment Register	Report displays voided payment information. Run by Void Date.
Invoice on Hold	Report displays invoices on hold.
Unaccounted Transactions	Report displays the invoices which have not or cannot be transferred to General Ledger.
Discounts Taken and Lost	Report displays discounts taken and lost.
Posted Invoice	Report displays the invoices transferred to General Ledger.
Posted Payment	Report displays the payments transferred to General Ledger.
Payables Approval	Concurrent process runs the invoice approval process for more than one invoice or one batch at a time.
Supplier Audit	Report displays possible duplicate suppliers.
Mass Additions Create	Transfers the invoice data to Oracle Fixed Assets for processing.

Exhibit 7.84 Oracle Payables Sample Reports

an unposted journal entry is created. A General Ledger responsibility should review the journal online and post the entries.

The period-end reconciliation process should include verification that the Oracle Payables subsystem agrees to the Oracle General Ledger or at least can be reconciled. Remember, Oracle General Ledger is the system of record for all financial transactions. The period-end process should reconcile the liability account, the cash account, and other key accounts.

The Oracle Payables period process is displayed in Exhibit 7.85. The period process includes resolving invoices on hold, closing the current period, and opening the new period. In addition, the closing reports should be run, and the journals created and posted in Oracle General Ledger. The reconciliation process should then occur.

Unaccounted Transactions Report

The Unaccounted Transactions report displays all invoices which have not been transferred to Oracle General Ledger (see Exhibit 7.86). The report replaces the old Posting Hold report.

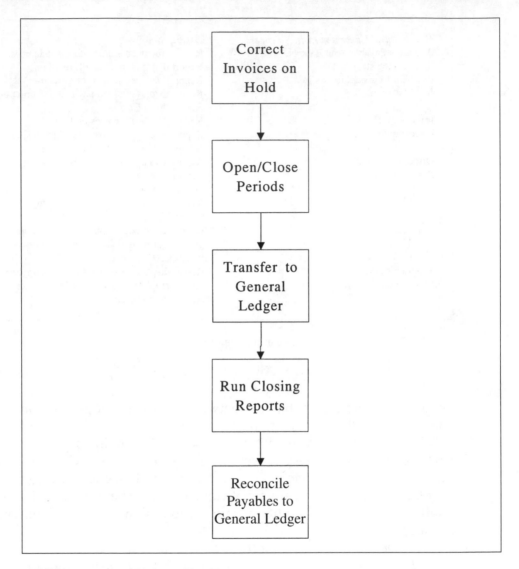

Exhibit 7.85   Payables Period Process

1. Run the **Unaccounted Transactions Report.** Enter a batch name and post through date. Accept the defaults for the remaining fields.
2. Review the report. Invoices or payments that were unable to post to the General Ledger are displayed. The invoices on this report should be corrected prior to closing. If the holds can't be resolved, the Un-

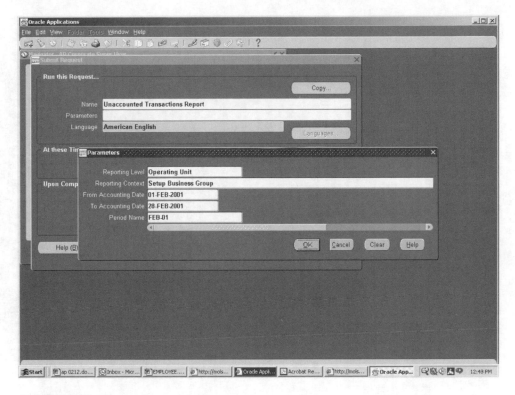

Exhibit 7.86 Reports

posted Invoice Sweep program will be required to transfer the invoices into the next period.

OPEN/CLOSE PERIOD

Typically, one period is open for processing to ensure the financial transactions are posted to the appropriate period (see Exhibit 7.87).

1. Select **Open** for the next period.
2. Select **Closed** for the current period. If any financial transactions have not been transferred to Oracle General Ledger, the system will prompt to start a concurrent process that transfers the current period transactions into the next open period. Enter the Sweep To Period. The concurrent program will transfer the transactions to the next period so the current period may be closed.

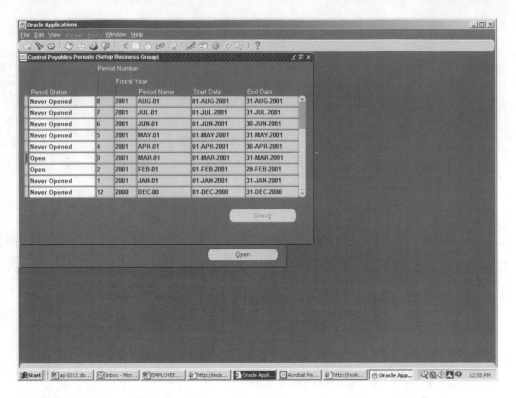

Exhibit 7.87 Open/Close Periods

Payables Accounting Process

The Payables Accounting Process includes the transfer to General Ledger process (see Exhibit 7.88).

1. Run the **Payables Accounting Process** concurrent program. Enter the From and To dates. Accept the defaults for the remaining fields.
2. Press **OK.**
3. Review all concurrent request processes and reports to confirm they completed successfully.

Review the Payables journals online in Oracle General Ledger (see Exhibit 7.89).

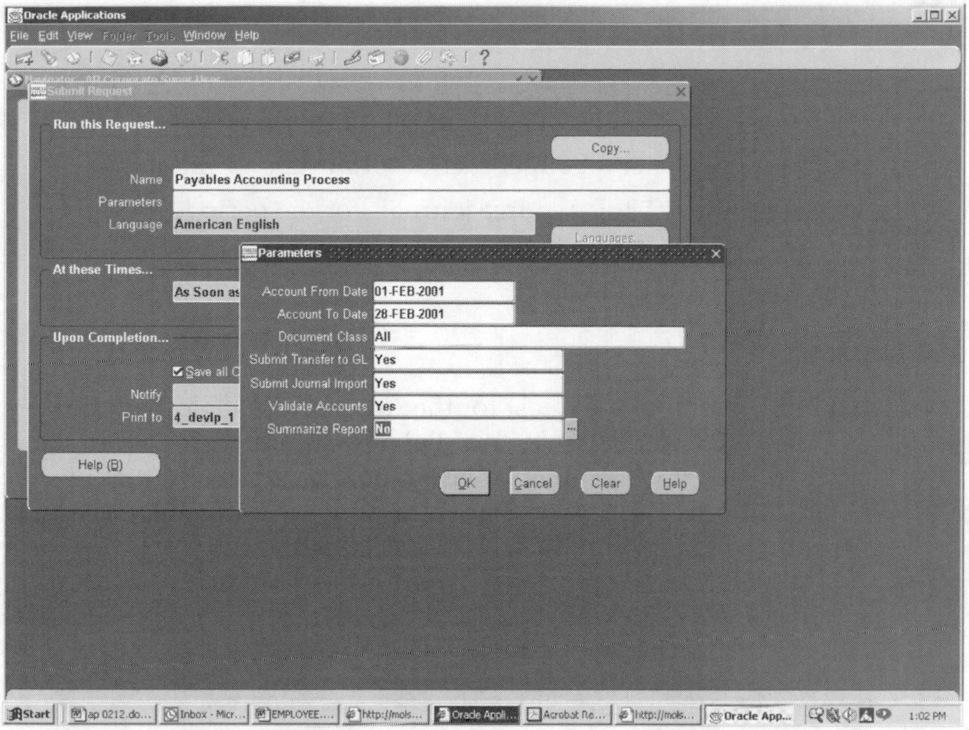

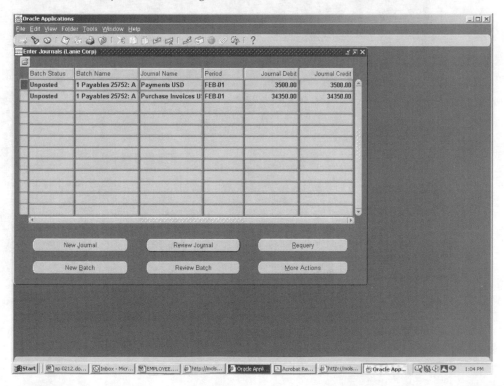

Exhibit 7.88 Payables Accounting Process

Exhibit 7.89 Payables Journals

1. From the **File** menu → **Switch Responsibility** → **GL Corporate Super User** responsibility.

2. From the General Ledger menu → **Journals** → **Enter.**

3. Query the Payables source journals for the period.

4. The journals must be posted as any other journal.

Run Reports

Exhibit 7.90 shows a request for the Accounts Payable Total Balance.

The Accounts Payable Trial Balance should agree with or be reconciled to the Oracle General Ledger accounts payable liability account. In addition, other Oracle Payables accounts—for example, Cash and Discounts Taken and Lost—should be reconciled to their respective

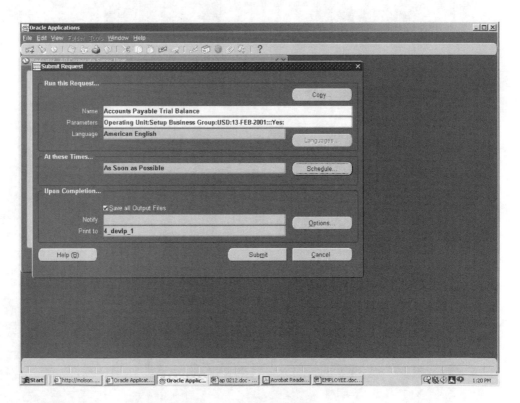

Exhibit 7.90   Payables Closing Reports Request

General Ledger accounts. Exhibit 7.91 lists the period-end reconciliation reports.

Period-End Reconciliation

Each organization should have period-end reconciliation procedures. These procedures should be followed *every* period for control and audit purposes.

1. The balance in the Accounts Payable Trial Balance report (see Exhibit 7.92) should agree to the accounts payable liability account in the General Ledger (see Exhibit 7.93).
2. The opening GL balance in the accounts payable liability account plus the total from the posted invoice register less the total from the posted payments register should tie to the ending GL balance in the accounts payable liability account (see Exhibit 7.93).

Report
Accounts Payable Trial Balance
Payables Accounts Analysis Report
Posted Invoice Register
Posted Payment Register

Discounts Taken and Lost
Void Payment Register

Exhibit 7.91   Payables Closing Reports

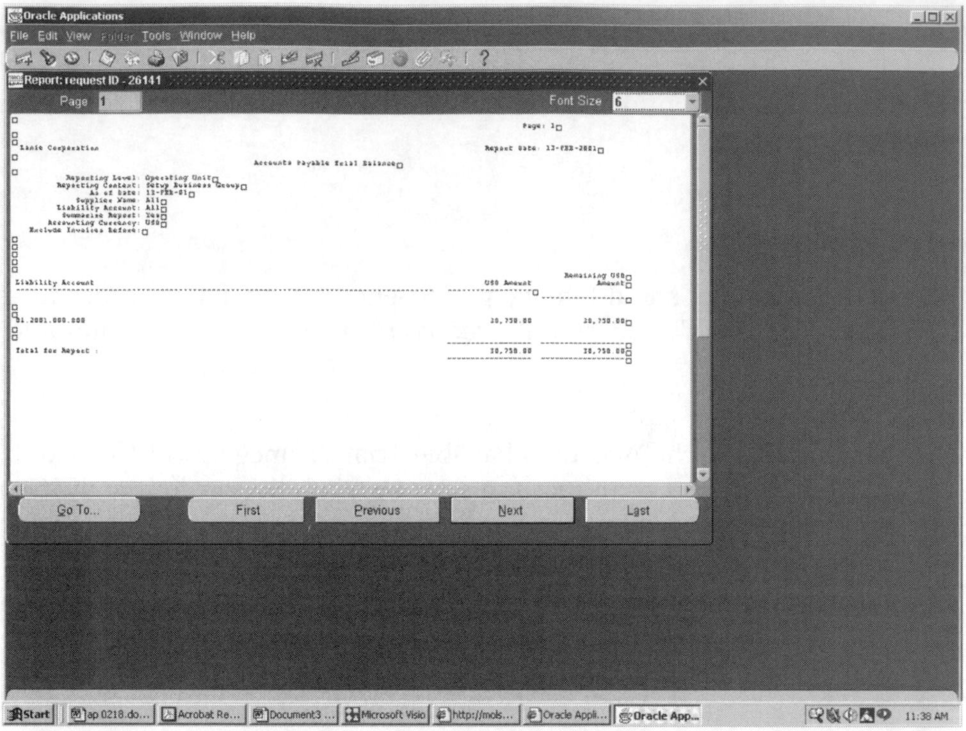

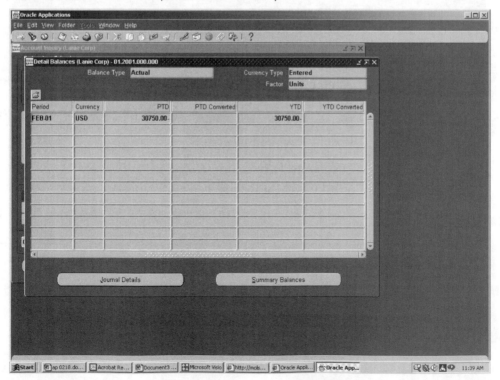

Exhibit 7.92 Accounts Payable Trial Balance Report

Exhibit 7.93 Accounts Payables Liability GL Account Balance

CHAPTER 8

Receivables

OVERVIEW

This chapter describes using the Oracle Receivables system to track customers, customer transactions, receipts, and collection activities. Oracle Receivables also prints invoices, credit memos, dunning letters, and statements. Full collection capabilities with a complete audit trail are also available.

Oracle Receivables is fully integrated with Oracle General Ledger. All accounting transactions flow to the General Ledger with full audit trail capabilities. Drill-down from the General Ledger journal entries to the Oracle Receivables accounting flexfield distribution details with full T-accounting and journal transaction detail accounting is available.

Oracle Receivables is fully integrated with Oracle Order Entry. All customer data is shared with Oracle Receivables. The Oracle Receivables AutoInvoice process imports orders into invoices and Return Material Authorizations (RMAs) into credit memos. Oracle Receivables provides online order inquiry capabilities within the invoice inquiry windows. The default invoice line transaction flexfield contains order number, order line number, ship date, and so on. See the *Oracle Receivables User Guide* Transactions Chapter under the Transaction Flexfields section.

Oracle Receivables is fully integrated with Oracle Cash Management. The cash forecasts from collection activities data in Oracle Receivables is imported into Oracle Cash Management. The Oracle Payables cash requirements data completes the cash forecast information by providing the anticipated cash disbursement data.

Oracle Receivables is an open item receivable system, not a balance forward receivable system (see Exhibit 8.1)

An open item receivable system links all receivable activities to the original transaction. For example, cash is applied to the invoice, not just the customer account. The original transaction has an open status until the sum of transaction activities equals zero, such as a full credit memo or a full receipt applied to an invoice. A transaction will be reopened if an activity causes the balance to not equal zero, such as reversed receipt.

A balance forward receivable system rolls forward all activities to an open balance. Receipts are applied to the customer account, not the invoice. For example, a credit card receivable system is a balance forward receivable system. Receipts are applied to the customer account, not to the individual credit card invoice transactions.

The open receivable methodology can impact the decision to convert and the conversion level. Converting all open detail can be cumbersome and time-consuming. Typically, open balances are converted into a beginning balance record per customer site. Users must refer back to hardcopy or the legacy system for the details if necessary. However, this is a one-time conversion issue, not an ongoing issue.

The typical Oracle Receivables business process flow is setup, cus-

Open Item	**Balance Forward**
Invoice 111 $1,000 Receipt 66 $<500> Net $500	Invoice 111 $1,000
Invoice 112 $1,000	Invoice 112 $1,000
Invoice 113 $1,000	Invoice 113 $1,000
	Receipt 66 $<500>

Exhibit 8.1   Accounts Receivable Methodologies

tomers, invoices, receipts, inquiry and reporting, and period processing (see Exhibit 8.2). The Oracle Receivables environment must be defined for the operating unit organization. Customers must be defined before an invoice and/or receipt may be entered. Likewise, if a receipt is to be applied to an invoice, the invoice must be entered first. Inquiry and reporting allow the collection personnel to record customer calls and other contact information. At period-end, the financial transactions should be transferred to create Oracle General Ledger journal entries.

SETUP

The minimal Oracle Receivables setup steps are displayed in Exhibit 8.3.

RECEIVABLES STEP 6.1: FLEXFIELDS

Oracle Receivables utilize predefined invoice descriptive flexfields.

Invoice Transaction Descriptive Flexfield

Oracle seeds the Oracle Receivables Invoice Transaction Flexfield with the Override Allowed field enabled. Therefore, the invoice transaction flexfield opens regardless if used or not. In order to avoid the window opening up, the Invoice Transaction Flexfield should be corrected and recompiled (see Exhibit 8.4).

Repeat for the Invoice Line Transaction flexfield.

1. From the **File** menu → **Switch Responsibility** → **AR Corporate Super User** responsibility.
2. From the Receivables menu → **Setup** → **Financials** → **Flexfields** → **Descriptive** → **Segments.**
3. Select the **Oracle Receivables Invoice Transaction Flexfield.**
4. Uncheck the **Freeze Flexfield Definition** box. The system displays a warning message.
5. Uncheck the **Override Allowed** box to disable opening during invoice data entry.
6. Check the **Freeze Flexfield Definition** box. The system displays a Compiling Flexfield Definition message. A concurrent process creates the invoice transaction flexfield view used by Oracle Receivables windows.

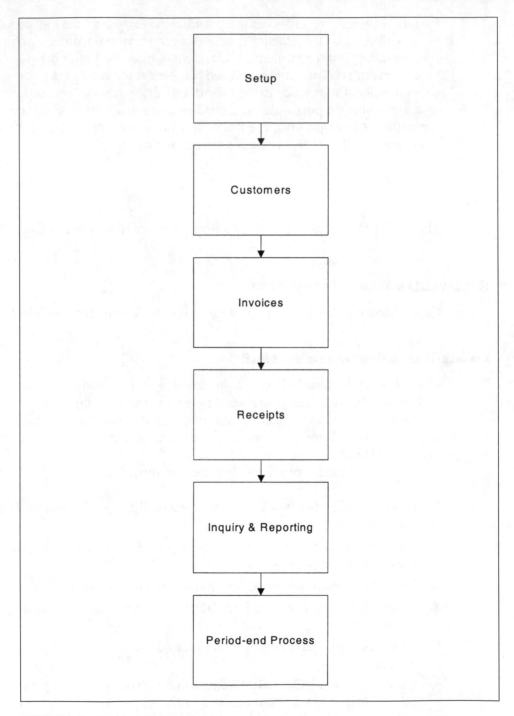

Exhibit 8.2 Receivables Business Process

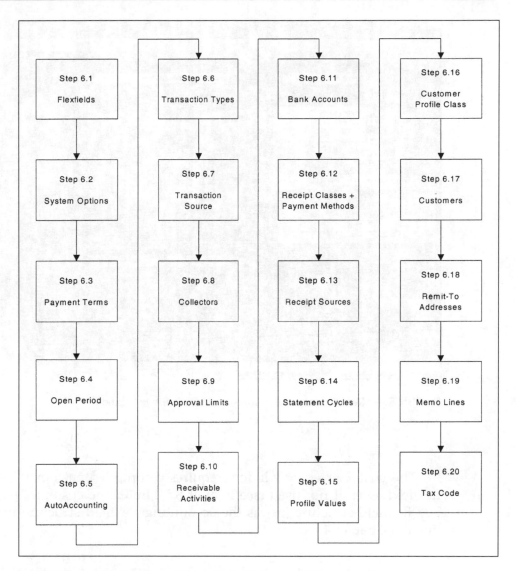

Exhibit 8.3   Oracle Receivables Setup Tasks

Customer Territory Key Flexfield

Oracle Receivables customer territories are a key flexfield used to define a reporting territory. For example, a territory may represent a rollup of locations; North America may be a customer territory. Customer territories must be defined, even if they are not used. Set up one structure and one value to complete the Oracle Receivables requirement.

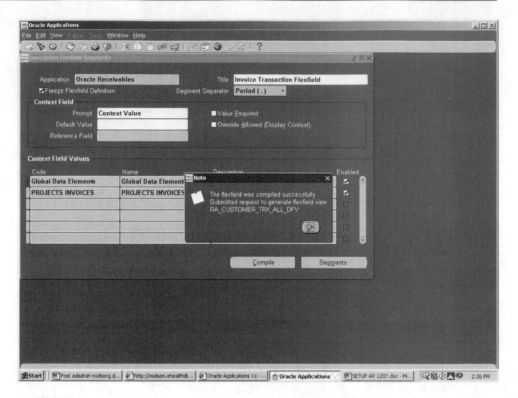

Exhibit 8.4   Receivables Invoice Transaction Descriptive Flexfield

The customer entry window requires a compiled customer territory flexfield, even if not used (see Exhibit 8.5). Enter the customer territory key flexfield structure just as the accounting flexfield structure was defined in Chapter 4.

1. From the Receivables menu → **Setup** → **Financials** → **Flexfields** → **Key** → **Segments.**

2. Query the **Oracle Receivables Customer Territory Flexfield.**

3. Enter the **Segments** and **Value Sets.**

4. Check the **Freeze Flexfield Definition** box.

5. Press **Compile.** The system displays a Compiling Flexfield Definition message and submits a concurrent request to create the customer territory flexfield view used by Oracle Receivables windows.

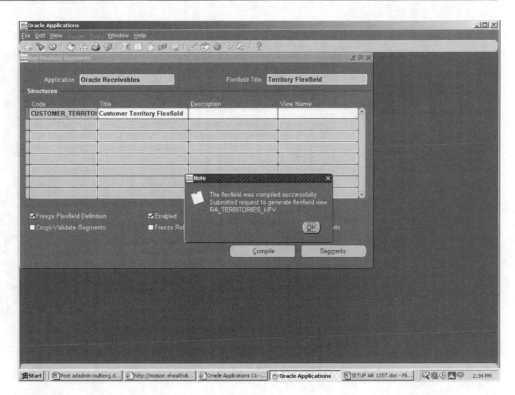

Exhibit 8.5   Receivables Customer Territory Key Flexfield

System Items Key Flexfield

Oracle application system items are a key flexfield defining the organization's inventory part number. For example, 162567 may be an inventory part number. System items must be defined, even if not used. Set up one structure to complete the Oracle Receivables requirement.

The transaction data entry window requires a compiled system item flexfield, even if not used (see Exhibit 8.6). Enter the system items key flexfield structure just as the accounting flexfield structure was defined in Chapter 4.

1. From the Receivables menu → **Setup** → **Financials** → **Flexfields** → **Key** → **Segments**.
2. Query the **Oracle Inventory System Items Flexfield**.
3. Enter the **Segments** and **Value Sets**.
4. Check the **Freeze Flexfield Definition** box.

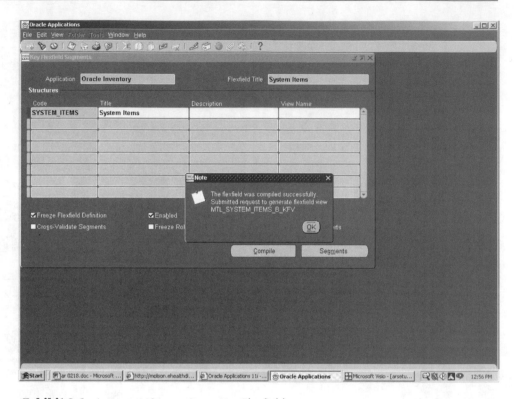

Exhibit 8.6   Inventory System Items Key Flexfield

5. Press **C**ompile. The system displays a Compiling Flexfield Definition message and submits a concurrent request to create the inventory system items flexfield view used by Oracle Receivables windows.

Sales Tax Location Key Flexfield

Oracle Receivables sales tax location is a key flexfield defining the sales tax methodology. Oracle Receivables seeds a variety of sales tax location structures. For example, a sales tax rate may be determined by the customer's state, county, and city. Typically, the tax rates are loaded from a tax service. Compile one of the seeded structures to complete the Oracle Receivables sales tax location requirement (see Exhibit 8.7).

1. From the Receivables menu → **Setup** → **Financials** → **Flexfields** → **Key** → **Segments**.
2. Select the **Oracle Receivables Sales Tax Location Flexfield.**

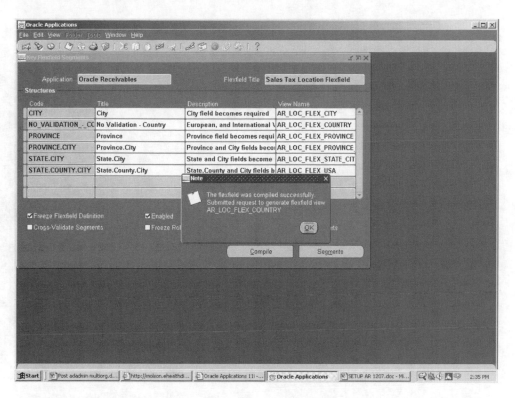

Exhibit 8.7   Receivable Sales Tax Location Key Flexfield

3. Highlight the appropriate sales tax location flexfield structure.
4. Check the **Freeze Flexfield Definition** box. The system displays a Compiling Flexfield Definition message.
5. Press **OK.**

RECEIVABLES STEP 6.2: SYSTEM OPTIONS

The Oracle Receivables system options define the Oracle Receivables system processing defaults (see Exhibit 8.8).

The Accounting options define the accounting method, whether the journal import should process immediately after the financial transactions have been transferred, and the default accounting flexfields.

1. From the Receivables menu → **Setup** → **System** → **System Options.**
2. Select the **Accounting Method.**

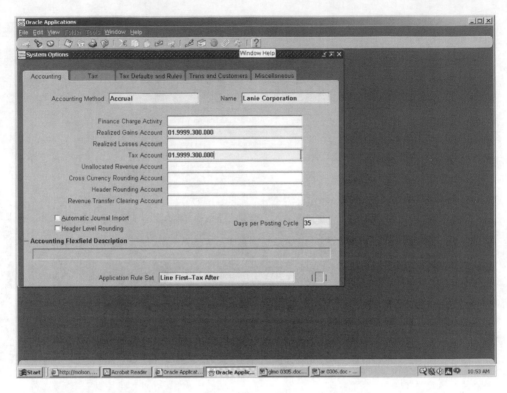

Exhibit 8.8   System Options: Accounting

3. Select the Set of Books **Name.**
4. Enter the **Realized Gains Account** accounting flexfield.
5. Enter the **Tax Account** accounting flexfield.
6. Check the **Automatic Journal Import** box.
7. Press the **Tax** tab.

The Tax options define the default tax processing options including the sales tax location flexfield structure, tax validation levels, and tax rounding options (see Exhibit 8.9).

1. Select the **Tax Method.**
2. Select the compiled sales tax **Location Flexfield Structure** compiled in the previous step. The Location Flexfield Structure must be unique and may not be shared with any other organization.
3. Select the **Address Validation** option.

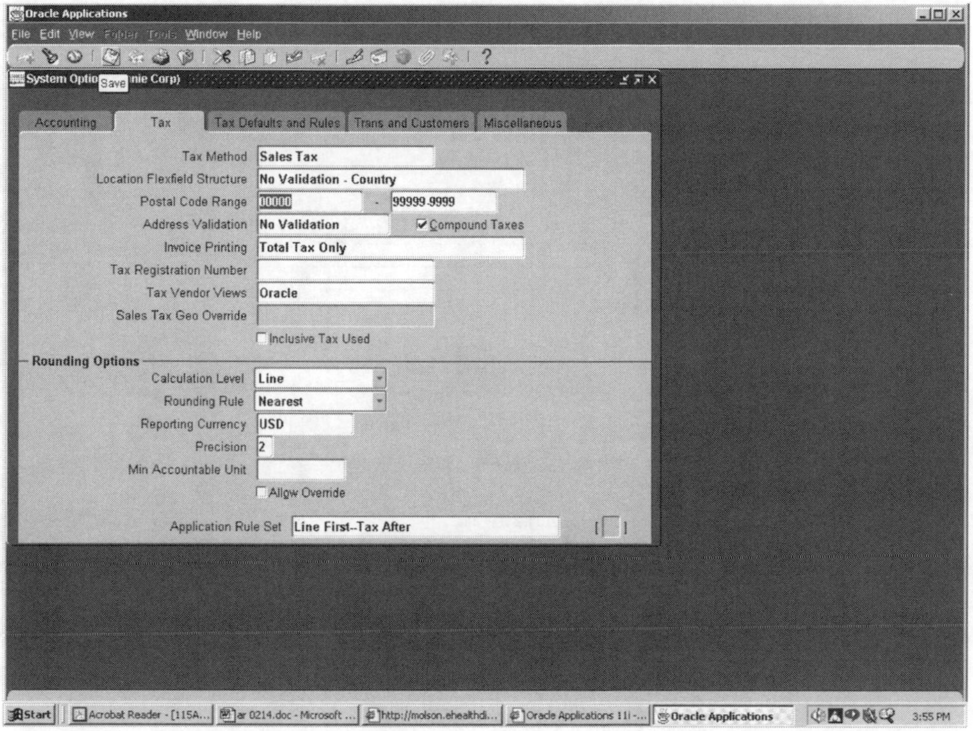

Exhibit 8.9   System Options: Tax

4. Select the **Invoice Printing** for taxes option.
5. Press the **Trans and Customer** tab.

The Transaction and Customer options define the customer numbering scheme, the customer site numbering scheme, and the ability to change printed transactions, as well as delete incomplete transactions (see Exhibit 8.10).

1. Check the **Allow Change to Printed Transactions** box.
2. Check the **Allow Transaction Deletion** box.
3. Check the **Automatic Customer Numbering** box to automatically number customers.
4. Check the **Automatic Site Numbering** box to automatically number customer sites.

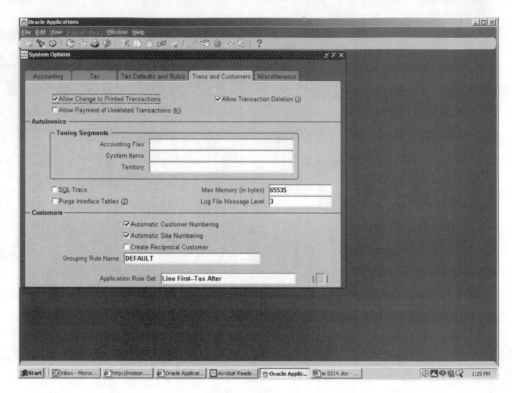

Exhibit 8.10 System Options: Trans and Customers

5. Select the **Grouping Rule Name.**
6. Press the **Miscellaneous** tab.

The Miscellaneous options define the source of the customer territory flexfield and other receivables processing options (see Exhibit 8.11).

1. Select the **Split Amount.**
2. Select the **Days in Days Sales Outstanding Calculation.** The default 90 days is displayed.
3. Select the **Discount Basis.** The default Lines Only is displayed.
4. Select the **Chargeback Due Date.** The default Deposit Date is displayed.
5. Select the **Default Country.**
6. Select the **Source of Territory.** The default Salesrep is displayed.
7. Select the **Application Rule Set.** The default Lines First—Tax After is displayed.

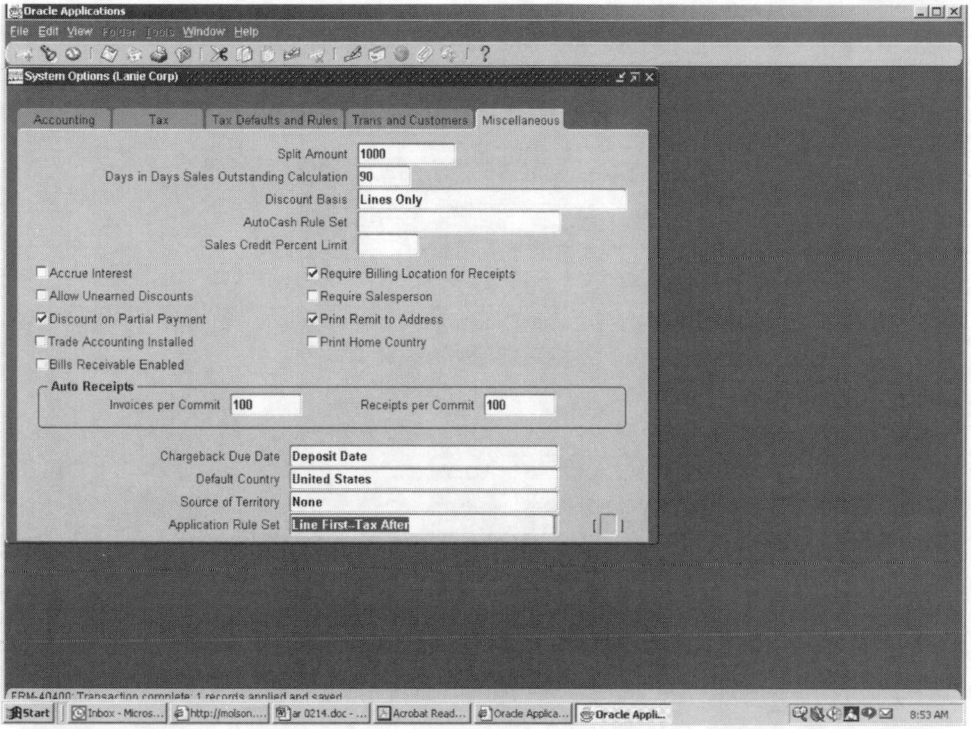

Exhibit 8.11 System Options: Miscellaneous

The system will send concurrent requests to compile the sales tax location structures.

RECEIVABLES STEP 6.3: PAYMENT TERMS

Oracle Receivables shares the payment terms with Oracle Payables (see Exhibit 7.7 in Chapter 7). The payment terms for Oracle Receivables are shown in Exhibit 8.12.

1. From the Receivables responsibility → **Setup** → **Transactions** → **Payment Terms.**
2. Query the payment terms defined in Payables Step 4.4.
3. Press the **Discounts** to review the discount percent.

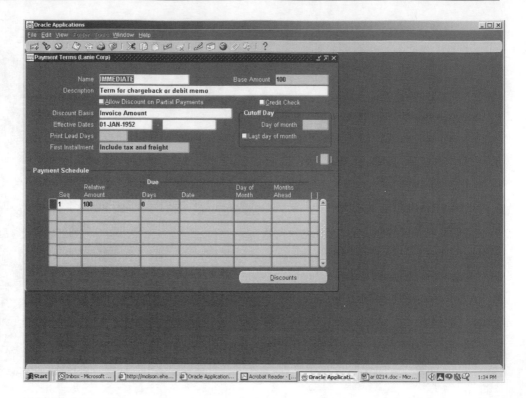

Exhibit 8.12   Payment Terms

RECEIVABLES STEP 6.4: OPEN PERIOD

The Oracle Receivables periods are displayed from the GL Set of Books calendar. Oracle Receivables periods may be opened or closed, independent of the other applications (see Exhibit 8.13). Typically, one period is open to ensure the financial transactions are posted to the appropriate period.

1. From the Receivables menu → **Control** → **Accounting** → **Open/Close Periods.**
2. Select **Open** in the Status field to open the first period for processing.

Multiple periods may be Open at once; however, the Accounts Receivable personnel must carefully watch the GL Date defaults. One period should be open at a time to ensure financial transactions are recorded to the proper accounting period and to assist the reconciliation process.

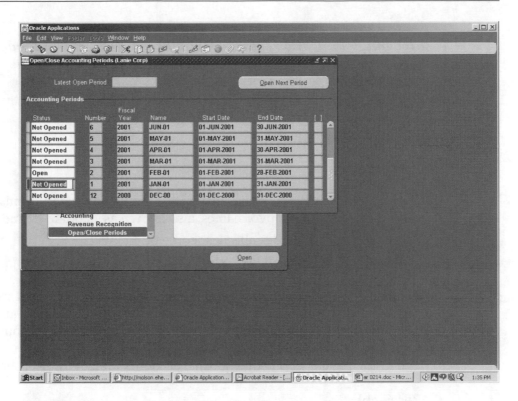

Exhibit 8.13　Receivables Open/Close Periods

RECEIVABLES STEP 6.5: AUTOACCOUNTING

AutoAccounting is used in Oracle Receivables to build the default journal entry accounts. Each accounting flexfield segment value may be derived from a variety of default values defined at the transaction type, transaction line, salesrep, or tax level. For example, the Receivables company and account segment values are derived from the transaction type parameters. The Revenue company and account segment values are derived from the transaction type and the product line is derived from the standard transaction line (see Exhibit 8.14).

Oracle Receivables allows the following AutoAccounting parameters:

- Constant which indicates keep the segment value the same
- Transaction Type (Trx Type) which includes invoices, credit memos, and debit memos

Account	Company	Account	Cost Center	Product Line
Receivables	Trx Type	Trx type	000	000
Revenue	Trx Type	Trx Type	000	Std lines

Exhibit 8.14 AutoAccounting

- Standard Memo Line (Std Line) which includes inventory items and user-defined standard invoice lines, also known as standard memo lines
- Salesreps which includes all salespeople or agents
- Taxes which includes all tax codes

Typically, a combination of transaction types and standard memo lines is used. Constants may be included. Salesreps and taxes are optional; therefore, they are less likely to be selected as AutoAccounting parameters.

The following General Ledger journal accounts utilize AutoAccounting:

- Receivable
- Revenue
- Freight
- AutoInvoice Clearing
- Unbilled Receivable
- Unearned Revenue

All accounts must have the AutoAccounting parameters defined prior to entering transactions.

The AutoAccounting parameters must be set for all Oracle Receivables accounts (see Exhibit 8.15).

1. From the Receivables menu → **Setup** → **Transactions** → **AutoAccounting**
2. Enter the AutoAccounting parameters for each Type.
3. For each Type, select either the Table Name or Constant Value. Table Names options vary dependent on the Type. Valid Table Names include: Transaction Types, Standard (Memo) Lines, Salesreps, and Taxes.

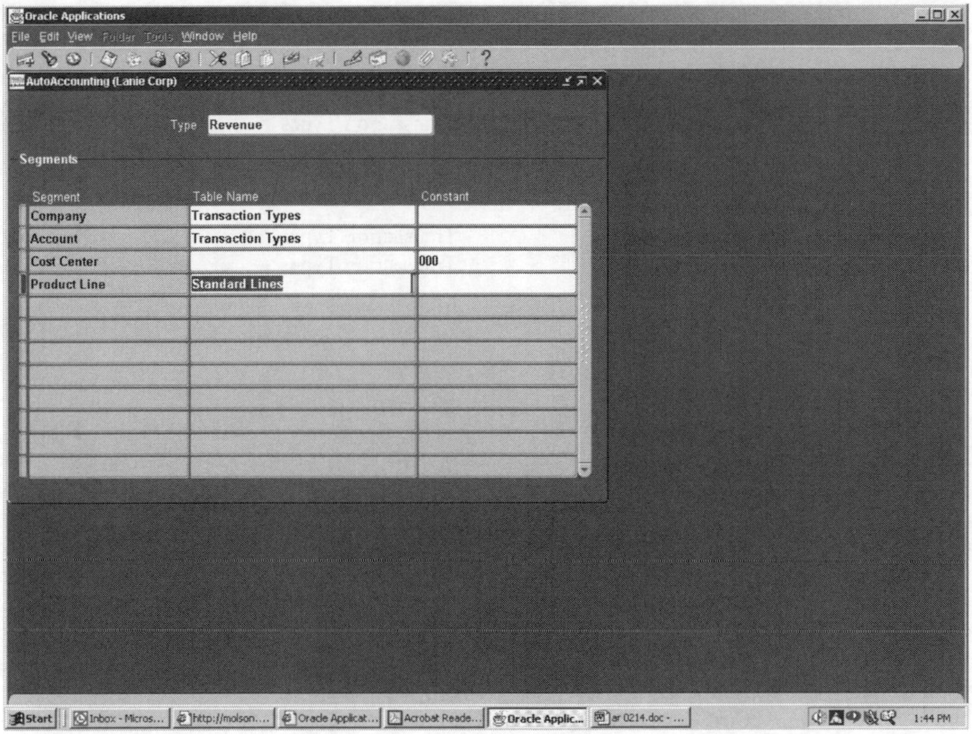

Exhibit 8.15 AutoAccounting: Revenue

Exhibit 8.16 displays the AutoAccounting parameters defined.

RECEIVABLES STEP 6.6: TRANSACTION TYPES: CREDIT MEMOS

During invoice entry, the user must select the transaction type. Transaction types dictate the invoice and credit memo capabilities, including posting to a customer account, posting to Oracle General Ledger, and the accounting flexfield values which may be called by AutoAccounting (see Exhibit 8.17).

1. From the Receivables menu → **Setup** → **Transactions** → **Transaction Types.**
2. Enter the credit memo transaction type first. Enter a **Name** and **Description** which reflect the type of transaction.
3. Select the appropriate transaction **Class.**

Account Type	Table Value	Constant Value
Revenue		
Company	Transaction Types	
Account	Transaction Types	
Cost Center		000
Product Line	Standard (Memo) Lines	
Receivables		
Company	Transaction Types	
Account	Transaction Types	
Cost Center		000
Product Line		000
AutoInvoice Clearing		
Company		01
Account		9999
Cost Center		300
Product Line		000
Freight		
Company		01
Account		6401
Cost Center		300
Product Line		000
Tax		
Company		01
Account		6501
Cost Center		300
Product Line		000
Unbilled Receivable		
Company		01
Account		9999
Cost Center		300
Product Line		000
Unearned Revenue		
Company		01
Account		9999
Cost Center		300
Product Line		000

Exhibit 8.16 Receivable AutoAccounting Parameters

4. Check the **Open Receivable** box to post the transaction to a customer's account.
5. Check the **Post To GL** box to post the transaction to General Ledger.
6. Select the **Printing Option** to **Print**.
7. Select the **Transaction Status** option to **Open**.
8. Select the **Creation Sign** of **Negative Sign.**

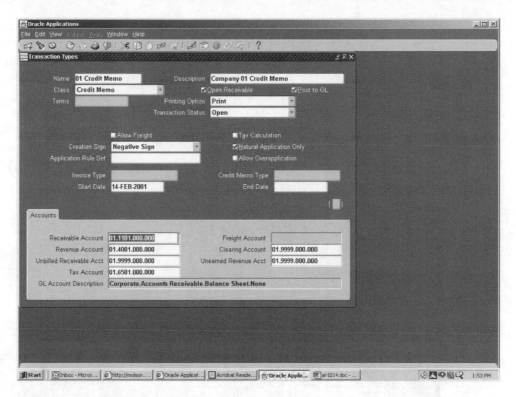

Exhibit 8.17 Transaction Types: Credit Memo

9. Check the **Natural Application Only** box to only allow amounts to bring the balance to zero. For example, an invoice is a positive amount and only negative amounts may reduce the balance to zero. If the Natural Application box is enabled, the **Allow Overapplication** box can't be enabled. In other words, a receipt can't be applied which would take the invoice balance over its natural (application) balance. A receipt of $200 can't be applied to an $100 invoice because the natural application rule states only a positive amount balance (or zero amount balance) may exist and the invoice may not be overapplied.

10. Enter the **Receivable Account.** Any AutoAccounting parameters of Transaction Type will use the applicable segment values.

11. Enter the **Revenue Account.** Any AutoAccounting parameters of Transaction Type will use the applicable segment values.

Enter the invoice transaction type after the credit memo transaction type has been defined, as the invoice transaction type references the credit memo transaction type. Enter a Name and Description which reflect the type of transaction. All AutoAccounting accounts which reference Trx Types will derive the segment value here (see Exhibit 8.18).

1. From the Receivables menu → **Setup** → **Transactions** → **Transaction Types.**

2. Enter the credit memo transaction type first. Enter a **Name** and **Description** that reflect the type of transaction.

3. Select the appropriate transaction **Class.**

4. Check the **Open Receivable** box to post the transaction to a customer's account.

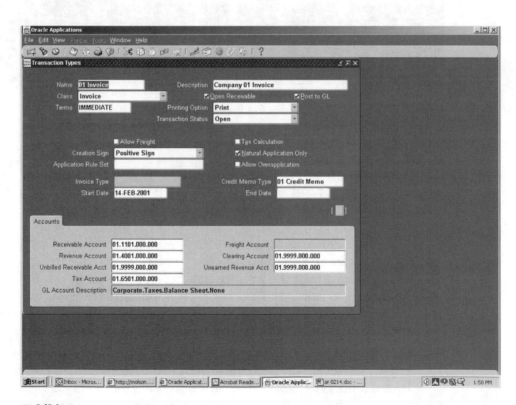

Exhibit 8.18   Transaction Types: Invoice

5. Check the **Post To GL** box to post the transaction to General Ledger.

6. Select the **Printing Option** to **Print.**

7. Select the **Transaction Status** option to **Open.**

8. Select the **Creation Sign** to **Positive Sign.**

9. Check the **Natural Application Only** box to only allow amounts to bring the balance to zero. For example, an invoice is a positive amount and only negative amounts may reduce the balance to zero. If the Natural Application box is enabled, the **Allow Overapplication** box can't be enabled. In other words, a receipt can't be applied which would take the invoice balance over its natural (application) balance. A receipt of $200 can't be applied to an $100 invoice because the natural application rule states only a positive amount balance (or zero amount balance) may exist and the invoice may not be overapplied.

10. Select the **Credit Memo Type.**

11. Enter the **Receivables Account.** Any AutoAccounting parameters of Transaction Type will use the applicable segment values.

12. Enter the **Revenue Account.** Any AutoAccounting parameters of Transaction Type will use the applicable segment values.

RECEIVABLES STEP 6.7: TRANSACTION SOURCE

Transaction sources define the invoice batching options. Batching options include the batch numbering scheme, the transaction numbering scheme, and the default transaction type. Oracle Receivables seeds transaction sources. In addition, the Oracle Receivables profiles can set the default transaction source by user (see Exhibit 8.19).

1. From the Receivables menu → **Setup** → **Transactions** → **Sources.**

2. Enter the transaction batch source **Name.**

3. Select the **Type.**

4. Check the **Automatic Batch Numbering** box and enter the **Last Number** used.

5. Check the **Automatic Transaction Numbering** box and enter the **Last Number** used.

6. Select the default **Standard Transaction Type.**

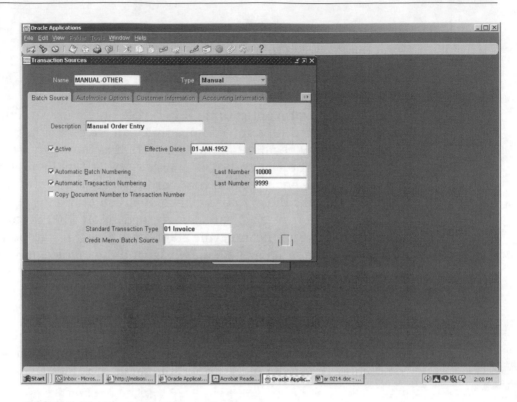

Exhibit 8.19   Receivables Transaction Sources

RECEIVABLES STEP 6.8: COLLECTORS

Collectors are the people who call customers to discuss their overdue accounts (see Exhibit 8.20).

1. From the Receivables menu → **Setup** → **Collections** → **Collectors**.
2. Enter the **Collector Name, Description, Correspondence Name,** and office **Telephone Number.** The Collector name must be unique.

RECEIVABLES STEP 6.9: APPROVAL LIMITS

Approval limits determine the adjustment limits by user (see Exhibit 8.21).

1. From the Receivables menu → **Setup** → **Transactions** → **Approval Limits.**
2. Select the Oracle Applications **Username.**

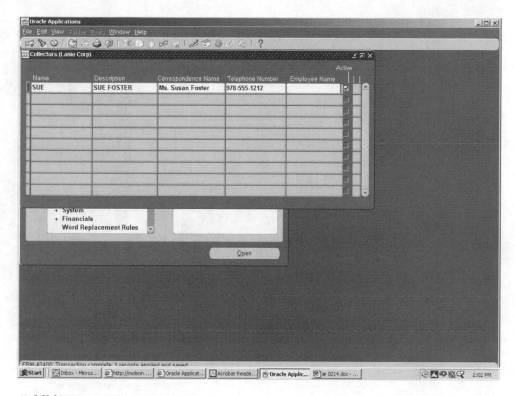

Exhibit 8.20 Collectors

3. Select the **Document Type.** The default **Adjustment** is displayed.
4. Select the **Currency.**
5. Enter the **From** and **To Amounts.** Typically, a negative amount to a positive amount is entered to allow both negative and positive adjustments amounts.

RECEIVABLES STEP 6.10: RECEIVABLE ACTIVITIES

Oracle Receivables uses receivable activities for noninvoice and noncustomer cash receipts, Receivable activities include:

- Adjustments
- Miscellaneous Cash
- Earned and Unearned Discounts

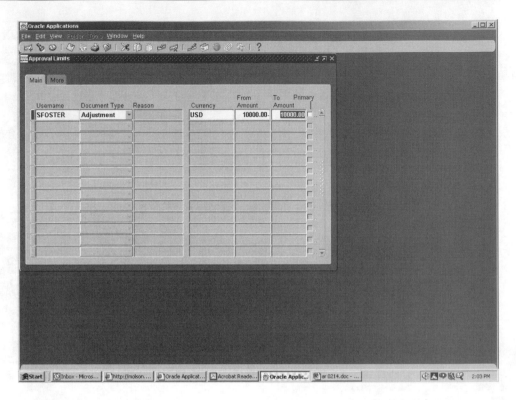

Exhibit 8.21   Approval Limits

- Finance Charges
- Bank Errors

The receivable activity of adjustment is shown in Exhibit 8.22 and involves four steps:

1. From the Receivables menu → **Setup** → **Receipts** → **Receivable Activities.**
2. Enter a receivable activity **Name** and **Description.**
3. Select a **Type** of **Adjustment.**
4. Enter the **Activity GL Account.** The accounting flexfield segment value descriptions are displayed.

Exhibit 8.23 shows the miscellaneous cash receivable activity. The procedure for miscellaneous cash contains four steps:

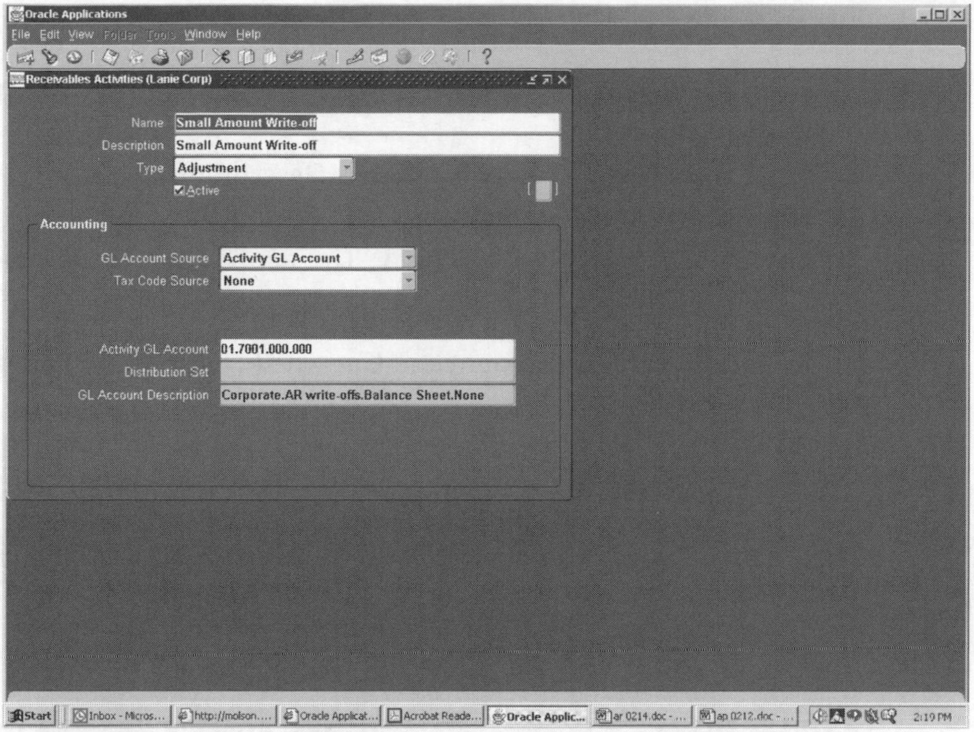

Exhibit 8.22 Receivable Activities: Adjustment

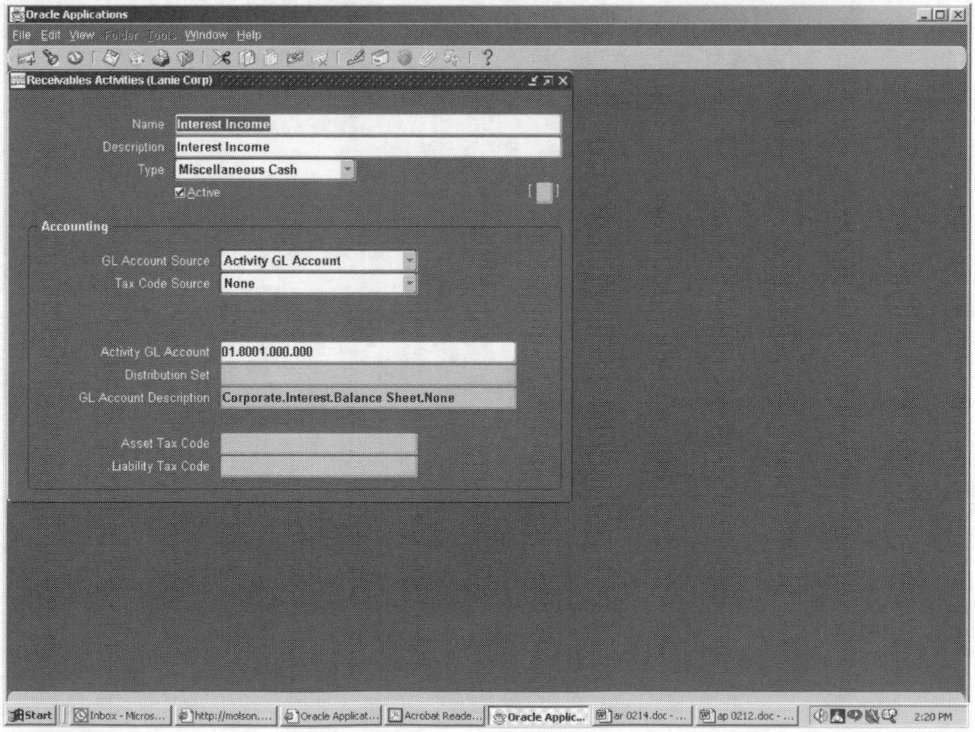

Exhibit 8.23 Receivable Activities: Miscellaneous Cash

1. From the Receivables menu → **Setup** → **Receipts** → **Receivable Activities.**

2. Enter a receivable activity **Name** and **Description.**

3. Select a **Type** of **Miscellaneous Cash.**

4. Enter the **Activity GL Account.** The accounting flexfield segment value descriptions are displayed.

Define the **Earned Discount** and **Unearned Discount** Activities before defining the bank accounts.

RECEIVABLES STEP 6.11: BANK ACCOUNTS

Bank data is shared with Oracle Payables (see Exhibit 8.24). Enter a new Bank or Bank Account following the Oracle Payables setup Step 5.4. For

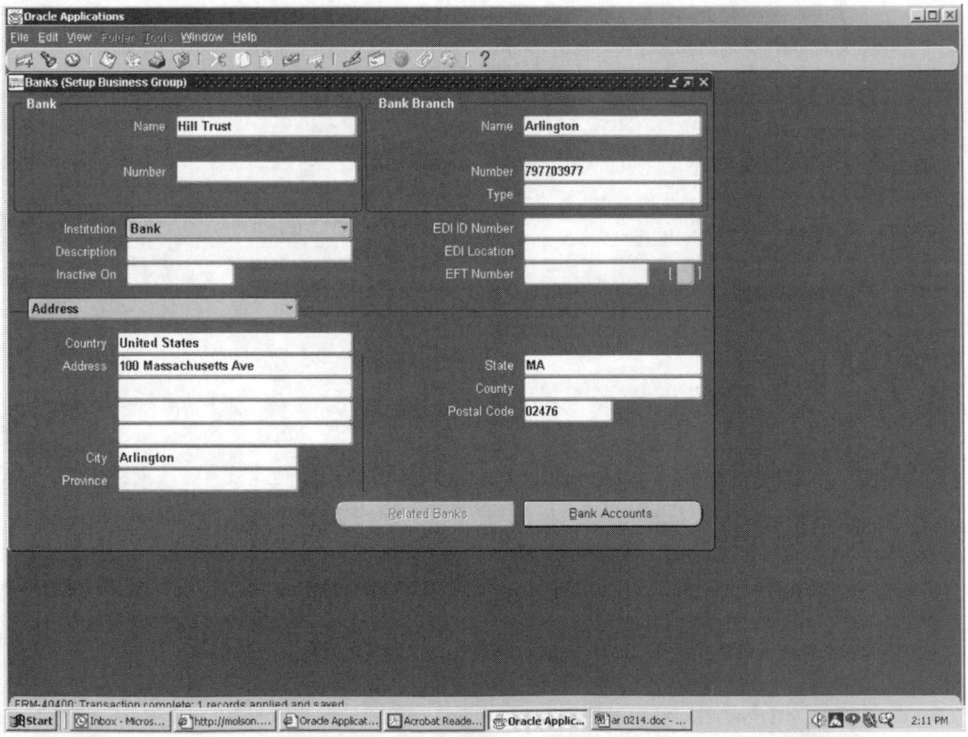

Exhibit 8.24   Banks

Oracle Receivables, enter the specific GL accounts in the More Receivables Options tab.

1. From the Receivables menu → **Setup** → **Receipts** → **Banks.**
2. Query the Bank.
3. Press **Bank Accounts.**

The bank account is Cash and is displayed in the GL Accounts tab (see Exhibit 8.25). Press the **More Receivable Options** tab.

The GL Accounts determine the accounting flexfields used during the journal creation process (see Exhibit 8.26).

Oracle Receivables utilizes a variety of accounting flexfields during the cash receipt process. The Oracle Receivables accounts include:

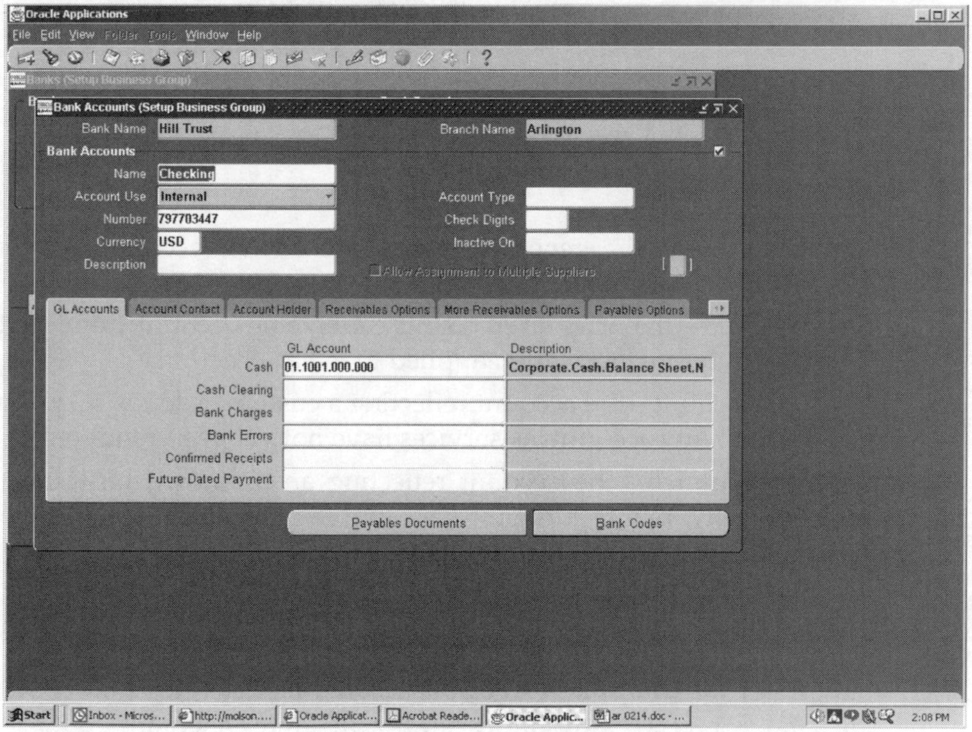

Exhibit 8.25 Bank Accounts

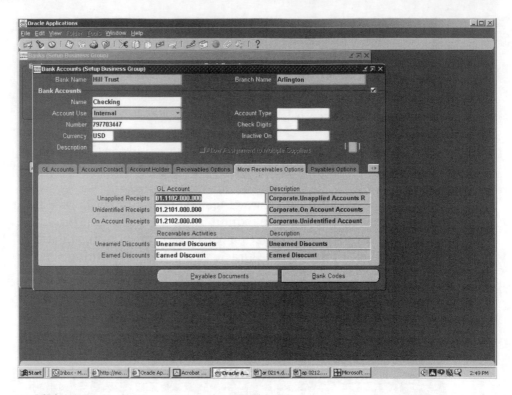

Exhibit 8.26   Bank Accounts: More Receivables Options

- Unapplied—the generic Accounts Receivable account to be credited during the receipt header process.
- Applied—the original Accounts Receivable account from the transaction to be credited when applied to the transaction.
- On Account—the account reflecting a customer deposit. Typically, this is a liability account, as services have not yet been rendered.
- Unidentified—the account reflecting an unknown customer receipt. Typically, this is a liability account, as the organization can't determine the origin.

To access the receivables options, follow these five steps:

1. Enter the **Unapplied Receipts** accounting flexfield.
2. Enter the **Unidentified Receipts** accounting flexfield.
3. Enter the **On Account Receipts** accounting flexfield.

4. Select the **Unearned Discounts** receivable activity defined in Accounts Receivable Step 6.10.

5. Select the **Earned Discounts** receivable activity defined in Accounts Receivable Step 6.10.

RECEIVABLES STEP 6.12: RECEIPT CLASSES AND PAYMENT METHODS

Receipt classes define the receipt methods such as manual receipts or automated receipts (see Exhibit 8.27).

1. From the Receivables menu → **Setup** → **Receipts** → **Receipt Classes**.

2. Enter the Receipt Class **Name**.

3. Select the **Creation Method**.

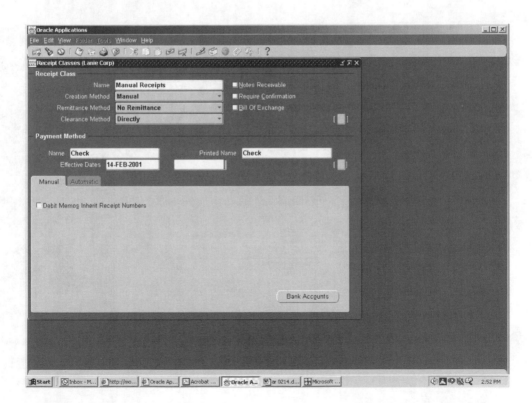

Exhibit 8.27   Receipt Classes

4. Select the **Remittance Method.**

5. Select the **Clearance Method.**

6. Enter the Payment Method **Name.** The Printed Name field will display the same value.

7. Press <u>Bank Accounts.</u>

In the Bank Account window,

1. Select the **Bank Name.**

2. Select the **Account Name.** The system will display the GL Accounts (see Exhibit 8.28).

RECEIVABLES STEP 6.13: RECEIPT SOURCES

The receipt sources define the receipt batching options. Batching options include the batch numbering scheme, the default bank account, and pay-

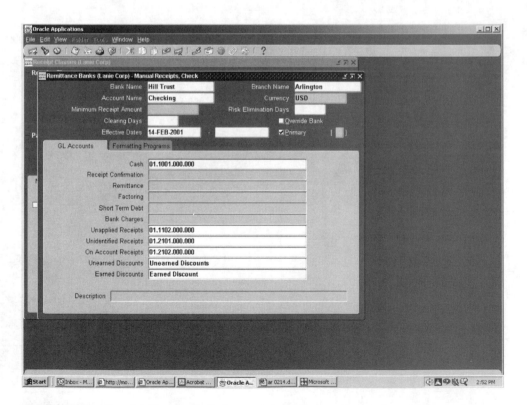

Exhibit 8.28   Receipt Classes: Bank Accounts

ment method. Oracle Receivables seeds receipt sources. In addition, the Oracle Receivables profiles can set the default receipt source by user (see Exhibit 8.29).

1. From the Receivables menu → **Setup** → **Receipts** → **Sources**.
2. Enter the receipt source **Name** and **Description**.
3. Select the **Receipt Source Type** of **Manual** or Automated by highlighting the appropriate option.
4. Select the **Receipt Class**.
5. Select the **Payment Method**.
6. Select the **Bank Account**.
7. Select **Batch Numbering** of Manual or Automatic by highlighting the appropriate option. If Automatic is selected, enter a **Last Number** used.

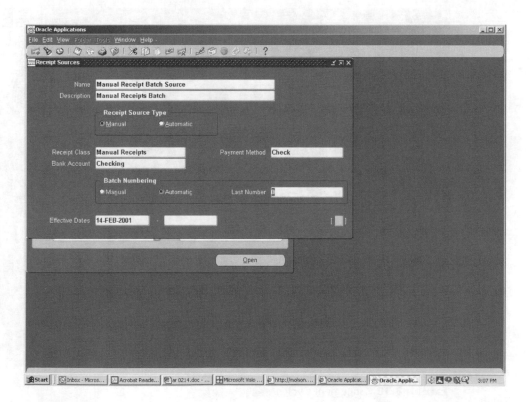

Exhibit 8.29   Receipt Sources

RECEIVABLES STEP 6.14: STATEMENT CYCLES

Statement cycles define the statement print dates. Typically, these are period or quarter end.

1. From the Receivables menu → **Setup** → **Print** → **Statement Cycles.**
2. Enter the statement cycle **Name** and **Description** (see Exhibit 8.30).
3. Select the **Interval.**
4. Enter the **Statement Dates.**
5. Check the Skip box to skip printing statements for the period.
6. Once the statements have been printed for the period, the Date Printed field will display.

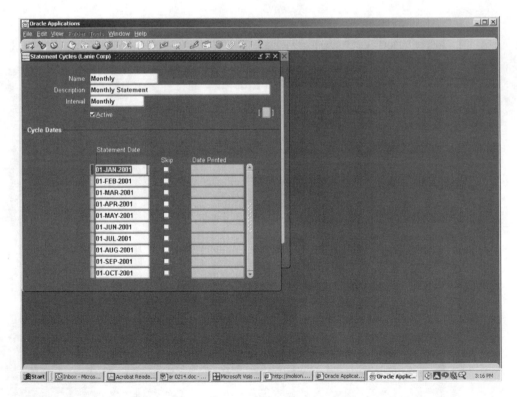

Exhibit 8.30   Statement Cycles

RECEIVABLES STEP 6.15: PROFILE VALUES

The most important Oracle Receivables user profile values are displayed in Exhibit 8.32.

1. From the **File** menu → **Switch Responsibility** → **System Administrator** responsibility.

2. From the System Administrator menu → **Profile** → **System**

3. Enter the **Profile Name** search criteria. Enter **AR%** and press the **Find** button. The system will display all profile values which begin with AR. Note all AR profiles don't begin with an AR prefix.

4. The system displays the query results (see Exhibit 8.31).

 Most Oracle Receivables profile values are not changeable at the user level. Only the System Administrator can change profile values above the user level. The Receivables profile options are discussed in *Oracle Receivables User Guide*, Appendix A.

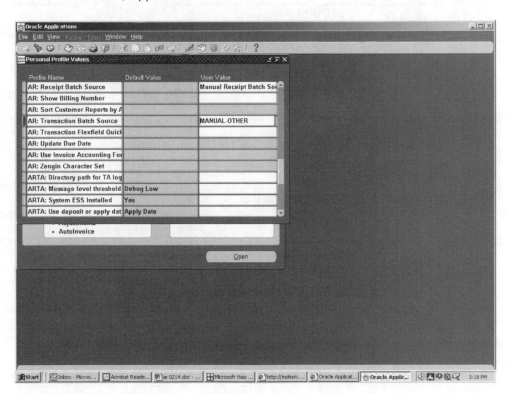

Exhibit 8.31 Receivables Profile Values

RECEIVABLES STEP 6.16: CUSTOMER PROFILE CLASS

The customer credit profile, set up during system definition, determines the credit process performed during the order entry process. Credit limits are set by currency, by order amount, and by total credit limit amount. Credit checking can occur at order entry or prior to pick release. Refer to the *Oracle Order Entry User Guide* for more information.

Either use the seeded DEFAULT profile class or define your own. If using the DEFAULT profile class, query the record and change the processing options as applicable.

1. From the **File** menu → **Switch Responsibility** → **AR Corporate Super User** responsibility.
2. From the Receivables menu → **Customers** → **Profile Classes.**

Profile	Use
AR: Cash Allow Actions	Allows entry of adjustments or chargebacks during cash receipt entry.
AR: Cash Default Amount Applied	Defaults the amount of unapplied cash in the cash receipts application window.
AR: Change Customer Name	Allows maintenance and changing of customer names.
AR: Change Customer on Transactions	Allows changing the customer on a transaction even after the transaction has been printed or had activities.
AR: Override Adjustment Activity	Allows the accounting flexfield to be overridden during adjustment data entry.
AR: Receipt Batch Source	Defaults the batch source during cash receipt entry.
AR: Transaction Batch Source	Defaults the batch source during invoice and credit memo entry.
AR: Update Due Date	Allows the invoice due date to be changed during invoice maintenance.
AR: Use Invoice Accounting for Credit Memos	Use the invoice accounting flexfields as the default values for the credit memo.
HZ: Generate Contact Number	Automatically numbers the customer contact.
HZ: Generate Party Number	Automatically numbers the customer party number.
HZ: Generate Party Site Number	Automatically numbers the customer party site number.
Indicate Attachments	Change to No per the User Guide.

Exhibit 8.32 Receivables Profile Values Uses

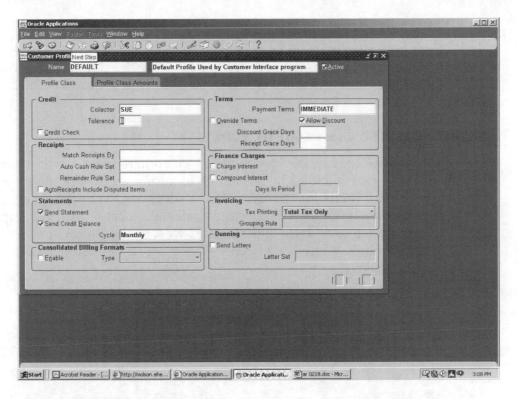

Exhibit 8.33   Customer Profile Classes: Profile

3. Query to retrieve the seeded Customer Profile Class Name of **DE-FAULT.**

4. Select the default **Collector.**

5. Check the **Send Statement** box to send statements.

6. Check the **Send Credit Balance** box to send statements with a credit balance.

7. Select the statement **Cycle.**

8. Select the default **Payment Terms.**

9. Uncheck the **Charge Interest** box.

10. The system will prompt for the update methodology. Select "Update All Profiles" as no customers have been defined.

RECEIVABLES STEP 6.17: CUSTOMERS

Customer sites must be set up before the specific Remit-To Address locations by state may be defined (see Exhibit 8.34). See the Customers section of this chapter for detailed customer data entry procedures.

RECEIVABLES STEP 6.18: REMIT-TO ADDRESSES

The Remit-To addresses define where customers should send their cash receipts (see Exhibit 8.35). The Remit-To addresses may represent a lockbox or may represent the organization's location. Multiple Remit-To addresses may be defined. For example, all states east of the Mississippi go to one Remit-To address and all states west of the Mississippi go to another Remit-To address. Customer sites must be defined before the State may be selected.

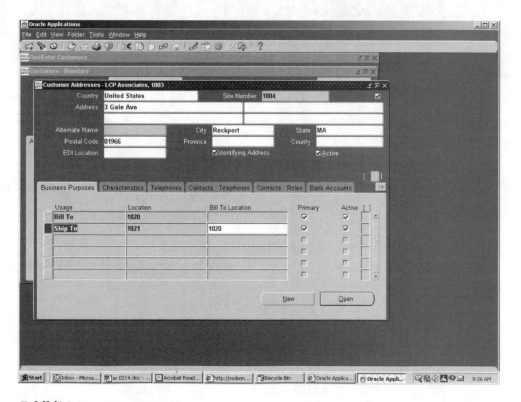

Exhibit 8.34   Customers

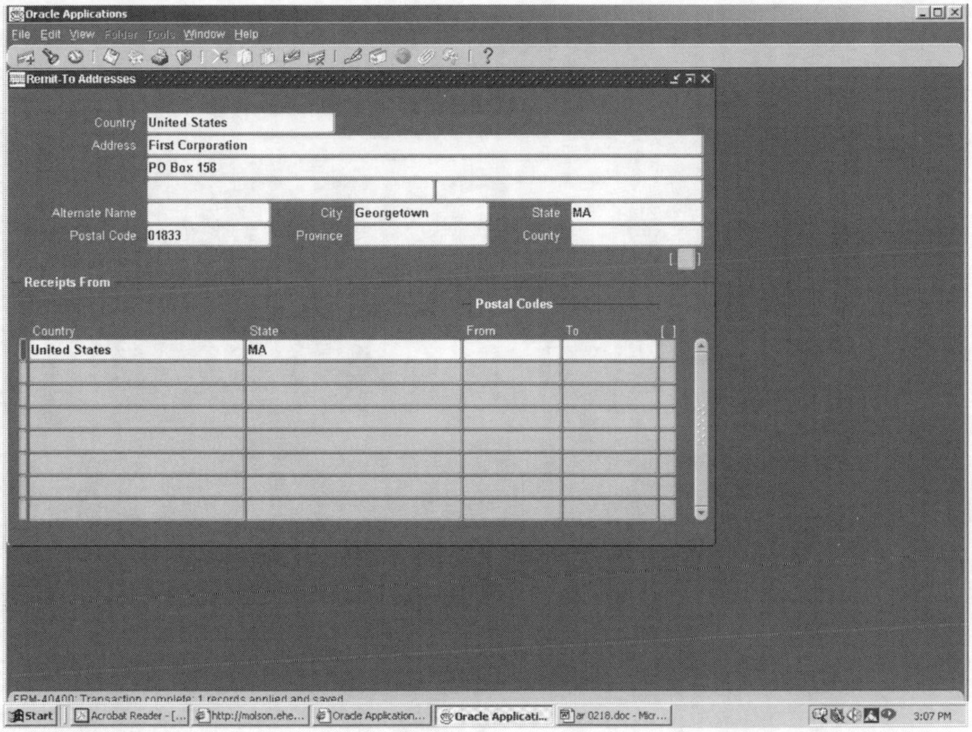

Exhibit 8.35   Remit-To Addresses

1. From the Receivables menu → **Setup** → **Print** → **Remit-To Addresses.**
2. Select the default **Country.**
3. Enter the **Remit-To Address, City, State,** and **Postal Code** fields.
4. Select the customer **Country** for this remit-to address. Specific states cannot be selected until a customer site record with the state has been defined.

RECEIVABLES STEP 6.19: (STANDARD) MEMO LINES

Standard memo lines speed transaction data entry by creating regularly used or standard transaction lines (see Exhibit 8.36). The standard memo lines may be selected from the List of Values in the transaction line description field.

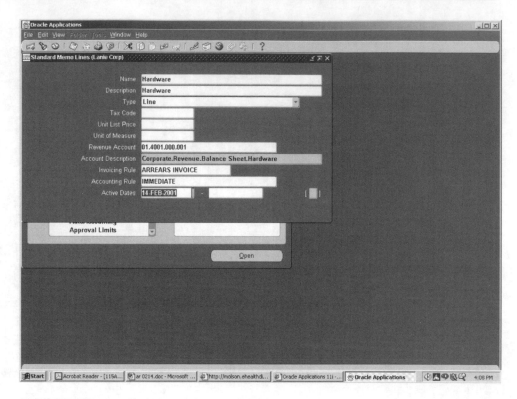

Exhibit 8.36 Standard Memo Lines

1. From the Receivables menu → **Setup** → **Transactions** → **Memo Lines.**

2. Enter the memo line **Name** and **Description.**

3. Select the **Type** of **Line.**

4. Enter the **Revenue Account** if AutoAccounting uses Standard (memo) Lines as source.

5. Select the **Invoicing Rule.** Invoicing rules define when the receivable is recorded.

6. Select the **Accounting Rule.** Accounting rules determine the revenue recognition periods. Typically, an organization sets the accounting rule to recognize the revenue immediately that, in turn, will recognize the receivable as well.

RECEIVABLES STEP 6.20: TAX CODES

Tax codes must be defined for the miscellaneous cash data entry process (see Exhibit 8.37).

1. From the Receivables menu → **Setup** → **Tax** → **Codes.**
2. Enter the tax code **Name.**
3. Select the **Tax Type.**
4. Select the **Taxable Basis.**
5. Enter the **Tax Rate.**

CUSTOMERS

Customer and customer sites define the customer name and address information to bill customers goods and services rendered. Minimally, cus-

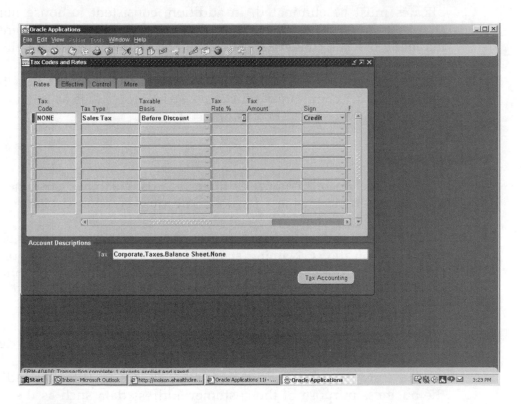

Exhibit 8.37 Tax Codes

tomer records have three components: a customer record, a customer site record, and a customer site business purpose record.

The one-customer-to-many-customer-sites architecture allows one customer record to have one or more site records. Understanding and utilizing the one-customer-to-many-customer-sites concept is critical for Oracle Receivables to run as efficiently and effectively as possible. Strict in-house naming standards, customer verification procedures, and data entry procedures will improve the Oracle Receivables system and in-house business processes.

Customer and customer site records may be converted or imported. A review of the active customer and address records in the legacy system should occur. The number of records should determine if the customer conversion process is manual or automated. Both conversion strategies require users to clean the data. The current customer data must be extracted and the users must review the data. The one-customer-to-many-customer-sites architecture must be established and duplicates must be eliminated. In addition, consistent in-house naming standards must be applied. Then the customer data may be entered manually or via a conversion program. Fortunately, there is a delivered customer interface. However, the customer conversion program must still be written in-house or delivered by a consulting organization. In addition, the user community must have strict procedures as to what system owns the customer and customer site data.

Customer Record

The customer record comprises three records: customer, customer site, and customer site business purpose. All must be defined before a customer transaction can occur (see Exhibit 8.38.)

The first record is the customer record. The customer record is shared by all organizations. Naming standards must reflect this level of data sharing. The customer data defaults to all sites during data entry, but only during the initial data entry.

The second record is the customer site record. The customer site is specific by individual operating unit organization in a multi-org environment. The customer site defines the address component and the default data applies only to the specific site.

The third record is the customer site use record. This data indicates the business purpose of the customer address data such as the bill-to address or the ship-to address data. The appropriate site will appear in

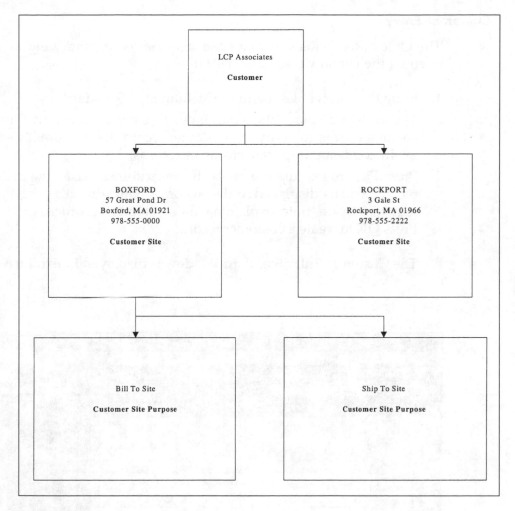

Exhibit 8.38 Customer Site Architecture

the List of Values during data entry. For example, in the bill-to customer site field, only the sites with a business purpose of Bill To will
display.

 Some of the Oracle Receivables table names start with the prefix "RA"
because prior releases of Oracle Receivables included the Oracle Revenue
Accounting (RA) application which is now included within the Oracle
Receivables application.

Customer Entry

The Oracle Receivables displays the customer entry find window when opening the window (see Exhibit 8.39).

1. From the Receivables menu → **Customers** → **Standard.**
2. The system displays the Find/Enter Customers window. Enter the customer name to verify the customer record doesn't already exist to avoid accidental duplicate customer records.
3. Press **F̱ind** to execute the query. If the customer exists, the matching records will be displayed. If the customer name doesn't exist, the system displays a note explaining the customer record doesn't exist. Press **O̱K** to create a customer record.

   The Customer Entry Standard Window is displayed in Exhibit 8.40.

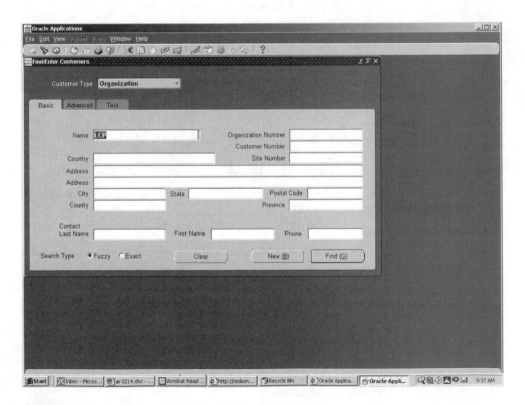

Exhibit 8.39   Customer Entry: Existing Customer

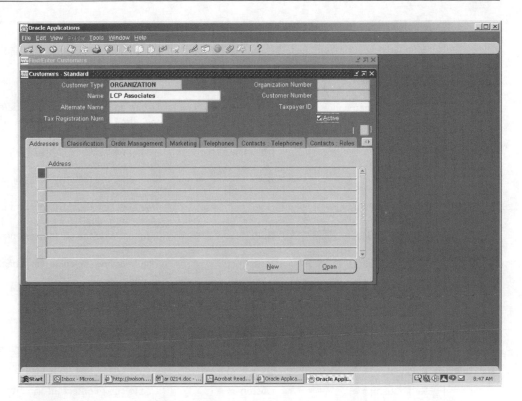

Exhibit 8.40 Customer Entry: Standard Window

1. Enter the **Customer Name.**
2. Leave the **Customer Number** blank to have the system generate the customer number. Otherwise, enter a Customer Number. Duplicate customer numbers are not allowed.
3. Press **New** to enter a new customer address.

 The System Options determine the customer numbering scheme.

Data entered at the customer level will cascade down to the site level during the initial definition process. Once a site has been established, changing the customer level record will not change the site level values. Each site must be modified individually after initial setup. See Exhibit 8.41 for a list of all the customer and customer site windows.

Optional Windows	Customer/Site Level	Use
Addresses	Customer	Use to define customer sites and site uses.
Classification	Customer	Use to define profile class and sales reps.
Order Management	Customer	Use to define the order entry defaults including order type, price list, and shipping information.
Marketing	Customer	Use to define customer data for marketing analysis.
Telephones	Both	Use to define the customer phone numbers.
Contact: Telephones	Both	Use to define the customer contact phone numbers.
Contact: Roles	Both	Use to define the customer contact positions.
Bank Accounts	Both	Use to define the customer's bank account.
Payment Method	Both	Use to define the payment method.
Profile: Transaction	Both	Use to define the profile class including the collector and the payment terms.
Profile: Document Printing	Both	Use to define if statements and/or dunning letters are sent.
Profile: Amounts	Both	Use to define the credit limits.
Relationships	Customer	Use to enter contact information.
Business Purpose	Site	Use to define the business need for the site such as a ship-to location or bill-to location.
Characteristics	Site	Use to define the territory flexfield for the site.

Exhibit 8.41   Customer/Customer Sites Windows

Exhibit 8.42 shows the Business Purpose Window under Customer Address.

1. In the Business Purposes tab, enter the **Customer Address.** The sales tax location flexfield structure selected in the System Options definition process will determine the required fields, such as county or postal code.

2. The **Country** defaults from the System Options.

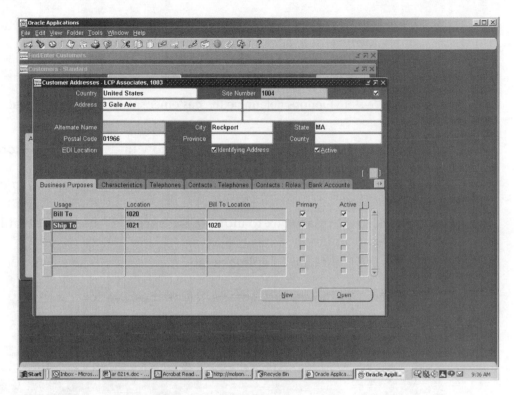

Exhibit 8.42 Customer Address Window: Business Purpose

3. Leave the **Site Number** blank to have the system generate the customer number. Otherwise, enter a Site Number. Duplicate customer numbers are not allowed.

4. The **Site Number** will be generated automatically if auto-numbering has been enabled. Otherwise, enter a Site Number.

5. Enter the **Address**, up to four lines. Enter the **City, State,** and **Postal Code.**

6. Check the **Identifying Address** box.

7. In the Business Purposes tab, select the **Bill To** usage. Minimally, a Bill To site must be entered to create transactions. In addition, the Ship To site references the Bill To Locations. Therefore, set up the Bill To location first and save the record. Then enter the Ship To address information. Oracle Receivables seeds business purposes, but additional values may be defined during system setup as a new Oracle Receivables Lookup Code.

8. Check the **Primary** box to have the customer site default in the data entry forms where site data is referenced. Save the record.

9. Press the **Telephones** tab.

 The System Options determine the customer site numbering scheme.

Exhibit 8.43 shows the telephones window under Customer Address.

1. Enter the customer site **Area Code, Telephone Number,** and telephone **Type.**

2. Check the **Primary** box to indicate this record is the site's default telephone information.

3. Press the **Contacts: Telephones** tab.

Exhibit 8.44 shows the Contacts Telephones window.

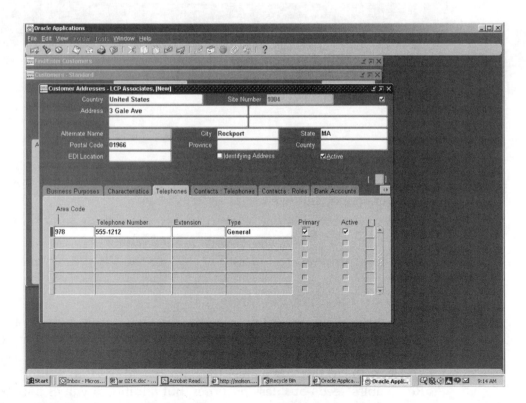

Exhibit 8.43   Customer/Addresses: Telephones Window

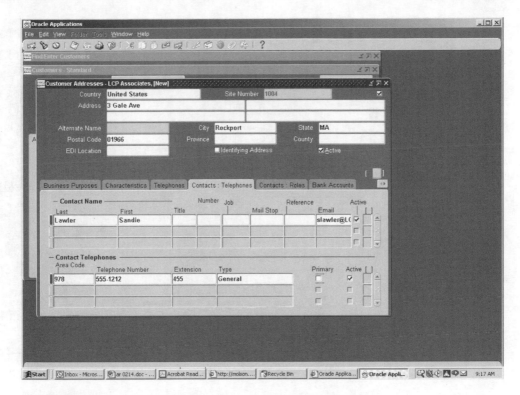

Exhibit 8.44   Customer Addresses: Contacts Telephones Window

1. Enter the **Last Name** and **First Name** of the customer site contact. Personnel at the site may include Accounts Payable personnel with whom the overdue account is discussed.

2. Enter the **Area Code** and **Telephone Number** of the contact.

3. Press the → to view the other Customer Address tabs.

4. Press the **Profile: Transaction** tab.

Oracle Receivables provides a DEFAULT profile class (see Exhibit 8.45).

1. The DEFAULT Customer **Profile Class** is displayed. Select another customer profile class if necessary.

2. Change the Profile: Transaction options to override the customer profile values. For example, enter the appropriate collector name.

3. Press the **Profile: Document Printing** tab.

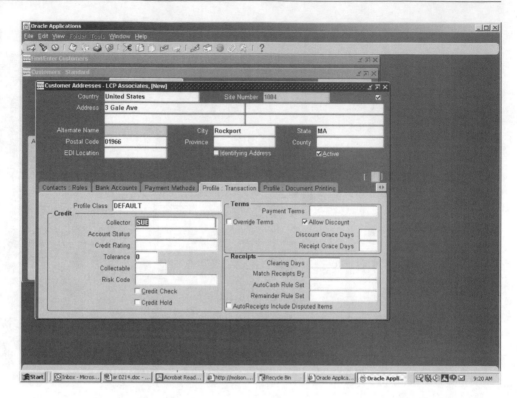

Exhibit 8.45   Customer Addresses: Transaction

Change the Customer Profile: Document Printing options to override the customer profile values. For example, select a different statement cycle (see Exhibit 8.46).

INVOICES

Oracle Receivables invoice process records the organization's billing for goods and services provided to customers. The typical Oracle Receivables transaction types include:

- Invoices
- Credit Memos
- Adjustments
- Chargebacks

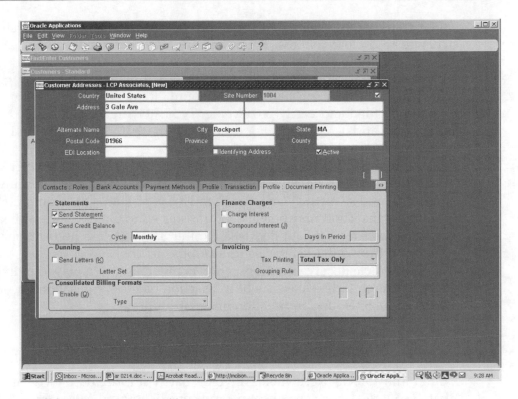

Exhibit 8.46 Customer Addresses: Document Printing

Invoices may be manually entered or automatically loaded via Oracle Receivables AutoInvoice process. AutoInvoice is used to load invoices from Oracle Order Entry as well as from an external billing system. AutoInvoice is an Oracle Receivables' open interface program and documented in the *Oracle Receivables User Guide*.

Credit memos represent the reduction of a transaction. Oracle Receivables credit memos may be applied to an invoice or entered as an on-account credit memo. On-account credit memos should be applied to an invoice to close the transaction.

Adjustments also represent an activity to an invoice such as a small amount write-off. Adjustments may increment or decrement the transaction. In addition, adjustments may be entered and have to go through an approval process based on the user approval limits.

Manually entered transactions should use transaction batches to ensure the financial integrity of the data entry process. Follow in-house transaction processing procedures. The control transaction count and the total transaction amount must balance before the transaction batch will change to a closed status. Break batches into reasonably sized batches. Count the number of transactions and amount of transactions. During the transaction data entry process, enter the batch name, if manually generated, and the control count and amount. Remember, the batch name should be filed and easily retrievable. Typically, organizations file by period name and batch name. For example, FEB-01 1001 where FEB-01 is the period name and 1001 is the batch name.

All manually entered transactions must run through an invoice completion process. The complete invoice process validates the dates, invoice amounts, and so forth. A transaction must have a status of "Complete" before the transaction may be viewed, transferred to Oracle General Ledger, or have cash receipts applied (see Exhibit 8.47). Online invoices may be imported from outside Oracle applications.

The Oracle Receivables transaction architecture is displayed in Exhibit 8.48. The architecture consists of transaction batches, transaction headers, transaction lines, and transaction line distributions.

Invoice Entry

Enter the Oracle Receivables invoice batch information including the batch source, dates, control count, and control amount (see Exhibit 8.49).

1. From the Receivables menu → **Transactions** → **Batches.**
2. The transaction **Source** name defaults from the AR: Transaction Source profile option. Select a new Source if necessary.
3. If the transaction source options indicate automatic batch numbering, the batch **Number** will be created when the record is saved. If the transaction source options indicate manual batch numbering, a unique batch Number must be entered.
4. The **Batch Date, GL Date,** and **Period** default to the system date. If the Oracle Receivables period doesn't have an Open status, the GL Date and Period must be entered.
5. The **Status** of New indicates a new batch. The Status will change to Open when transactions are entered, and Closed when the Control Count and Amount equal the Actual Count and Amount.
6. Enter the **Control Count** for the batch.
7. Enter the **Control Amount** for the batch.
8. Press **Transactions.**

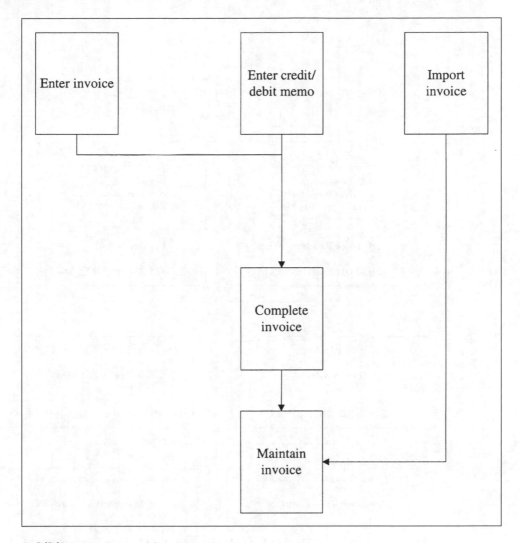

Exhibit 8.47 Receivables Transaction Process

Enter the Oracle Receivables invoice header information including the batch source, dates, control count, and control amount (see Exhibit 8.50).

1. If the transaction source options indicate automatic transaction numbering, the transaction **Number** will be created when the record is saved. If the transaction source options indicate manual

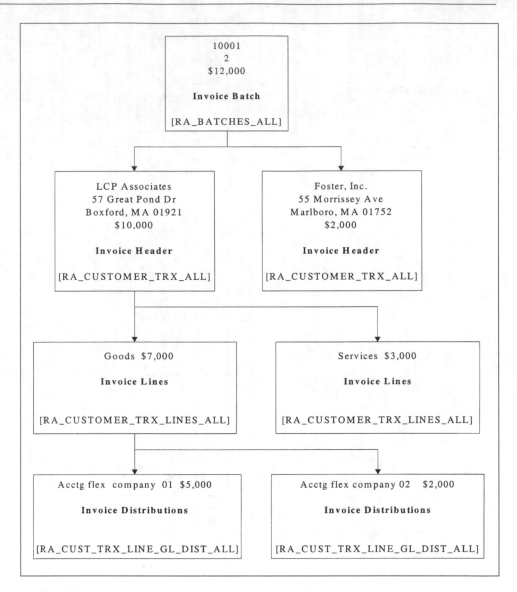

Exhibit 8.48 Invoice Architecture

transaction numbering, a unique transaction Number must be entered.

2. The **Invoice Date** will default to the system date.
3. In the Main tab, select the customer **Name** in the Bill To region. The primary customer site bill to address will default.
4. Press **Line Items** to enter the transaction lines.

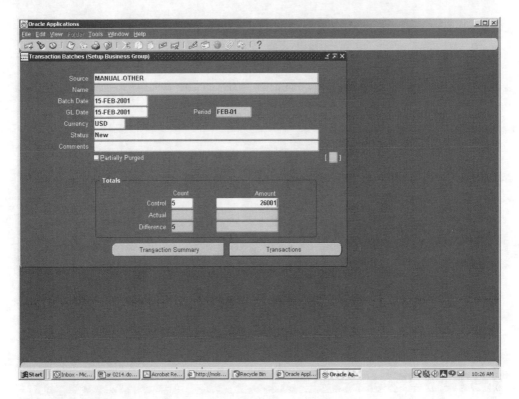

Exhibit 8.49 Invoice Batch

Line Items

1. In the Main tab, the line **Num**ber 1 defaults (see Exhibit 8.51).

2. Select the **Description** to choose a standard memo line. Otherwise, enter the transaction line description. AutoAccounting uses standard memo lines to build the distribution accounting flexfields.

3. Enter the **Quantity**.

4. Enter the **Unit Price**.

5. The system displays the Amount field which is calculated by multiplying the Quantity by the Unit Price.

6. Press **Distributions** to enter or review the accounting flexfields for the transaction. If all the segment values have been determined by AutoAccounting, review the accounting flexfield distributions. If AutoAccounting has not built all the segment values, the remaining segment values must be entered.

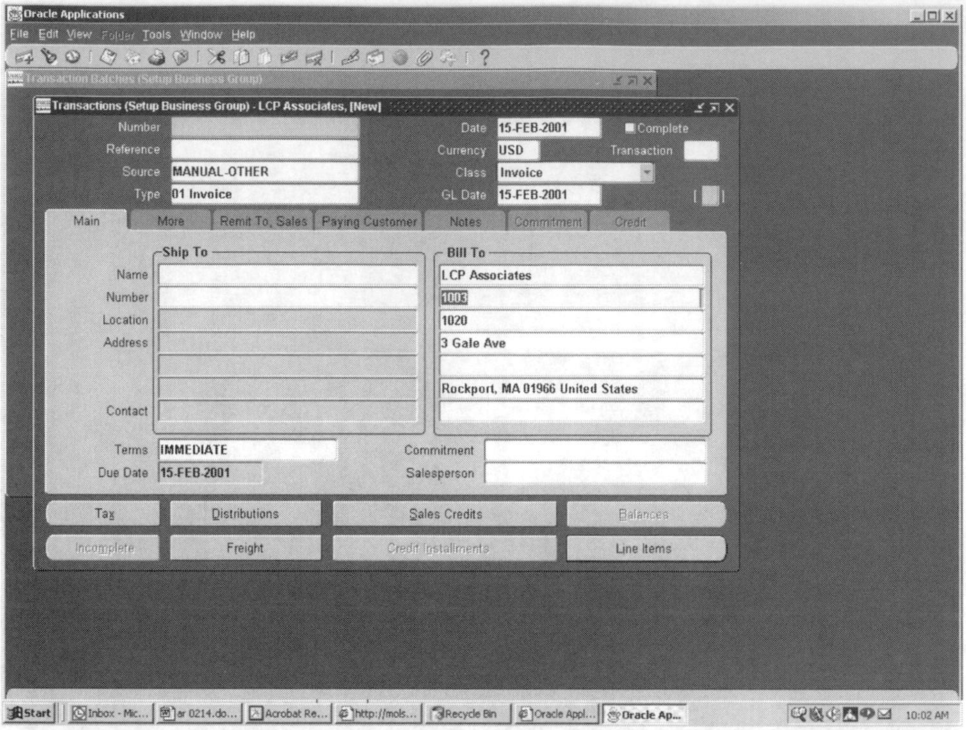

Exhibit 8.50 Invoice Header

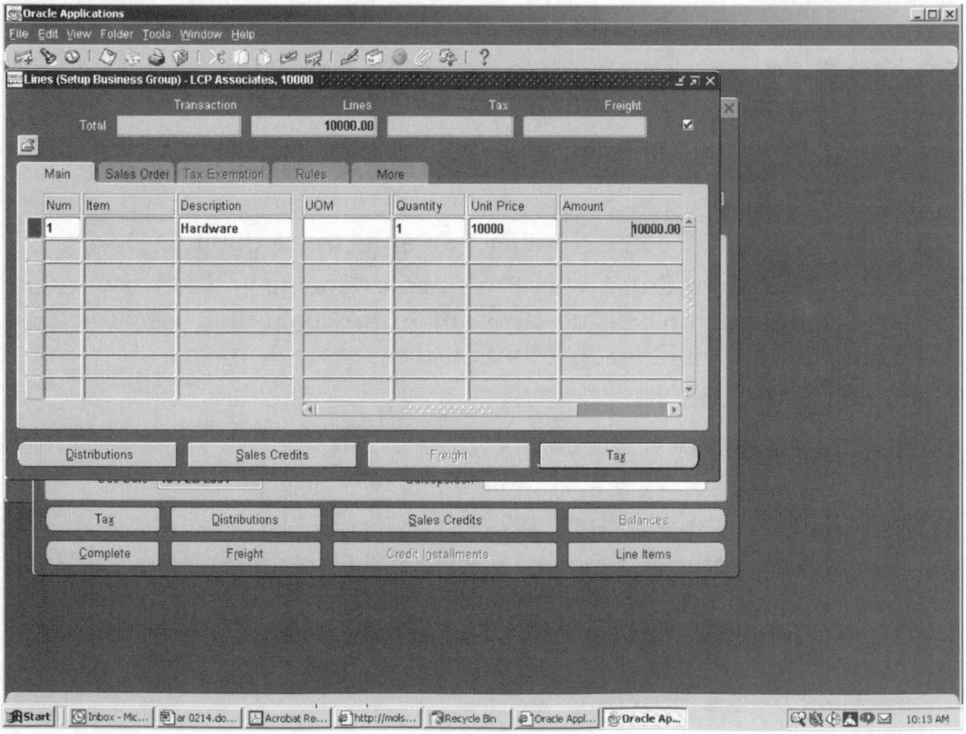

Exhibit 8.51 Invoice Line Items

1. By default, the form displays the revenue **Accounts For This Line** (see Exhibit 8.52). Valid accounting flexfields must be created for each journal line before an invoice may be completed and passed to Oracle General Ledger.

2. Optionally, choose the **All Accounts** option to see the balanced Oracle General Ledger journal transactions by account Class.

3. Return to the Transaction Header window to "Complete" the invoice. Invoices must be completed before they will be available for viewing and receipt application. All invoices must be reapproved after corrections or modifications have been entered.

Press **Complete** to enable the transaction for inquiry and receipts application (see Exhibit 8.53).

The Complete box in the upper right-hand corner of the window

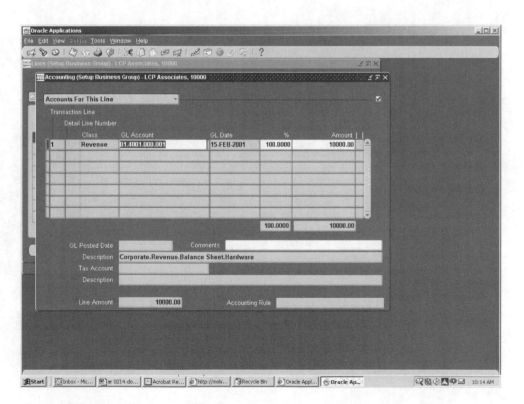

Exhibit 8.52 Invoice Line Distributions

should be checked, indicating the invoice is complete. In addition, the Complete button should now display "Incomplete."

CREDIT MEMOS

Oracle Receivables provides both credit memos and debit memos. Oracle Receivables credit memos represent reductions to transactions. Remember, Oracle Receivables is an open-item receivable system, so credit memos are applied to the invoice to close the transaction. In addition Oracle Receivables provides on-account credit memos. Eventually, these on-account credit memos are applied to invoice transactions.

In addition, if Oracle Order Entry is installed, an RMA may be linked to the original order and therefore the original Oracle Receivables transac-

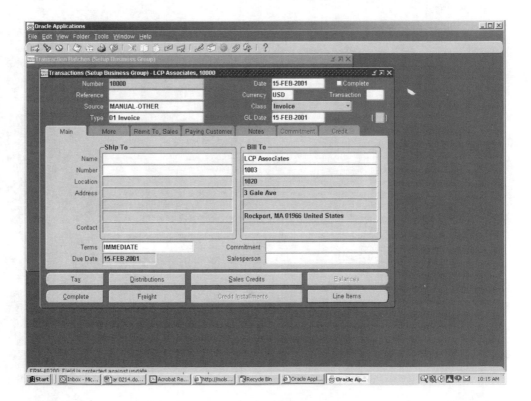

Exhibit 8.53 Invoice Completion

tion. The order to invoice link will continue through the RMA process. The credit memo received through AutoInvoice will reference the RMA and be applied to the original invoice.

Adjustments

Oracle Receivables provides adjustments to transactions. These adjustments may increment or decrement the original transaction. In other words, they may add or subtract from the original transaction balance. In addition, adjustments may be manual or automatic. User-defined adjustment amounts may be set as a run-time parameter to determine the potential adjustments. Furthermore, personnel may be given approval limits (Receivables Step 6.9). Pending adjustments and rejected adjustments must be monitored and addressed. Examples of typical adjustments include small amount write-offs, tax adjustments, and freight adjustments.

Chargebacks

Oracle Receivables provides chargebacks to close the original transaction and create a new transaction. Think of chargebacks as another transaction type as they have their own source and numbering schemes.

Credit Memo Entry

1. From the Receivables menu → **Transactions** → **Credit Transactions**
2. The Find Transaction window opens (see Exhibit 8.54).
3. Enter the invoice transaction **Number** to match to the credit memo.
4. Press **Find**.

The credit memo header links to the original transaction.

1. The original invoice transaction will be displayed (see Exhibit 8.55).
2. Enter the **Credit Memo %** or **Amount** to credit the invoice.
3. Press **Credit Lines.**

Credit memo line items represent the detail goods and services being billed to the customer.

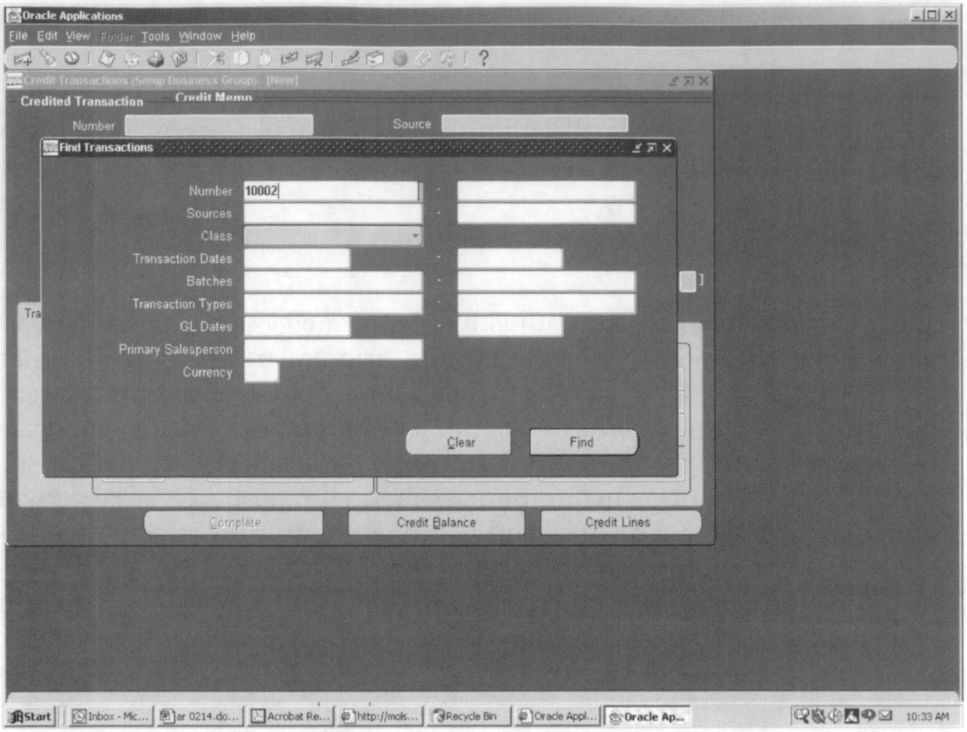

Exhibit 8.54 Credit Memo Match to an Invoice

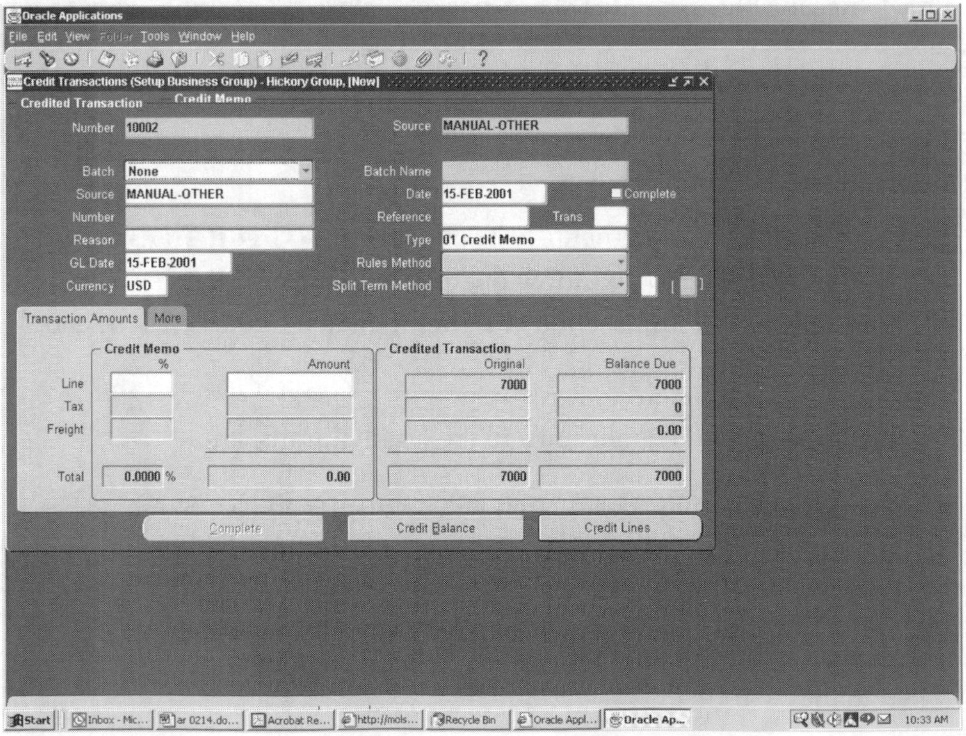

Exhibit 8.55 Credit Memo Header

1. Enter the credit memo line **Number, Description**, and a negative **Amount** (see Exhibit 8.56).

2. Press **Distributions** to review or enter the accounting flexfield distributions.

Return to the credit memo transaction window.

1. Press **Complete** to enable the transaction for inquiry and receipts application (see Exhibit 8.57).

The Complete box in the upper right-hand corner of the window should be checked, indicating the credit memo is complete. In addition, the Complete button should now display "Incomplete."

On-Account Credit Memo

1. From the Receivables menu → **Transactions** → **Transactions.**

2. Enter the On-account credit memo header just as with any other transaction.

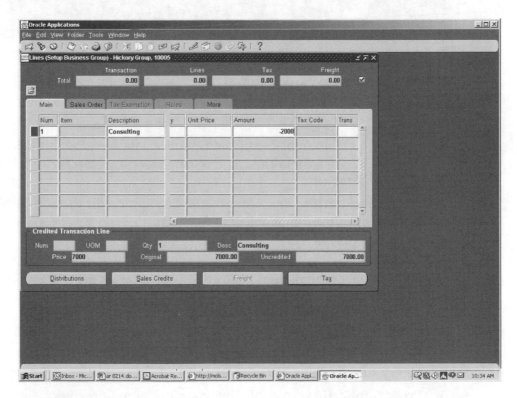

Exhibit 8.56   Credit Memo Lines

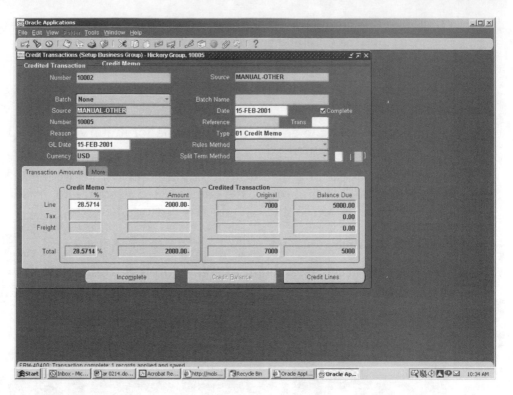

Exhibit 8.57   Credit Memo Complete

3. Enter the On-account credit memo lines data (see Exhibit 8.58). The line **Num**ber will default to 1. Select or enter the **Description.** Enter a negative **Amount.**

4. Press **Distributions** and enter the on-account credit memo line **Num**ber, **Description,** and a negative **Amount.**

5. Return to the invoice header window and press **Complete.**

On-account credit memos should be applied to an invoice transaction, when appropriate.

1. From the Receivables menu → **Transactions** → **Transactions Summary.**

2. Query the on-account credit memo (see Exhibit 8.59).

3. Press **Applications** to apply the on-account credit memo.

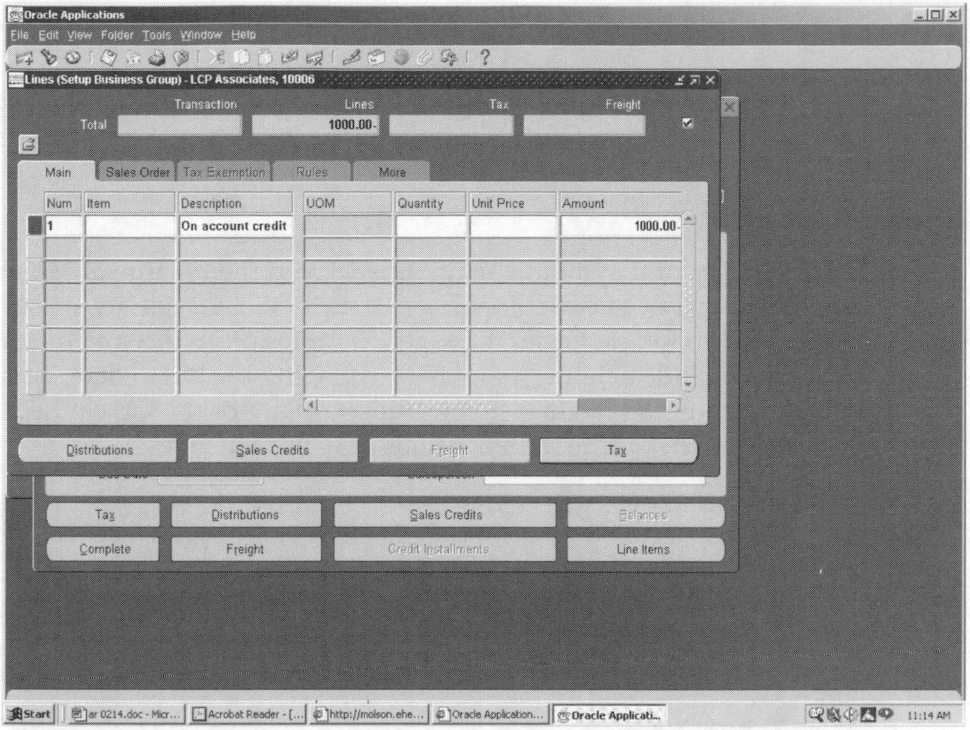

Exhibit 8.58   On Account Credit Memo Lines

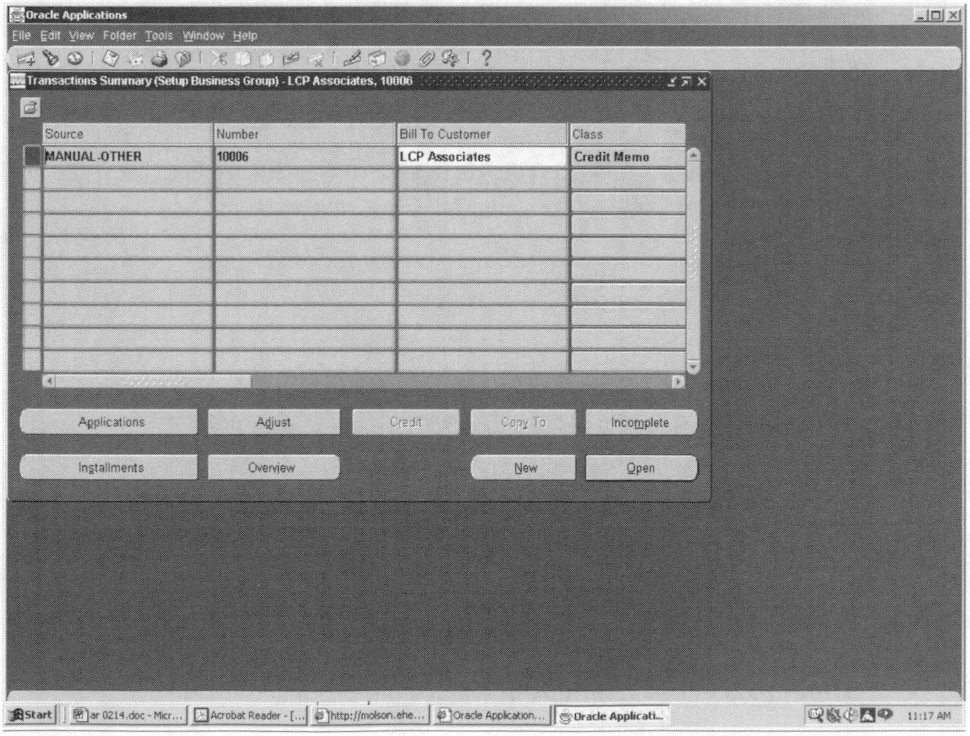

Exhibit 8.59   On Account Credit Memo Application to an Invoice

Check the **Apply** box to apply the on-account credit memo (see Exhibit 8.60).

Invoice Maintenance

Invoices may or may not be maintained given their status of "Complete," whether they have been printed, whether they have activity, or have been transferred to Oracle General Ledger. Samples of invoice maintenance capabilities include deleting an invoice, changing the bill to data, and updating the accounting flexfields. In addition, many of the Oracle Receivables System Options dictate if transactions may be changed.

 Review *Oracle Receivables User Guide*, Maintaining Transactions, for the complete invoice maintenance list.

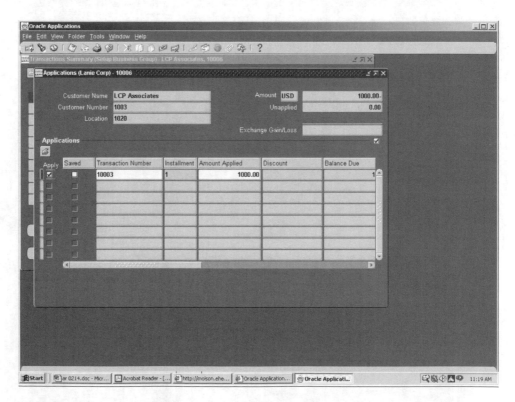

Exhibit 8.60   On Account Credit Memo Applied to an Invoice

PRINTING

Oracle Receivables prints invoices, credit memos, dunning letters, and statements.

Predefined print formats are provided, but typically organizations modify these print formats to conform with their in-house formats. These format changes can include company logos, removal of tax information, and so on.

Printing Transactions

Invoice print is run as an Oracle Receivables Standard Report Submission (SRS) concurrent program (see Exhibit 8.61). Print the invoices to the appropriate printer following in-house procedures.

1. From the Receivables menu → **Print Documents** → **Invoices.**
2. Select the **Invoice Print** program.

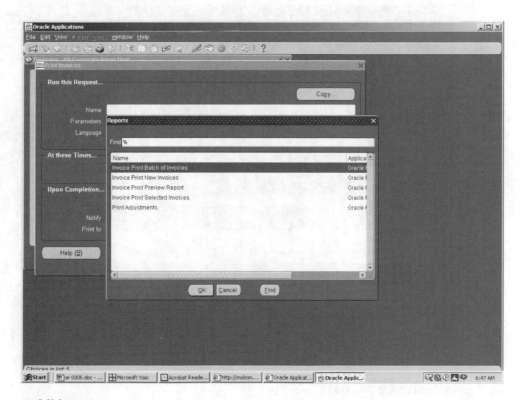

Exhibit 8.61 Printing Transactions

3. Select the **Invoice Print** parameters.

4. Press **Submit** to submit the Invoice Print concurrent request. Follow in-house invoice print procedures.

Printing Statements

If the customer Profile determines statements are to be sent, the Print Statements concurrent process should be run according to the statement cycle (see Exhibit 8.62).

1. From the Receivables menu → **Print Documents** → **Statements**.

2. Select the statement **Option**.

3. Select the statement aging **Bucket**.

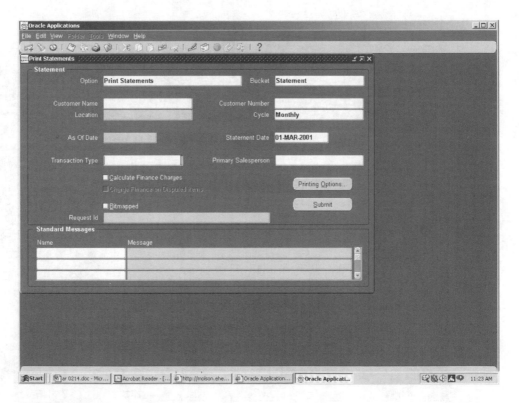

Exhibit 8.62 Printing Statements

4. Select the **Statement Cycle** as defined in Accounts Receivable Step 6.14.

5. Press **Submit** to submit the concurrent request. Follow in-house statement print procedures.

RECEIPTS

Oracle Receivables provides a variety of receipt methods. Receipts methods include manual receipts and automated receipt runs, such as lockbox. Lockbox processing has the customers remit their payments to a bank's lockbox. The bank deposits the checks. In addition, in a manual lockbox environment, the bank makes a copy of the checks and remittance advices. The bank forwards the copies to the organization for data entry into the Oracle Receivables system.

Alternatively, Oracle Receivables provides automatic lockbox processing. The bank sends a file detailing the remittance data including the customer, invoice number, amount, and so forth. Oracle Receivables must be configured to accept automatic lockbox processing. In addition, the programming staff must develop the programs to load and accept the bank file.

In conjunction with lockbox processing, Oracle Receivables provides AutoCash processing. The user-defined order of AutoCash rules have Oracle Receivables determine how to apply the receipt. For example, first try to automatically match the receipt to the invoice based on amount, and second try to apply the receipt to the oldest invoice.

Oracle Receivables utilizes a variety of accounting flexfields during the customer cash receipt process. The Oracle Receivables receipt statuses include:

- Unapplied
- Applied

Oracle Receivables creates two journal transactions for each customer cash receipt applied to a transaction. The first journal transaction records the cash and the unapplied receivable account. For example:

Dr Cash
    Cr Unapplied Receivable

The second journal transaction records the application of the receipt to the invoice Receivable account and the reversal of the unapplied accounts receivable account. For example:

Dr Unapplied Receivable
        Cr Accounts Receivable (from the actual invoice having receipt applied)

Noncustomer cash receipts, such as investment income or an employee return of an employee advance, are considered miscellaneous receipts. They are not applied to a customer or customer transaction.

The Oracle Receivables cash receipts business flow is depicted in Exhibit 8.63. Receipts are entered manually or automatically through a

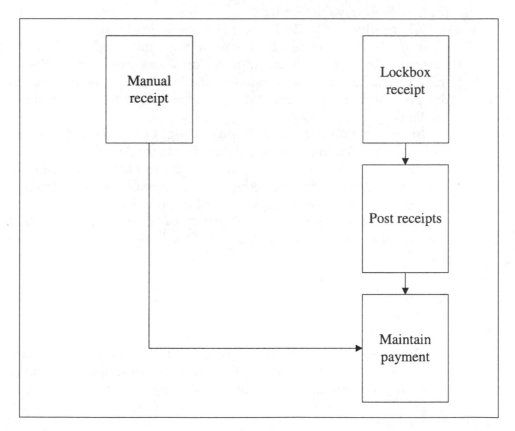

Exhibit 8.63   Receipts Business Flow

lockbox process. Receipt batches entered through the lockbox process must be posted. Receipt maintenance includes receipt reversal and receipt reapplication.

The Oracle Receivables receipts architecture consists of batches, checks, and applications (see Exhibit 8.64). The receipt batch records the batch name, control count, and control amount. The receipt check records the customer and receipt amount. The application records the receipt applied to the specific transactions.

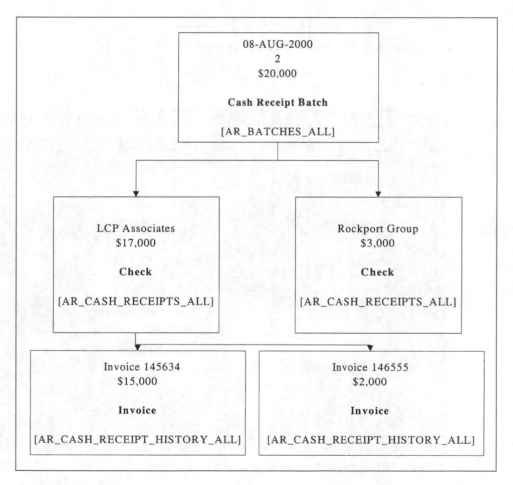

Exhibit 8.64 Receipts Architecture

Receipt Entry

The receipt batch data includes the batch name, the batch dates, and the batch control count and amount (see Exhibit 8.65).

1. From the Receivables menu → **Receipts** → **Batches.**
2. The **Batch Source** defaults from the AR: Receipt Source profile option. Select a new Source if necessary.
3. The **Batch, GL,** and **Deposit** dates default to the system date. Verify the dates are correct and the receipts are entered in the appropriate GL period.
4. Enter the **Control Count** for the batch.
5. Enter the **Control Amount** for the batch.

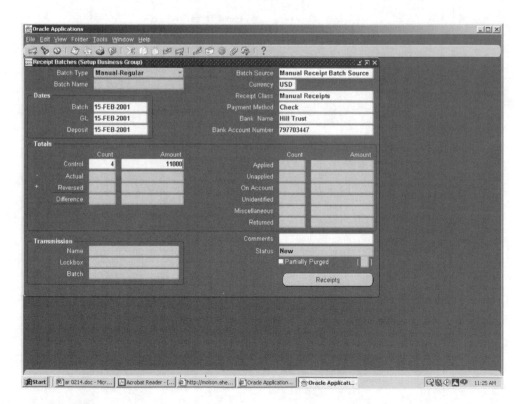

Exhibit 8.65   Receipts Batch

6. The **Status** is New, indicating a new batch. The Status will change to Out of Balance when receipts are entered, and Closed when the Control Count and Amount equal the Actual Count and Amount.

7. Press **Receipts** to enter receipt transactions.

The receipt data includes the cash receipt number, the receipt type, the receipt dates, and the receipt amount (see Exhibit 8.66).

1. Enter the **Receipt Number,** such as check number.
2. Select the **Type** of receipt. Cash will be displayed.
3. The Receipt Date defaults from the Receipt Batch.
4. The GL Date defaults from the Receipt Batch.
5. Enter the receipt **Amount.**
6. Press **New** to enter the new receipt.

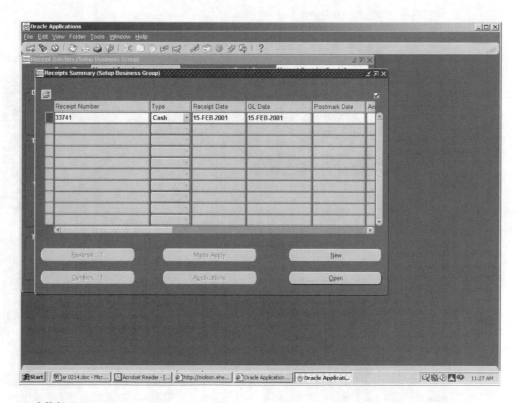

Exhibit 8.66   Receipt Data

1. In the Cash Receipts tab, enter the **Customer Name** or Customer Number (see Exhibit 8.67).
2. Press **Applications** to apply the receipt.

   A receipt must be applied to a transaction.

1. Select the **Transaction Number** or On-Account (see Exhibit 8.68).
2. The **Amount Applied** defaults from the AR: Cash Applied profile option. Change if necessary.
3. Press **Adjustments** to enter invoice adjustments if necessary.

   Typically, adjustments increment or decrement an original transaction. Adjustments made during the cash receipt process are usually for small amount write-offs (see Exhibit 8.69).

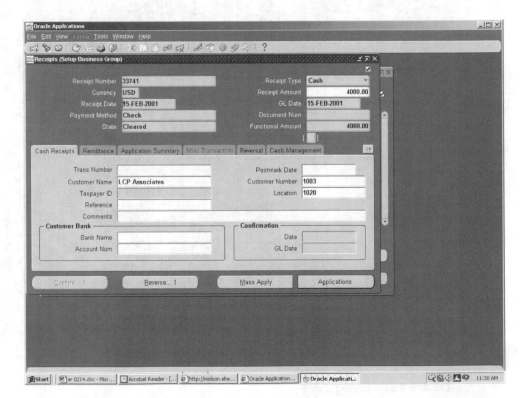

Exhibit 8.67   Receipt

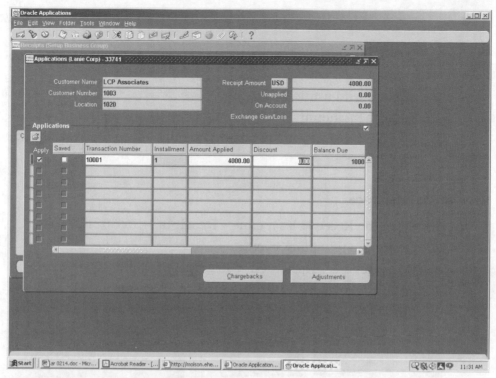

Exhibit 8.68 Receipt Application

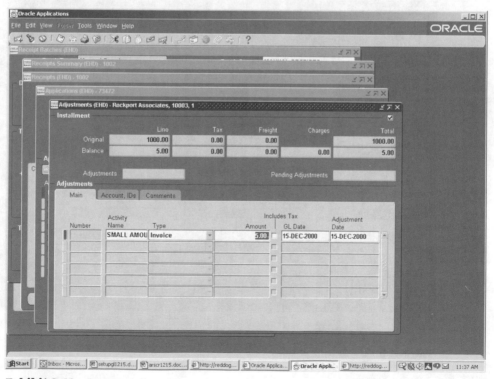

Exhibit 8.69 Receipt Adjustment

1. Select the adjustment **Activity Name** defined during the setup process.
2. Select the adjustment **Type.**
3. Enter the **Amount.**
4. The **GL Date** and **Adjustment Date** default to the system date. Modify if necessary.

Receipt Maintenance

1. From the Receivables menu → **Receipts** → **Receipts.**
2. Query the receipt to reverse.
3. Press **Reverse.** The system will display Exhibit 8.70.
4. Enter the reversal **Date, Category,** and **Reason.**
5. Press **Reverse** again.

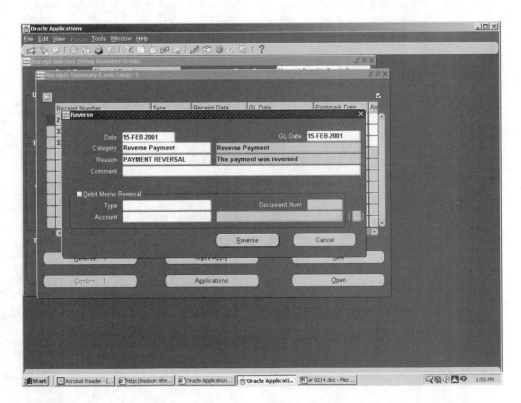

Exhibit 8.70   Reverse Receipt

Once a receipt has been reversed, it may be reapplied to another transaction.

1. From the Receivables menu → **Receipts** → **Summary.**
2. Query the receipt to reapply.
3. Press **Applications.** The system will display Exhibit 8.71.
4. Uncheck the **Apply** box to unapply the cash receipt to the transaction.
5. Select a **Transaction Number** to apply the receipt to, if applicable.

Miscellaneous Receipt

A noncustomer cash receipt is considered a miscellaneous receipt (see Exhibit 8.72).

1. Enter the receipt batch as normal.
2. During the cash receipt data entry process, select the **Receipt Type** of Misc.

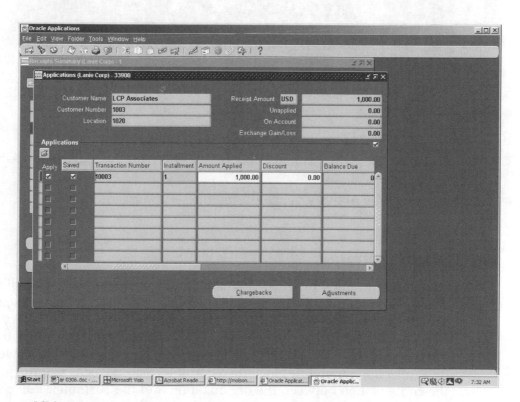

Exhibit 8.71 Reapply Receipt

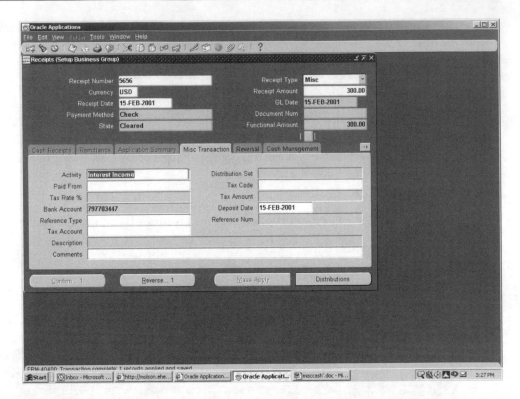

Exhibit 8.72   Miscellaneous Receipt

3. Press the **Misc. Transaction** tab to enter the noncustomer cash receipt.

4. Select the **Activity** define during the setup process.

INQUIRY AND REPORTING

Oracle Receivables provides robust inquiry and reporting capabilities. The Collections menu provides an in-depth inquiry and collection activity capabilities. Online inquiry capabilities include customer summary displays with drill-down to the transactions and activities applied to the transactions. Online user-defined customer agings are available as well.

Collection capabilities include recording customer calls that document the conversation between the organization and the customer. Full collection activity documentation includes the collector, the customer contact, conversational notes, and the cash forecast information. In addition, Oracle Receivables can create the collector to-do list from the customer call responses. For example, if the customer says "call back in three days," the system can remind the collector that the three days have passed and to follow up.

Oracle Receivables provides standard receivable reporting capabilities including aging reports, transaction and receipt reports, and the journals to Oracle General Ledger.

Customer calls allow the discussion information to be stored online (see Exhibit 8.73).

1. From the Receivables menu → **Collections** → **Customer Calls.**
2. Select the **Collector** name.
3. Select the **Customer Name** and **Location.**

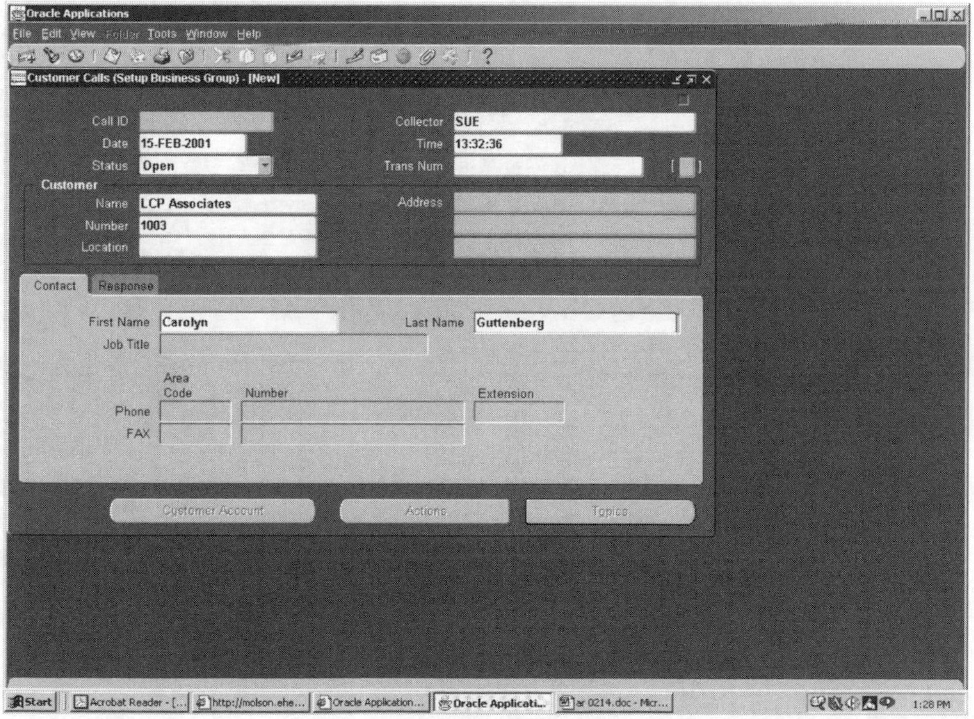

Exhibit 8.73 Customer Calls

4. In the Contact tab, either select a customer contact **First** and **Last Names** or enter a new customer contact record.

5. Press the **Response** tab to enter the discussion notes.

Enter the customer **Response** and **Notes** (see Exhibit 8.74).

1. From the Receivables menu → **Collections** → **Aging**.

2. The system displays the Find Aging window. Enter the search criteria including the Aging Bucket.

3. Press **Find**.

4. The customer aging is displayed (see Exhibit 8.75).

5. Press **Account Details** to view the transactions which compose the aging bucket balances (see Exhibit 8.76).

The open transactions are displayed, with original amounts and balance due amounts for the customer.

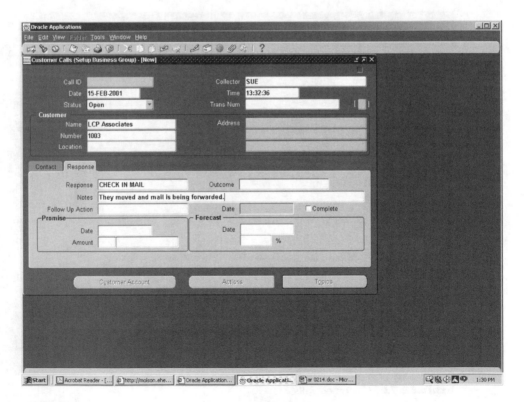

Exhibit 8.74   Customer Calls: Response and Notes

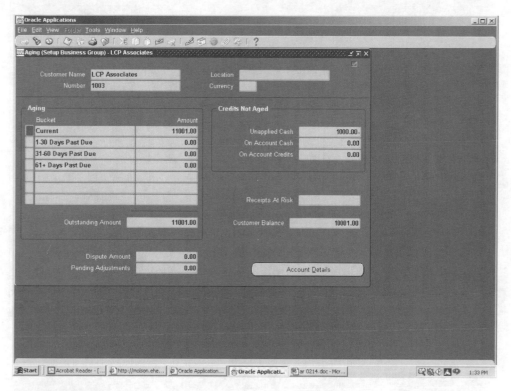

Exhibit 8.75 Aging

1. The transactions are displayed.
2. Press **Activities** to view all activities against a transaction.

   The Activities for the transaction are displayed (see Exhibit 8.77).

Reports

Oracle Receivables utilizes Oracle applications Standard Report Submission (SRS) for submitting concurrent reports, listings, and processes (see Exhibit 8.78).

1. From the Receivables menu → **Control** → **Request** → **Run**.
2. Enter the report **Name** and **Parameters**.
3. Press **Submit**.

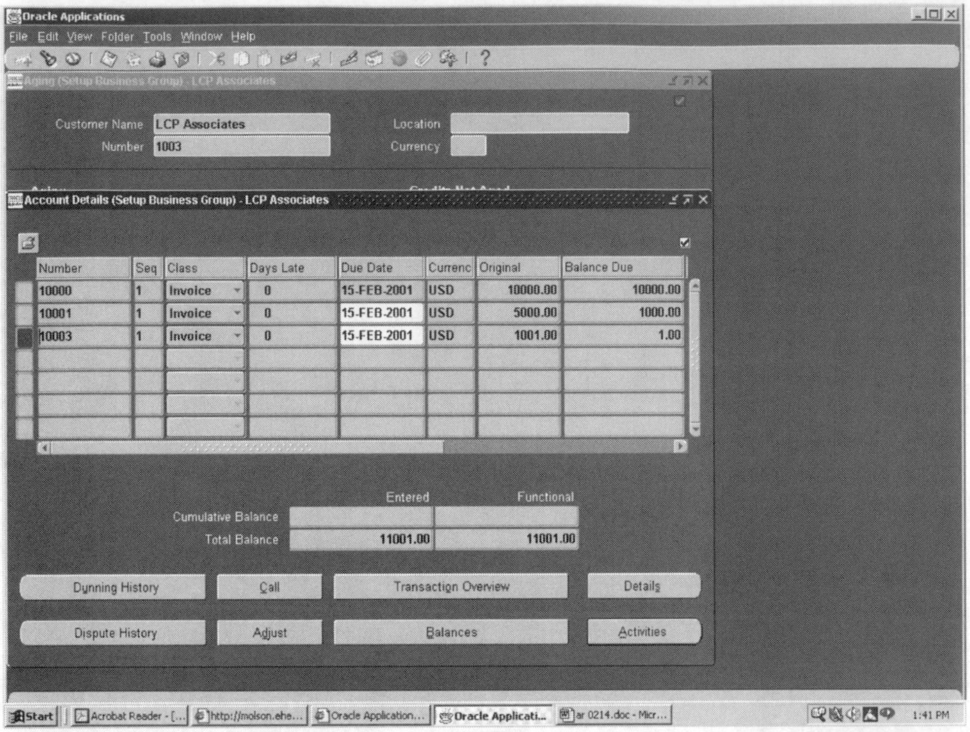

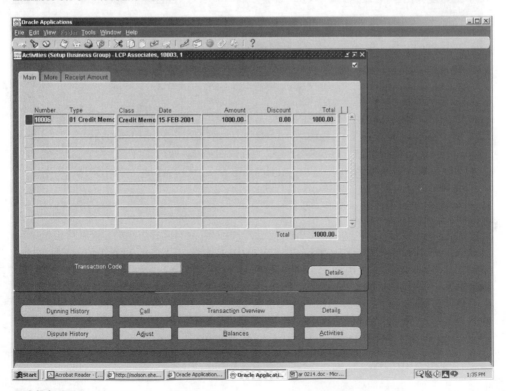

Exhibit 8.76 Account Details

Exhibit 8.77 Activities

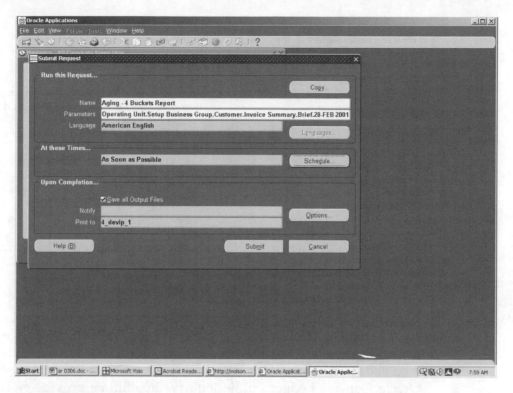

Exhibit 8.78 Oracle Receivables Closing Process

Exhibit 8.79 displays a sample of Oracle Receivables reports.

 There are two navigation menus for running Oracle Receivable reports. Use the Control →Requests →Run navigation path, which allows all reports to be run for the responsibility. The Reports menu options are specific reports.

 See the *Oracle Receivables User Guide* for a complete list of reports, listings, and concurrent processes.

PERIOD PROCESS

Periodically, Oracle Receivables transactions should be posted to Oracle General Ledger. Typically, these receivable journals are posted to General Ledger either weekly or at period-end.

Oracle Receivables Report	*Description*
Transaction Register	Report displays the invoice and credit memo transactions.
Adjustment Register	Report displays the adjustments.
Unapplied Receipt Register	Report displays the unapplied cash receipts.
Applied Receipt Register	Report displays the cash receipts applied to a customer account.
Receipt Register	Report displays the cash receipts.
Journal Entries	Report displays GL journal entries.
Receipt Journal	Report displays the cash receipt journal.
Sales Journal by GL Account	Report displays the transaction journal.
Aged Trial Balance	Report displays the open customer accounts.
AR Reconciliation	Report displays the AR reconciliation
Aging	Report displays the open customer accounts by aging period.

Exhibit 8.79   Oracle Receivables Standard Reports

The rule of thumb is to summarize subledger detail to General Ledger. This holds true for Oracle Receivables. The Oracle General Ledger Accounts Analysis reports provide a clear audit trail of the Oracle Receivables subledger detail.

Oracle General Ledger online inquiry capabilities provide full drill-down capabilities for either Summary or Detail journals. Recommend summarizing journal entries to minimize the reconciliation and performance issues associated with too much detail Oracle Receivables data in General Ledger. As the number of unique journal lines is smaller with summarized journal lines, reconciliation will be easier, reports will be smaller, and performance should be better.

The Oracle Receivables transactions are run through the Receivables Transfer to GL concurrent program. Once the concurrent process is complete, an unposted journal entry is created. Switch to an Oracle General Ledger responsibility to review the journal online. The journal should be posted.

The Oracle Receivables closing process is displayed in Exhibit 8.80. The preliminary closing reports should be run to verify the transactions will transfer properly (see Exhibit 8.81). The current period status should be changed to "close pending" and the next period opened. The Oracle Receivables financial transactions should be transferred to Oracle General Ledger. The final closing reports should be produced and the Oracle Receivables system should be reconciled to Oracle General Ledger for key accounts. The "close pending" period should be changed to closed.

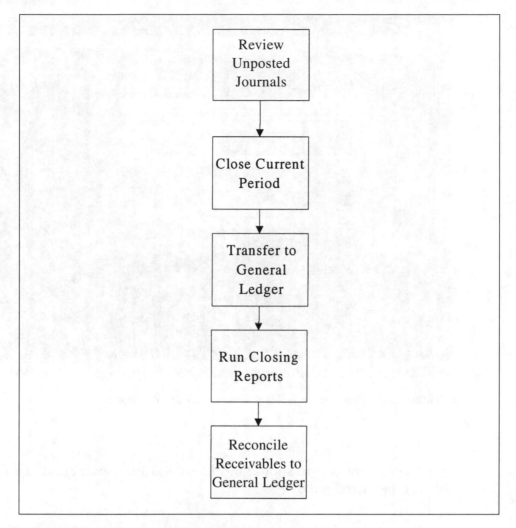

Exhibit 8.80 Oracle Receivables Closing Process

Run the Journal Entries report to view unposted Oracle Receivables transactions.

1. From the Receivables menu → **Control** → **Request** → **Run**.
2. Enter the report **Name** of Journal Entries and Journal Entries report **Parameters.**
3. Press **Submit.**

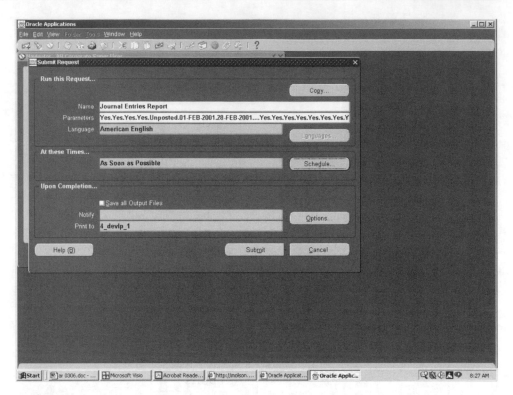

Exhibit 8.81 Oracle Receivables Preliminary Closing Reports

The current period should be closed and the next period should be opened (see Exhibit 8.82).

1. From the Receivables Menu → **Accounting** → **Open/Close Periods.**
2. Select **Closed Pending** for the current period.
3. Select **Open** for the next period.

The Oracle Receivables financial transaction should be transferred to Oracle General Ledger periodically (see Exhibit 8.83).

1. From the Receivables Menu → **Interfaces** → **General Ledger.**
2. Change **Posting Detail** to **Summary.**
3. Enter the **GL Dates** to transfer.

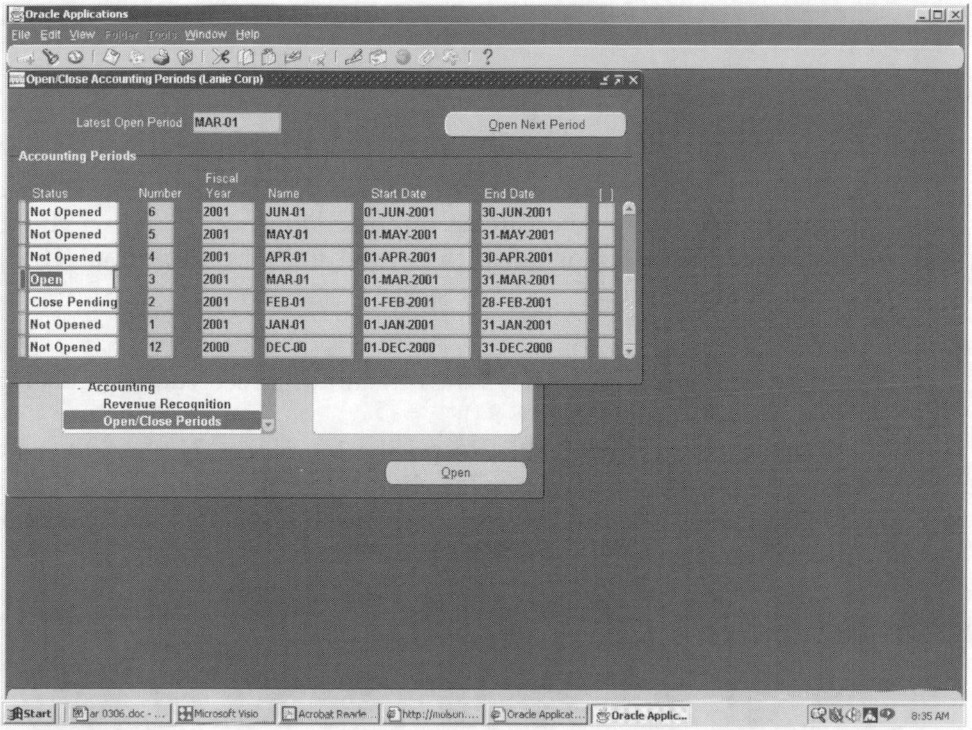

Exhibit 8.82 Control Receivables Periods

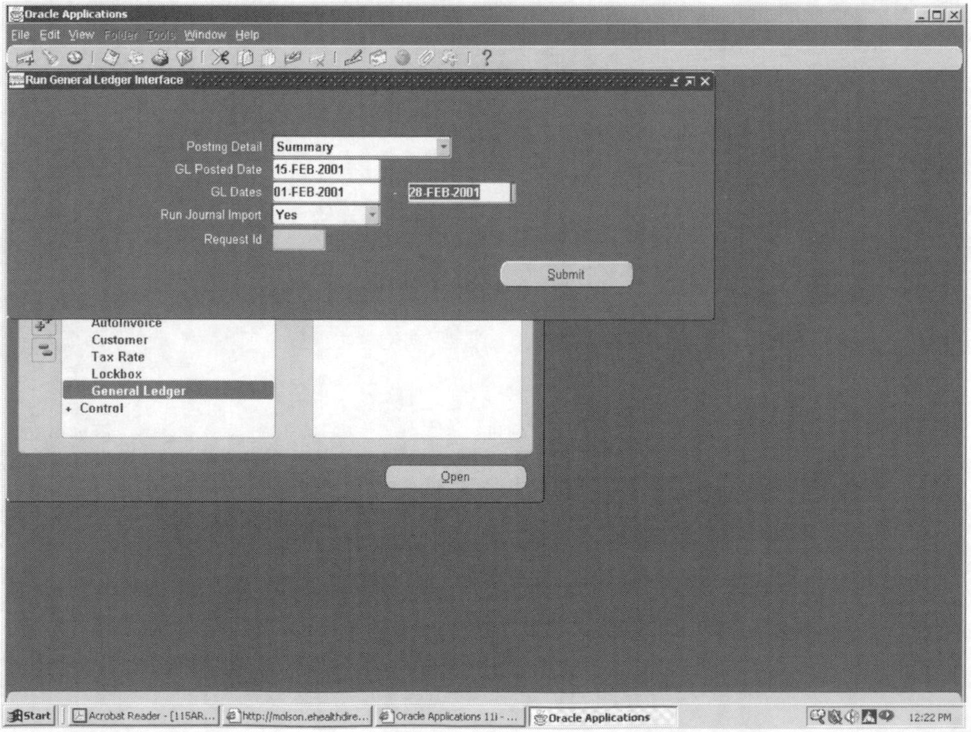

Exhibit 8.83 Receivables GL Interface

4. Press **Submit.**

5. Review the Receivables Transfer to GL and Journal Import reports.

6. Once the Receivables Transfer to GL report has completed, the Journal Import process will create an unposted journal entry. Switch to a General Ledger responsibility to review the journal online. The journal should be posted.

The Aging report displays the outstanding receivables in user-defined aging buckets (see Exhibit 8.84).

The Accounts Receivable Reconciliation report displays the receivable account inflows and outflows (see Exhibit 8.85).

The General Ledger report displays the receivable account inflows and outflows (see Exhibit 8.86).

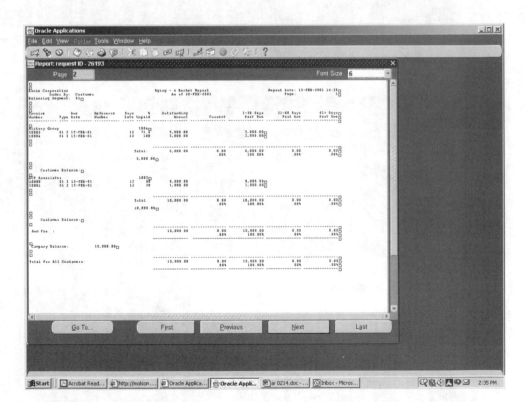

Exhibit 8.84   Aging Report

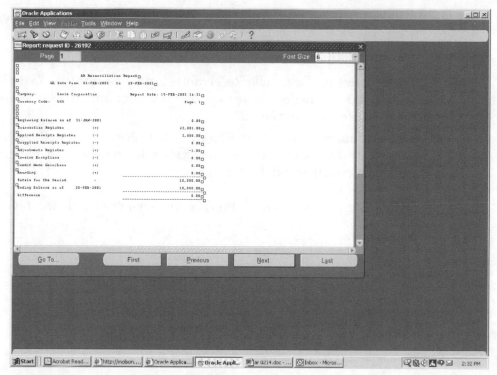

Exhibit 8.85 AR Reconciliation Report

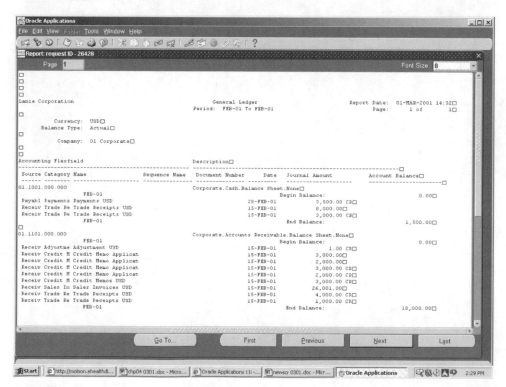

Exhibit 8.86 General Ledger Report

Receivables Reconciliation Process

1. The balance in the Oracle Receivables Aging report (see Exhibit 8.84) should be reconciled to the receivables account in Oracle General Ledger (see Exhibit 8.86).

2. The Accounts Receivable Reconciliation Report (see Exhibit 8.85) should be reconciled to the GL receivables balances in the General Ledger report (see Exhibit 8.86).

Repeat for all key reconciliation accounts, such as cash and revenue.

Index

% percent sign, 48-50, 72

A

Accessing Oracle Applications, 29–32
Account Analysis reports, 104, 240,328
Account Generator, 20
Adadmin utility, 153–155
Adjustments, 305,318–320
Application Desktop Integrator (ADI), 112, 117
Applied receipt, 276, 313–314
Approval limit, 270–271
AutoAccounting, 263–265
AutoCash, 313
AutoInvoice, 297

B

Bank accounts
    Payables, 173–176
    Receivables, 274–277

Budgets, 116–
    Budget, 119–120
    Entry, 120–125
    Organization, 117–119
    Transfer, 125–126
Business Group, 145–146

C

Calendar, 94–96
Calls, 323–324
Cash Management, 158, 249
Chargeback, 305
Code combinations, 73–75
Column, 24–26
Collectors, 270
Concurrent processing, 19, 59
    Submitting report, 59–61
    Viewing report, 61–64
Conversion, 10, 183–184, 288
Contacts, 183–185, 294–295

Credit memos
    Payables, 202–206
    Receivables, 304–310
Cross-Validation Rules, 73–74,
       88–89
Customers, 284,287–296
    Architecture, 288–289
    Entry, 290–296
    Sites, 291–296
Customer Profile Class, 282–283

D

Data, 9
Data entry mode, 48
Data field colors, 45–46
Data flows, 9–10
Data naming standards,
       13
Database Administrator (DBA),
       19–20
Debit memos
    Payables, 202–203
    Receivables, 304
Documentation, 4–5
Downloading a concurrent request,
       64–65
Dynamic Insertion, 73

E

Earned Discount, 274,
       277
Employee expense reporting
    Expense report entry, 210–215
    Expense report template,
       172–173

F

Financial Options, 158–161,166–171,
       184, 192, 208
Financial Statement Generator (FSG)
    Architecture, 133–135
    Request, 135–136
    Sample, 136
Fixed Assets, 158
Flexfields, 20,67–89
    Descriptive Flexfields, 67,
       75–77
       Invoice Transaction, 251
    Key Flexfields
       Accounting, 67, 68–75
       Analysis, 69
       Design, 70
       Segment values, 72,
       85–88
       Setup, 77–89
       Structure, 70–72,
       77–85
       Customer Territory, 67,
       253–254
       Sales Tax Location, 67,
       256–257
       System Item, 67, 255–256
    Qualifiers, 71–72

G

General Ledger, 91–139
    Business Process, 93
    Integration, 17–18
    Overview, 91–93
    Setup , 94–103
    Using , 93–94
GRE/Legal entity,
       145–148

H

Hardware, 2
Home Page List of Responsibilities, 32
Housekeeping, 8–9
Human Resources, 142, 157–158, 170–171, 211–213

I

Icons, 34, 44, 47
Inquiries
General Ledger, 126–128
Account , 128–133
Payables, 233–239
Distribution, 238–239
Invoice, 234–235
Payment, 235–237
Supplier , 233–234
Receivables, 322–326
Account Details, 325–326
Activities, 325–326
Aging, 324–325
Calls, 323–324
Intercompany account, 101–102
Interfaces, 10
Inventory organization, 151
Invoices
Payables, 190–202
Approval/Hold, 196–199
Architecture, 191–193
Business Process, 191–192

Entry, 191–195
Maintenance, 199–202
Printing, 311–312
Recurring, 215–216
Receivables, 296–313
Architecture, 298–300
Business Process, 298–299
Completion, 303–304
Entry, 298–304
Maintenance, 310
Printing, 311–313

J

Journal import, 112–114
Journals, 104–116
Architecture, 105–107
Business process, 105
Entry, 107–109
Maintenance, 108
Post, 109–111
Recurring, 115–116

K

Keyboard mapping, 3, 43

L

Legal entity, 147–148
List of Values, 48
Location, 144
Lookup codes, 162–163

M

Manual payment, 228–230
Mass Allocations,
        114–115
Matching, 206–208
Menu, 35–41
Metalink, 6
Miscellaneous cash receipt,
        321–322
Multi-org (Multiple-organization),
        141–155
    Architecture, 22–25
    Overview, 141
    Setup, 141–155

O

On-account receipt, 276
Operating unit, 148–150
Optimizer, 89, 138
Oracle Application User Group
        (OAUG),
        6
Oracle Support, 4–6
Order Entry, 249, 304–305
Organization, 145–151

P

Parent account, 70–72, 87–88
Passwords, 55
Patches/Upgrades, 6, 9
Payables, 157–248
    Business process, 158–159
    Overview, 157–158
    Setup, 158–183

Payables Options, 112, 158–161,
        176–181, 184, 192, 198, 209,
        240
Payment terms, 165–166,
        261
Payments, 216–233
    Architecture, 216–218
    Automatic payment process
        Cancel, 227–228
        Confirm, 224–227
        Modify, 221–222
        Print and Format, 222–224
        Select, 218–220
    Business process, 216–217
    Manual , 228–230
    Void, 230–233
People, 11
Period End Process
    General Ledger, 139
    Payables, 240–248
    Receivables, 327–334
Periods
    General Ledger, 102–104
    Payables, 182–183, 243–244
    Receivables, 262–263,
        330–331
Personal Computer, 7
Post
Prepayment, 208–210
Printer, 3, 56–57
Procedures, 13
Profile values, 57–58
    General Ledger, 98–100
    Multi-Org, 142–143,
        152–155
    Payables, 164–165
    Receivables, 281–282
Project methodology,
        14–16
Projects, 157, 210
Purchasing, 158, 206–208

Q

Query mode, 48

R

Receipt class, 277–278
Receipt source, 278–279
Receipts, 313–322
    Architecture, 315
    Business process, 314–315
    Entry, 316–322
    Maintenance, 320–321
    Miscellaneous, 321–322
Receivables, 249–334
    Business process, 251–252
    Methodologies, 250
    Overview, 249–251
    Setup, 251–287
Receivables activity, 271–274
Reconciliation
    Payables, 247–248
    Receivables, 334
Relational database architecture, 9,
    23–27
Remit-to address, 284–285
Reporting entity, 181–182
Reports
    General Ledger, 133–138
    Multi-org, 154
    Payables, 239–240, 246–248
    Receivables, 325–327, 328,
        332–333
    System Administrator,
        59–63
Reprinting, 64–65
Responsibility, 19, 53–55, 151–152,
    154
Row, 24–26

S

Security, 75
Self-Service , 157, 210
Set of Books
    Architecture, 20–22
    General Ledger, 96–98, 104
    Multi-org, 147–150
    Payables, 163–164, 177
    Receivables, 258
Single organization architecture,
    22
Sizing, 3
Software, 4
Standard memo lines, 285–286
Statements
    Cycles, 280
    Printing, 312–313
Summary accounts, 70
Suppliers, 183–189
    Architecture, 184–185
    Entry, 184–189
    Sites, 188–190
System Administrator, 19, 31–32,
    53–60
System Options, 257–261

T

Table, 24–27
Tax codes, 287
Testing, 7–8
Toolbar, 42–44
Top Ten List, 34
Training, 12–13
Transaction Source, 269–270
Transaction Types
    Credit memo, 265–267
    Invoice, 268–269

U

Unapplied receipt, 276, 313–314
Unearned Discount, 274, 277
Unidentified receipt, 276
User, 55–56

W

Web browser, 29
Wild card search, 49–50
Window, 42, 45–49